In this timely collection of essays, prominent historians survey the Hiroshima story from the American decision to drop the first atomic bomb to the recent controversy over the Enola Gay exhibit in Washington, D.C. The essays analyze the American resort to atomic warfare in 1945 and show how that decision resonates in American and Japanese memory. The first essay surveys the literature on the atomic bombing of Japan, while the second and third essays evaluate the decisions that led to that event. The remaining essays discuss how the Japanese and American people have remembered Hiroshima in the years since the end of World War II. They emphasize the construction of an official memory of Hiroshima, the challenge posed by alternative or countermemories, and the tension between history and memory in the Hiroshima story. The collection thus unites up-to-date scholarship by diplomatic historians with the recent interest in memory that has emerged as part of the new cultural history.

Hiroshima in History and Memory

HIROSHIMA

IN HISTORY AND MEMORY

Edited by

MICHAEL J. HOGAN

The Ohio State University

CAMBRIDGE
UNIVERSITY PRESS

CAMBRIDGE UNIVERSITY PRESS
Cambridge, New York, Melbourne, Madrid, Cape Town, Singapore,
São Paulo, Delhi, Dubai, Tokyo, Mexico City

Cambridge University Press
32 Avenue of the Americas, New York, NY 10013-2473, USA

www.cambridge.org
Information on this title: www.cambridge.org/9780521566827

First published 1996
14th printing 2010

A catalog record for this publication is available from the British Library.

ISBN 978-0-521-56206-5 Hardback
ISBN 978-0-521-56682-7 Paperback

To my Father
and other veterans of World War II

Contents

Illustrations

Following Page 142

1. Wartime *Enola Gay*.
2. "Little Boy" type nuclear weapon.
3. "Fat Man" type nuclear weapon.
4. Atomic explosion over Nagasaki.
5. Atomic bomb damage to Hiroshima.
6. Atomic bomb damage to Nagasaki.
7. Atomic bomb damage to Nagasaki.
8. The head of one of the Saints lying by the front gate of the Urakami Cathedral, Nagasaki.
9. Japanese Premier Shigemitsu signs the formal document of surrender.
10. Racist wartime propaganda.
11. *36 Hour War*.
12. A sit-in in front of the Hiroshima peace park.
13. Wartime "comfort women" demonstrating in Tokyo.
14. The restored fuselage of the *Enola Gay*.

Preface and Acknowledgments

Most of the essays in this volume first appeared in the Spring 1995 issue of *Diplomatic History*, the journal of record for specialists in the history of American foreign relations. The response to that publication was so favorable that I decided to bring the essays together in a book that could reach an even larger audience. All of the original essays were reedited for this purpose and one of them, the essay by Barton J. Bernstein, was revised and shortened. In addition, I prepared a new introduction for this book and added a long essay of my own on the controversy that surrounded recent plans by the National Air and Space Museum to commemorate the fiftieth anniversary of Hiroshima and Nagasaki. I am grateful to the authors for the hard work that went into their excellent essays, to the Society for Historians of American Foreign Relations for permission to republish those essays, and to Pauline Testerman and Anita Smith of the Truman Library for help in locating photographs.

I am also grateful to Amy L. S. Staples, Bruce Karhoff, Bruce Khula, Nathan Citino, and Rowland Brucken for help in preparing the introductory chapter to this volume; to Amy Staples, Bruce Karhoff, and Stuart Hilwig for assistance with my essay on the *Enola Gay* controversy; and to Ann Heiss for her expertise as a proofreader and copyeditor. Finally, I owe a special debt to my editor, Frank Smith of Cambridge University Press, and to Professor Michael Kammen of Cornell University, for their critical reading of my contribution to this volume.

This book is dedicated to the veterans of World War II, especially my father, Eugene J. Hogan, who served on board the *U.S.S. Minneapolis* during the Battle of Leyte Gulf and other engagements.

The Authors

BARTON J. BERNSTEIN is professor of history at Stanford University, where he codirects the International Relations Program and the International Policy Studies Program. He writes on nuclear history, Cold War policies, and science and technology policy, including medical issues. He has published *The Atomic Bomb: The Critical Issues* (1976), among other volumes, and has recently published "Seizing the Contested Terrain of Early Nuclear History: Stimson, Conant, and Their Allies Explain the Decision to Use the Atomic Bomb," *Diplomatic History* (Winter 1993).

HERBERT P. BIX, who lives in Wintrop, Massachusetts, is the author of *Peasant Protest in Japan, 1590–1884* (paperback, 1992) and many essays and translations on Japanese social and political history, including "The Showa Emperor's 'Monologue' and the Problem of War Responsibility" in *The Journal of Japanese Studies* (Summer 1992). His essay in this book will be the basis of a chapter in his forthcoming history of the Japanese monarchy in war and peace, 1868–1989.

PAUL BOYER is Merle Curti Professor of History and director of the Institute for Research in the Humanities at the University of Wisconsin-Madison. His books include *By the Bomb's Early Light: American Thought and Culture at the Dawn of the Atomic Age* (1984; reissued with a new introduction by the author, 1994).

JOHN W. DOWER, Henry Luce Professor of History and International Cooperation at the Massachusetts Institute of Technology, is the author of *War without Mercy: Race and Power in the Pacific*

War (1986) and, most recently, *Japan in War and Peace: Selected Essays* (1994).

MICHAEL J. HOGAN is professor and chair of history at The Ohio State University. Since 1987 he has also been editor of *Diplomatic History*. He is the author of *Informal Entente: The Private Structure of Cooperation in Anglo-American Economic Diplomacy, 1918–1928* (1977) and *The Marshall Plan: America, Britain, and the Reconstruction of Western Europe, 1947–1952* (1987). His edited works include *Explaining the History of American Foreign Relations*, with Thomas G. Paterson (1991) and *America in the World: The Historiography of U.S. Foreign Relations since 1941* (1995).

SEIITSU TACHIBANA is professor of international relations at Yamanashi Women's Junior College, Kofu City, Japan. His works in English include *At the Mercy of Nuclear Weapons: Origins of U.S. Nuclear Policy, 1939–1945* (1979), "SDI: Ten Fundamental Contradictions – The Need for a Real Alternative to the Nuclear Predicament – A View from Nagasaki" (1989), "A New World Order: The Nuclear Dimension" (1993), and other articles on related issues.

J. SAMUEL WALKER is historian of the Nuclear Regulatory Commission, where his job is to write a scholarly history of the regulation of nuclear power (but not nuclear weapons). His most recent book is *Containing the Atom: Nuclear Regulation in a Changing Environment, 1963–1971* (1992). His interest in the use of the atomic bomb is an extension of his training in U.S. diplomatic history at the University of Maryland, where he studied with Wayne S. Cole.

Hiroshima in History and Memory

1

Hiroshima in History and Memory: An Introduction

MICHAEL J. HOGAN

The story is a familiar one, though nonetheless dramatic. In the early morning of 6 August 1945, an American B-29 bomber, the *Enola Gay*, lifted off a runway on Tinian Island in the Pacific. Piloted by Colonel Paul W. Tibbets, who had named the giant Superfortress after his mother, the *Enola Gay* carried a ten-thousand-pound atomic bomb known as "Little Boy." At 8:15 A.M., the crew of the *Enola Gay* covered their eyes with dark glasses and the bombardier, Thomas Ferebee, released the huge orange and black bomb over Hiroshima, Japan, a city of 250,000 people, many of whom were starting their last day on earth. The bomb exploded over the city with a brilliant flash of purple light, followed by a deafening blast and a powerful shock wave that heated the air as it expanded. A searing fireball eventually enveloped the area around ground zero, temperatures rose to approximate those on the surface of the sun, and a giant mushroom cloud roiled up from the city like an angry gray ghost. Within seconds Hiroshima was destroyed and half of its population was dead or dying. Three days later, a second atomic bomb destroyed the Japanese city of Nagasaki, killing more than 60,000 people.

The bombings of Hiroshima and Nagasaki were the final acts in an Asian war that had its origins in the 1930s, specifically in Japan's efforts to forge an empire in east Asia and the western Pacific. Japanese expansion threatened American interests, particularly in the economically and strategically important area of Indochina. When diplomatic warnings failed to deter the Japanese, the government in Washington decided in July 1940 to embargo the export of critical materials to Japan, especially oil, which sustained Japanese industry and fueled the Japanese military. Confronted with the choice between curbing its expansionist ambitions or confronting the United States, the Japanese government responded on 7 December 1941 with a surprise attack on the American fleet at Pearl Harbor.

Pearl Harbor brought the United States into the Second World War, not only against Japan in Asia but also against Germany and Italy in Europe. It was a long and bloody struggle. By the time the United States had fully mobilized, most of Southeast Asia had fallen to Japan, including the Philippines, which the Japanese overran in the first months of 1942. Ferocious battles of attrition marked the American struggle to regain lost ground and defeat Japan. Japanese forces waged a stubborn, often suicidal resistance in places like Guadalcanal, Midway Island, Bougainville, Tarawa, Saipan, Corregidor, Iwo Jima, and Okinawa. With each battle the death toll mounted, not only of Japanese and American soldiers but also of civilians caught up in the fighting or massacred, as in the Philippines, by retreating Japanese forces. The Japanese "rape of Nanking" and the American firebombing of Tokyo symbolized the incredible brutality of the Pacific war and set the stage for the destruction of Hiroshima and Nagasaki.

Amid the carnage, both sides began planning for the final battle. The Japanese stockpiled aircraft, expanded conscription, and amassed a formidable force to meet the Allied armies that would invade their homeland. The Americans expanded their bombing operations, destroyed what remained of Japan's naval fleet, blockaded the Japanese islands, and raced to complete the production of an atomic bomb that could end the war without a costly invasion. American scientists and engineers, organized by the War Department in the so-called Manhattan Project, had been working to manufacture an atomic bomb since the early days of the war. President Harry S. Truman learned of the bomb shortly after becoming president. Neither then nor later did he reexamine the original assumptions behind the Manhattan Project, which held that the atomic bomb was a legitimate weapon and should be used to end the war as soon as possible.

In Japan, meanwhile, government officials debated whether or not to negotiate an end to the conflict. A peace faction urged this course as the only alternative to a doomed resistance to American power. The Japanese government even went so far as to approach the Soviet Union, an American ally in the European theater, about mediating a negotiated peace with the United States. At stake was its desire to modify the American demand for unconditional surrender in order to safeguard Japan's political system and the postwar position of Emperor Hirohito. As it turned out, divisions within the government prevented the Japanese from pursuing these peace initiatives with enough resolve to end the war before the atomic bombing. In the United States, on the other hand, the very existence of the bomb made policymakers less inclined to modify their demand for unconditional surrender. So did the possibility that a quick end to the war would preclude the Soviet Union from entering the battle against Japan, deny the Soviets any part in the postwar occupation of that country, and enhance the diplomatic leverage that American leaders could bring to bear in negotiating postwar issues with their counterparts in Moscow.

With Japanese leaders dithering over the terms of a satisfactory settlement, and with American officials contemplating the diplomatic as well as the military advantages of the atomic bomb, no obstacle emerged to stop the B-29 crews from flying their deadly missions, or to extend by even one day the lives of those in Hiroshima and Nagasaki who were not party to the policy debates in Tokyo and Washington. Instead, the Japanese government surrendered on 10 August 1945, four days after Hiroshima, one day after Nagasaki. The Second World War was over; the atomic age had begun.

II

What is the meaning of Hiroshima and Nagasaki? How have historians explained the American resort to atomic warfare, and how does that decision resonate in American and Japanese memory? These and other questions are addressed in the following essays, which were solicited to commemorate the fiftieth anniversary of the atomic bombing of Japan. The first three essays deal with Hiroshima and Nagasaki as topics of historical analysis. This sort of analysis is ongoing, of course; its conclusions are open to debate and constant revision, as the essays make clear. The remaining essays deal with how Hiroshima and Nagasaki have been remembered in the United States and Japan. The study of memory, as a form of scholarship, emerged in the 1980s as part of the new cultural history. The emphasis was often on the social construction of memory, particularly on efforts by the state and powerful political groups to forge historical traditions that could serve their interests. According to Michel Foucault, historical memories are constantly refashioned to suit present purposes. They are also socially acquired and collective. Individual memories gradually fold together into a collective memory of the group. Embedded in the social fabric, they become idealized memories and their ability to survive in the face of alternative memories, or countermemories, depends on the power of the group that holds them. Seen in this light, history and memory are in a fundamental state of tension. History is "an intellectual and secular production" that subjects the past to critical scrutiny, whereas memory, as Pierre Nora explains, "installs remembrance with the sacred." Whereas history is objective, memory is subjective, selective, and present minded.[1]

The second set of essays in this volume deal with the tension that can exist between history and memory. They recount the efforts in Japan and the United States to suppress the history of Hiroshima and Nagasaki – that is, to forge an officially sanctioned memory of the atomic bombings. They also describe how groups in both countries sought to uncover the past, or at least to forge a countermemory. Finally, they trace the efforts on both sides to make history and memory the vehicles for constructing a particular national identity and for advancing important political goals.

The book begins with an excellent historiographical overview by J. Samuel Walker, a historian of the U.S. Nuclear Regulatory Commission. Walker's essay introduces the reader to the literature on the American decision to drop the atomic bombs on Japan. It traces the evolution of that literature in the years since 1945, identifies the issues in contention, and outlines what has become the

1 Pierre Nora, "Between Memory and History: *Les Lieux de Memoire*," *Representations* 26 (Spring 1989): 7–25. The entire Spring 1989 issue of *Representations* is devoted to the subject of "Memory and Counter-Memory." See also for background on the study of memory the excellent book by Patrick H. Hutton, *History as an Art of Memory* (Hanover, VT, 1993), esp. 1–26.

dominant view of historians. According to Walker, the literature deals with two essential questions. The first is whether the bombing was necessary to end the war quickly and thereby save the lives that would have been lost in an American invasion of the Japanese homeland. The second concerns the motives behind the American decision to drop the bomb and why policymakers found this strategy for ending the war more attractive than others, such as a test demonstration of the bomb or some modification of the American demand for Japan's unconditional surrender.

Initially, at least, most scholars agreed with former president Harry S. Truman and other policymakers, who explained the decision to use the bomb as the best way to end the war quickly, avoid an invasion of Japan, and save thousands of American and Japanese lives. Gar Alperovitz challenged this view in *Atomic Diplomacy*, a brilliantly provocative book published in 1965. According to Alperovitz, American decision makers were aware of alternative strategies for ending the war without dropping the atomic bombs or launching a bloody invasion. They ruled out these alternatives, however, relied instead on the atomic bomb, and did so less for military than for political reasons – namely, to preclude Soviet entry into the war against Japan and to give the Truman administration the military leverage it needed to deal successfully with the Soviet Union on postwar issues. The bomb, Alperovitz concluded, made Truman and other American leaders more aggressive negotiators. It gave them the confidence to reverse earlier understandings with the Soviet Union and contributed to the origins of the Cold War.

With Alperovitz's book, scholarship on the atomic bombing of Japan would never be the same again. Although a later generation of historians would not go as far as Alperovitz, they were ready to concede that political considerations played an important part in the way American leaders thought about the bomb. They raised doubts about the number of lives that would have been lost in an invasion of Japan and about whether the atomic bombing was the only other way to end the war. As the war neared an end, according to Walker's summary of the recent scholarship, the military justification for using the bomb was less compelling than had once been the case. Nevertheless, "there were no moral, military, diplomatic, or bureaucratic considerations that carried enough weight to deter dropping the bomb and gaining its projected military and diplomatic benefits."

Walker's survey of the literature is followed by two additional essays on the events surrounding the American resort to atomic warfare and the Japanese decision to surrender. The first of these essays is by Barton J. Bernstein, a historian at Stanford University and a prominent figure in the historiographical debates over the atomic bombing of Japan. Bernstein begins his essay by arguing that American leaders saw the atomic bomb as a legitimate weapon of war. Because of this, and because Truman's military advisers did not present alternative strategies for ending the war short of a bloody invasion of Japan, the president's decision to use the bomb was virtually inevitable. Truman would have authorized the bombing "even if the Soviet Union had not existed," Bernstein concludes, although the political and diplomatic advantages to be gained reinforced what the president saw as a military necessity.

From this point Bernstein goes on to evaluate the various strategies for ending the war without a costly invasion or the atomic bombing of Japan. He finds little reason to believe that any one of these strategies would have brought the war to a end prior to the planned invasion. Some combination of alternatives might have worked, however, and Bernstein finds no military justification for dropping the second atomic bomb on Nagasaki. His conclusions amount to speculation and second-guessing, of course. American leaders at the time, Bernstein admits, had no reason to believe that Japan would surrender after the Hiroshima bombing and were convinced that bombing both cities was necessary. This also became the prevailing view in Washington and among the American people in the years after Hiroshima, when it was attached to the notion that nuclear weapons, or rather the fear of nuclear war, contributed to a prolonged period of peace between the superpowers.

Bernstein's article strikes a middle ground between the original accounts of the atomic bombing and the revisionist arguments of Alperovitz and others. Much the same can be said of the provocative essay by Herbert P. Bix, an independent scholar who specializes in Japanese social and political history. Bix argues that historians have slighted the Japanese military and political context to the

atomic bombing of Hiroshima and Nagasaki and misunderstood
the role that Emperor Hirohito played in the closing months of the
war. Contrary to much of the current scholarship, Bix claims that
Hirohito was completely in control of the war and its ending. He
shows, for example, that Hirohito was actively involved in plans to
resist an American invasion of Japan. He claims as well that Japan's peace overtures in Moscow were little more than a tactic to
delay a Soviet invasion of Manchuria, not a serious effort to negotiate an end to the war. Bix blames Hirohito's "reluctance to face
the fait accompli of defeat" for prolonging the war, not Truman's
unwillingness to consider terms other than unconditional surrender. Only after the war did Japanese leaders seek to shield the
emperor from popular blame for his wartime leadership – in part
by concocting a picture of Hirohito as a great savior who intervened in the political process in order to end the war and protect
the Japanese people from further death and destruction. In truth,
Bix argues, Hirohito and other leaders were less concerned with
protecting their people than with finding a reason to surrender that
would save face and prevent a violent popular reaction against
their leadership. The atomic bombing of Hiroshima and Nagasaki
gave them that reason.

III

The Japanese constructed a memory of the war that was flawed in
other ways as well. John W. Dower takes up this issue in the first of
several essays that deal not so much with the Hiroshima bombing
as a historical episode as with the ways in which the Japanese and
the Americans have confronted the past in the years since 1945. In
the immediate postwar period, according to Dower, the Japanese
reacted to the bombing with a deep sense of rage, first against the
United States and then against their own government for involving
them in a suicidal war with a technologically superior nation
armed with atomic bombs. The atomic bomb, in this sense, became a symbol not only of Japan's victimization but of its inferior-
ity, a view that helped to drive both the postwar peace movement
in Japan and Japanese efforts to build a technologically superior
economy.

Although the victims of Hiroshima and Nagasaki received little attention in the early postwar era, in part because of American censorship during the occupation period, a new genre of atomic bomb literature and art began to emerge once the occupation came to an end. As memories of the horror were rekindled, they combined with the Cold War and the nuclear arms race to forge a countermemory that further fueled the peace movement in Japan. At the same time, however, the Japanese had to come to grips with the realization that the atomic bomb had claimed other victims as well, including thousands of conscripted Korean workers who were, in effect, the victims of Japanese imperialism as well as the American bombing. For the first time, the Japanese were forced to reconcile their sense of themselves as victims with their role as wartime victimizers, not only in Korea but in China and elsewhere. As Dower concludes, the act of reconstructing Japan's memory of the war and the process of reconciling memory and identity continue today.

In his contribution to this volume, Seiitsu Tachibana, a Japanese scholar who specializes in international relations, reinforces the conclusions we find in Dower's essay. Although most Japanese came to see themselves as the victims of World War II, according to Tachibana, the demands for compensation by the victims of Japanese aggression and by the survivors of Hiroshima and Nagasaki have reawakened the country to its wartime role as victimizer. Tachibana traces the important part played by the survivors of Hiroshima and Nagasaki in recovering Japan's memory of the war and challenging its identity as victim. They became peace crusaders, he argues. They organized an active movement against nuclear war and the nuclear arms race, and they urged their government to aid the victims of Japanese aggression in Southeast Asia. As both Dower and Tachibana admit, the Japanese have been slow to reconstruct their memory of the war, particularly their identity as victimizer. The government has been reluctant to compensate the victims of Japanese aggression, to acknowledge Japan's wartime atrocities, or to admit its responsibility for the war and the atomic bombings of Hiroshima and Nagasaki. Nevertheless, Tachibana is hopeful of changes to come, out of which might emerge a genuine peace culture and an honest encounter with Japan's past.

In his essay, Paul Boyer, a historian at the University of Wisconsin, surveys the role of Hiroshima and Nagasaki in American memory. At one end of the spectrum of meaning, he notes, Hiroshima became a symbol of righteous vengeance, a demonstration of America's technological and scientific superiority, a savior of American and Japanese lives that would have been lost in an invasion of the Japanese homeland. As noted earlier, this was the official memory of the atomic bombings. It was offered by President Truman, Secretary of War Henry L. Stimson, and other decision makers in the immediate aftermath of the war and was protected by a pattern of censorship that prevented the emergence of an alternative narrative. Nevertheless, a different history, a countermemory, eventually emerged at the other end of the spectrum of meaning. In this history, Hiroshima and Nagasaki became studies in flawed decision making and symbols of the fate that awaited all mankind if the superpowers did not disarm.

As this suggests, the meaning of Hiroshima has been contested in the United States, as it has been in Japan, where it now calls up the image of Japan as both victim and victimizer. Religious beliefs and generational differences, as well as political ideology, colored American perceptions of the event. The view embraced by antinuclear activists, a dark view of atomic holocaust, rose and fell with the rhythms of the peace movement in the postwar period. The official view, protected by government censorship and actively promoted by public officials, became the view of most Americans. Eventually challenged by scholarly monographs, it remained part of the collective memory as encoded in high school textbooks. Even most college textbooks, as J. Samuel Walker shows in his second contribution to this volume, continued to view the atomic bombing of Japan as the only alternative to a costly invasion.

Although memories of the actual event have begun to fade with the passing of the war generation, Hiroshima has lost none of its symbolic power, as I try to show in my essay on the controversial plans to mount a public display of the *Enola Gay* at the Smithsonian Institution's Air and Space Museum. On one level, that controversy highlights the tension that often exists between history and memory. Involved, in other words, was a clash between a historical analysis of the Hiroshima and Nagasaki bombings, particularly of the death and destruction at ground zero, and a collective memory that essentially idealized those events. What is more, the debate over the exhibit clearly illustrated how powerful groups can appropriate the past for political purposes. More was involved in this case than what the Hiroshima narrative had to say about the heroism of American veterans. At stake as well was what contemporary representations of the past should say about American identity and national purpose.

Taken together, the essays in this volume should make for interesting and stimulating reading. The authors often take sides in the historiographical and political controversies that have followed in the wake of Hiroshima and Nagasaki. But the essays are not intended to force the reader into the same corners occupied by the authors. Instead, they are published here so that the reader can see how those corners are drawn. They give readers less familiar with the subject a picture of how scholarship on the atomic bombing of Japan has changed over time. They also provide a good introduction to the study of memory, to the opposition that can exist between history and memory, and to the politics that often surrounds the representation of historical events in contemporary society.

2

*The Decision to Use the Bomb: A Historiographical Update**

J. SAMUEL WALKER

To commemorate the fiftieth anniversary of the end of World War II, the National Air and Space Museum, a part of the Smithsonian Institution, made plans for an exhibit featuring a section of the fuselage of the *Enola Gay*, the plane that dropped the atomic bomb on Hiroshima in August 1945. Curators consulted with an advisory committee of experts on the use of the bomb in an effort to ensure that the exhibit was historically accurate and consistent with recent scholarly findings. Although museum officials were acutely aware that the subject was controversial, they were ill-prepared for the outrage that early drafts of the script triggered. Veterans' groups led a fusillade of attacks that accused the Smithsonian of making the use of the bomb appear aggressive, immoral, and unjustified. The *Wall Street Journal*, for example, condemned "scriptwriters [who] disdain any belief that the decision to drop the bomb could have been inspired by something other than racism or blood-lust."

The Smithsonian modified its script in response to the complaints of veterans, members of Congress, and a chorus of other critics, and eventually drastically scaled back the planned exhibit to eliminate any analysis of the reasons that the bomb was used. This elicited protests from scholars that the museum had sacrificed historical accuracy to accommodate political pressures. The outcry over the Smithsonian's exhibit plans vividly demonstrated that the decision to use the bomb remained an emotionally charged issue,

*This article expresses the personal views of the author. It does not represent an official position of the U.S. Nuclear Regulatory Commission or any other agency of the federal government.

even nearly half a century after the end of World War II. It also graphically illustrated the wide gap between popular and scholarly views of the reasons for the atomic attacks on Japanese cities. In an article on the "new battle of Hiroshima," *Newsweek* magazine summarized the interpretation that prevailed in popular perceptions: "The U.S. calculation, grimly momentous though it was, seems inescapable: an invasion of Japan would have been bloodier than the bombing." Scholarly investigations, however, have shown that President Harry S. Truman never faced a categorical choice between an invasion and the bomb and that the issues surrounding the use of atomic weapons were much more complex. Those studies have produced a rich and controversial historiography.[1]

Questions about the wisdom and morality of using the bomb arose shortly after Hiroshima. The central issue in a rather sporadic debate among scholars, journalists, former government officials, and publicists was whether the bomb was necessary to end the war against Japan promptly or whether other means were available to achieve the same goal. The prevailing view, advanced by former policymakers and supported by most scholars, held that the bomb obviated the need for an invasion of Japan, accelerated the conclusion of the war, and saved a vast number of American lives. But several writers, including Norman Cousins and Thomas K. Finletter, P. M. S. Blackett, Carl Marzani, William Appleman Williams, and D. F. Fleming, suggested that the bomb was not essential for a rapid end to the war and/or that its use was dictated more by political than by military considerations.[2]

1 *Wall Street Journal*, 29 August 1994; *Washington Post*, 26 and 30 September 1994; *New York Times*, 11 October 1994 and 31 January 1995; Bill Powell with Daniel Glick, "The New Battle of Hiroshima," *Newsweek*, 29 August 1994, 36. For a discussion of popular views of the decision to use the bomb see J. Samuel Walker, "History, Collective Memory, and the Decision to Use the Bomb," in this volume.
2 For a valuable detailed essay on the literature before 1974 see Barton J. Bernstein, "The Atomic Bomb and American Foreign Policy, 1941–1945: An Historiographical Controversy," *Peace and Change* 2 (Spring 1974): 1–16. This essay focuses on publications that have appeared since that time.
    The orthodox position on the use of the bomb is clearly outlined in Henry L. Stimson, "The Decision to Use the Atomic Bomb," *Harper's* 197 (February 1947): 97–107; Harry S. Truman, *Memoirs: Year of Decisions* (Garden City, 1955); and Samuel Eliot Morison, "Why Japan Surrendered," *The Atlantic* 206 (October 1960): 41–7. For early dissenting views see Norman Cousins and Thomas K. Finletter, "A Beginning for Sanity," *Saturday Review of Literature* 29 (15 June 1946): 5–9; P. M. S. Blackett, *Military and Political Consequences of Atomic Energy* (London, 1948); Carl Marzani,

In the first scholarly treatment of the subject based on extensive research in primary sources, Herbert Feis supplied an authoritative, though not definitive, evaluation of those issues. He declared without equivocation in 1961 that the bomb was not needed to force Japan's surrender "on [American] terms within a few months." Feis endorsed the U.S. Strategic Bombing Survey's conclusion that the war would have been over no later than the end of 1945 even without the bomb, Soviet entry into the war, or an invasion of the Japanese islands. But he argued that even though the bomb was not essential to end the war, its use was justified. American policymakers, he maintained, were convinced that dropping the bomb would save "probably tens of thousands" of American lives. Feis insisted that "the impelling reason for the decision to use [the bomb] was military – to end the war victoriously as soon as possible."[3]

Gar Alperovitz's *Atomic Diplomacy*, published in 1965, directly challenged Feis's conclusions and triggered a sharply contested historiographical dispute. Alperovitz contended that political rather than military considerations were the key to understanding the use of the bomb; he insisted that it was dropped primarily to impress the Soviets rather than to defeat the Japanese. His book received far more attention and stirred far greater discord than earlier works that had argued along the same lines, in part because he drew from recently opened sources to reconstruct events in unprecedented detail, in part because of growing uneasiness about the conduct of U.S. foreign policy in Vietnam, and in part because of the emerging scholarly debate over the origins of the Cold War.

Alperovitz agreed with Feis that the bomb was not needed to end the war in Asia but differed with him about the reasons that it was used. In his view, President Truman and his advisers saw the bomb as a diplomatic lever that could be employed to thwart Soviet ambitions in Eastern Europe and Asia. Soon after taking office, Truman reversed Franklin D. Roosevelt's efforts to cooperate with the Soviets by condemning them for their actions in Poland. After learning about the prospects for the bomb, however, he

We Can Be Friends (New York, 1952); William Appleman Williams, *The Tragedy of American Diplomacy* (Cleveland, 1959); and D. F. Fleming, *The Cold War and Its Origins* (Garden City, 1961).

3 Herbert Feis, *Japan Subdued: The Atomic Bomb and the End of the War in the Pacific* (Princeton, 1961).

adopted a "strategy of a delayed showdown" in order to avoid a confrontation with the Soviets and postpone the Potsdam meeting until the bomb was tested. If it proved successful, it could not only strengthen the diplomatic position of the United States in opposing Soviet policies in Eastern Europe but also end the war against Japan before the Soviets invaded and gained control of Manchuria.

Alperovitz argued that political considerations, not military ones, explained why the Truman administration did not explore alternatives to using the bomb to end the war, such as investigating the seriousness of Japanese peace initiatives, moderating the demand for unconditional surrender, or waiting for the Soviets to declare war on Japan. He further asserted that the bomb raised the confidence of American policymakers that they could successfully challenge Soviet expansionism in Europe and Asia, and that armed with the bomb, they mounted a "diplomatic offensive" after Hiroshima. In short, Alperovitz emphasized three main themes: the prospect of having the bomb was the guiding factor in the U.S. posture toward the Soviet Union in the spring and summer of 1945; the anticipated impact of the bomb on Soviet-American relations was crucial in motivating the Truman administration to use it; and the monopoly of atomic technology brought about policy shifts by the United States that played an important role in causing the Cold War.[4]

Alperovitz's "revisionist" thesis provoked a spirited reaction from a diverse array of scholars who agreed on little except that he was wrong. Gabriel Kolko, the most doctrinaire of New Left interpreters of the beginning of the Cold War, did not view use of the bomb as a major policy or moral issue and dismissed it as a factor in causing U.S.-Soviet discord. From a quite different perspective, Thomas T. Hammond, who found it "almost incredible that the United States failed to take fullest advantage of its atomic monopoly in 1945," described Alperovitz's findings as "implausible, exaggerated, or unsupported by the evidence." Perhaps the harshest attack came from Robert James Maddox, who, after checking Alperovitz's footnotes, called *Atomic Diplomacy* a piece of "creative writing." He thought it "disconcerting . . . that such a work

4   Gar Alperovitz, *Atomic Diplomacy: Hiroshima and Potsdam* (New York, 1965).

could have come to be considered a contribution to the historical literature on the period." Despite the criticism, many scholars took Alperovitz's arguments seriously. His book spurred a great deal of scholarly effort that was designed, implicitly or explicitly, to test his hypothesis.[5]

By the mid-1970s, several important new studies, aided by the opening of key primary sources, had discounted parts of Alperovitz's position but substantiated others. Lisle A. Rose defended the Truman administration against some of Alperovitz's criticisms. He disagreed that Truman adopted a "strategy of delay" by postponing the Potsdam Conference in hopes that the bomb would be tested by the time the meeting began. He denied that the United States practiced any form of atomic diplomacy at Potsdam or bombed Hiroshima for political reasons. Despite his generally sympathetic view of Truman, however, Rose condemned the administration for attempting to take advantage of its atomic monopoly after the war to win diplomatic gains from the Soviet Union, and he denounced the destruction of Hiroshima and Nagasaki as "vile acts."[6]

Martin J. Sherwin found Alperovitz's interpretation more persuasive than did Rose, but he also took issue with some of the key points in *Atomic Diplomacy*. In *A World Destroyed*, Sherwin stressed that a full understanding of U.S. atomic policies required an examination of Roosevelt's as well as Truman's actions. He showed that from the beginning of the Manhattan Project, senior policymakers viewed the bomb as only a potential weapon and left any decisions about how it would be used for the future. They never seriously questioned whether it would be used at all if it became available. Roosevelt was secretive in his treatment of atomic energy issues, and he ruled out sharing information about the bomb project with the Soviet Union. After assuming the presidency, Truman quickly adopted a firmer posture toward the Sovi-

5 Gabriel Kolko, *The Politics of War: The World and United States Foreign Policy, 1943–1945* (New York, 1968); Thomas T. Hammond, " 'Atomic Diplomacy' Revisited," *Orbis* 19 (Winter 1976): 1403–28; Robert James Maddox, "*Atomic Diplomacy*: A Study in Creative Writing," *Journal of American History* 59 (March 1973): 925–34; idem, *The New Left and the Origins of the Cold War* (Princeton, 1973); Bernstein, "Atomic Bomb and American Foreign Policy," 10–12.

6 Lisle A. Rose, *Dubious Victory: The United States and the End of World War II* (Kent, OH, 1973).

ets than Roosevelt had taken, but Sherwin found no evidence of an elaborately planned showdown or "strategy of delay" in dealing with them.

Sherwin argued that the principal motive for using the bomb was to end the war as soon as possible. Policymakers saw no reason to reassess their assumption that the bomb would be dropped once it was ready. Sherwin agreed with Alperovitz that high-level officials viewed the bomb as a political weapon that could provide diplomatic leverage, but he regarded such considerations as secondary to the military ones. While denying any "diabolical motivations" on the part of the Truman administration, he regretted that it did not seriously weigh alternatives to the bomb. He suggested that modifying the unconditional surrender terms might have made the bombing of Hiroshima unnecessary and submitted that the attack on Nagasaki was indefensible.[7]

In an article published in 1975, Barton J. Bernstein, addressing Alperovitz's interpretation more directly than Sherwin, arrived at similar conclusions. Bernstein also emphasized the influence and momentum of Roosevelt's legacy in effectively narrowing the options available to Truman in dealing with the bomb. Like his predecessor, Truman assumed that the bomb was a legitimate weapon of war and was unlikely to change long-standing policies without any compelling reason to do so. Bernstein considered five possible alternatives to using the bomb to end the war: waiting for Soviet entry into the Far Eastern conflict; demonstrating the power of the bomb by setting off a warning shot in an uninhabited area; mitigating the demand for Japan's unconditional surrender; exploring the proposals of Japanese "peace feelers"; and relying solely on conventional weapons. He argued that each alternative seemed to policymakers to be less desirable, less feasible, or riskier than the atomic bomb option.

Bernstein emphasized that policymakers saw no reason to avoid dropping the bomb. They used it primarily to end the war and save American lives. They hoped the bomb would provide political

7   Martin J. Sherwin, *A World Destroyed: The Atomic Bomb and the Grand Alliance* (New York, 1975). Sherwin introduced his major arguments in "The Atomic Bomb and the Origins of the Cold War: U.S. Atomic Energy Policy and Diplomacy, 1941–1945," *American Historical Review* 78 (October 1973): 945–68.

gains by helping win diplomatic concessions from the Soviets, but this was, in Bernstein's estimation, "a bonus." He concurred with Alperovitz that the Truman administration wielded the bomb as a part of its diplomatic arsenal after the war, which he believed intensified but did not in itself cause the Cold War. Although he accepted parts of Alperovitz's thesis, Bernstein cast doubt on many of the arguments in and the emphasis of *Atomic Diplomacy*. Oddly enough, for a prominent Cold War revisionist, Bernstein came off in this article as a defender of the Truman administration, at least from much of the criticism that Alperovitz leveled against it.[8]

Other scholars who examined the question of the use of the bomb in the context of the developing Cold War agreed with the major points made by Sherwin and Bernstein. Several major works, in brief discussions of the decision to drop the bomb, supported the thesis that the Truman administration used it primarily for military reasons but also hoped that an additional result would be increased diplomatic power. Thus, John Lewis Gaddis, in a book that preceded the appearance of Sherwin's and Bernstein's analyses, and Daniel Yergin and Robert J. Donovan, in books that followed their publication, largely rejected Alperovitz's specific arguments but still accepted a key part of his overall framework. Gregg Herken concurred that the bomb served both military and diplomatic purposes and stressed how Truman and Secretary of War Henry L. Stimson carefully weighed its political implications. In a study of James F. Byrnes, the most unabashed proponent of atomic diplomacy, Robert L. Messer took a similar view. While denying Alperovitz's contention that the bomb was a major consideration in American planning for the Potsdam Conference, he criticized Truman and Byrnes for harboring illusions that possession of it "would save China, preserve the Open Door, make the Russians more manageable in Europe, and allow American leaders to dictate their own terms for the peace."[9]

8 Barton J. Bernstein, "Roosevelt, Truman, and the Atomic Bomb, 1941–1945: A Reinterpretation," *Political Science Quarterly* 90 (Spring 1975): 23–69.

9 John Lewis Gaddis, *The United States and the Origins of the Cold War, 1941–1947* (New York, 1972); Daniel Yergin, *Shattered Peace: The Origins of the Cold War and the National Security State* (Boston, 1977); Robert J. Donovan, *Conflict and Crisis: The Presidency of Harry S. Truman, 1945–1948* (New York, 1977); Gregg Herken, *The*

Long after its publication, the impact of Alperovitz's *Atomic Diplomacy* on serious historical writing was apparent. In important ways, it shaped the debate over the bomb and how historians approached it. Before the book appeared, few scholars took seriously the argument that political objectives had played a vital role in the decision to use the bomb. After it appeared, a broad consensus viewed diplomatic considerations as an important part of the administration's view of the bomb's value. This would have been inconceivable before *Atomic Diplomacy*. The book redirected the focus of questions that scholars asked about the bomb. The major issue was no longer whether the bomb was necessary to end the war as soon as possible. Rather, the central questions had become: What factors were paramount in the decision to use the bomb and why was its use more attractive to policymakers than other alternatives? The best historical scholarship on the subject drew on a rich lode of recently opened sources, including the diary of Henry L. Stimson, the records of the Manhattan Project, the papers and diary of Joseph Davies, the notes of Byrnes's aide Walter Brown, and portions of the Roosevelt and Truman papers, to address those questions.

Scholars working on the subject did not offer unqualified comfort either to supporters or detractors of Alperovitz's point of view. They sharply criticized his thesis in some respects, especially his emphasis on the "strategy of delay," the primacy of diplomatic goals, and the carefully plotted coherence of the Truman administration's policies. In general, they found that Alperovitz had exaggerated the impact of the bomb on the thinking of American leaders. But most scholars still subscribed to important elements of his interpretation, especially his claims that the bomb influenced American attitudes toward the Soviet Union and that diplomatic considerations played a role in deliberations on using the bomb against Japan.

At that point, despite differences of opinion over some specific issues, the historiographical debate over the bomb seemed largely settled. The latest scholarship combined the traditional view that

Winning Weapon: The Atomic Bomb and the Cold War, 1945–1950 (New York, 1980); Robert L. Messer, *The End of an Alliance: James F. Byrnes, Roosevelt, Truman, and the Origins of the Cold War* (Chapel Hill, 1982).

the United States dropped the bomb primarily for military reasons with the revisionist assertion that its inclusion in America's diplomatic arsenal aggravated tensions with the Soviet Union. The consensus did not go unchallenged for long, however. Important new evidence – Truman's handwritten diary notes of the Potsdam Conference, which were published in 1980, and private letters he had written to his wife, which were published in 1983 – prompted a reexamination of some important questions.

Truman's diary notes and letters provided the best available evidence about his understanding of and thoughts on the implications of the bomb at the time of Potsdam. But the new materials did not offer clear answers to the questions that had intrigued scholars. Indeed, as Robert Messer pointed out in a special issue of the *Bulletin of the Atomic Scientists* on the fortieth anniversary of Hiroshima, their implications for the historiographical debate over the use of the bomb were decidedly ambivalent. For example, after meeting with Josef Stalin for the first time, Truman recorded in his diary that the Soviet premier promised to enter the war against Japan on 15 August 1945, and added: "Fini Japs when that comes about." Here, then, was striking testimony that the president knew that the bomb was not needed to end the war quickly. This and other notations supported Alperovitz's contention that military requirements were not the primary reasons for using the bomb.[10]

But as Messer suggested, other statements Truman made seemed "to disprove the revisionist contention that he did not want 'the Russians' in the war at all." For a time, the president continued to express hope that the Soviets would enter the war promptly, which appeared to contradict the claim that one purpose of dropping the bomb was to keep the Soviets out of the war. This discrepancy can

10 Robert L. Messer, "New Evidence on Truman's Decision," *Bulletin of the Atomic Scientists* 41 (August 1985): 50–6. The diary notes are printed in Eduard Mark, "Today Has Been a Historical One: Harry S. Truman's Diary of the Potsdam Conference," *Diplomatic History* 4 (Summer 1980): 317–26; Barton J. Bernstein, "Truman at Potsdam: His Secret Diary," *Foreign Service Journal* 57 (July/August 1980): 29–36; and Robert H. Ferrell, ed., *Off the Record: The Private Papers of Harry S. Truman* (New York, 1980). Ferrell made no comment on the implications of the diary for the debate over the use of the bomb, but he did suggest that it provided evidence of duplicity on the part of Stalin. See Ferrell, ed., "Truman at Potsdam," *American Heritage* 31 (June/July 1980): 36–47. Truman's letters to his wife are published in Robert H. Ferrell, ed., *Dear Bess: The Letters from Harry to Bess Truman, 1910–1959* (New York, 1983).

be resolved by the fact that Truman and his advisers decided shortly after learning details about the power of the bomb tested in New Mexico that Soviet entry into the war was neither necessary nor desirable.

Yet other Truman statements in his diary and his letters from Potsdam raise further questions about his views. He told his wife on 18 July (before receiving details about the test shot): "I've gotten what I came for – Stalin goes to war August 15 with no strings on it." He added: "I'll say that we'll end the war a year sooner now, and think of the kids who won't be killed!" Did Truman at that time really believe that the war could last another year? If so, in contrast to other of his comments, it could support the traditional argument that his principal motive for using the bomb was to shorten the war. But on the same day that the president wrote to his wife about ending the war a year early, he recorded in his diary: "Believe Japs will fold before Russia comes in. I am sure they will when Manhattan appears over their homeland." This seems to suggest that Truman saw the bomb as a way not only to end the war sooner than expected but also to keep the Soviets out of it. The Truman documents are fascinating but inconclusive and sometimes contradictory. As Messer pointed out: "The evidence of the Potsdam diary and letters does not close the book on the question of why the bomb was dropped. Rather it opens it to a previously unseen page."[11]

If Truman's notes and letters muddied the historiographical waters, three books published around the fortieth anniversary of Hiroshima did little to clear them. Each was written by a professional journalist who regretted the use of the bomb but did not directly address the issues debated by historians. The best of them was Richard Rhodes's *The Making of the Atomic Bomb*, which focused on the scientific and technical complexities that had to be overcome to build an atomic bomb. Rhodes delivered an absorbing narrative of the problems and personalities involved in the Manhattan Project but discussed the decision to drop the bomb only briefly. He maintained that once the weapon proved successful, "men discovered reasons to use it." In a brutal and barbaric

11 Messer, "New Evidence on Truman's Decision," 55–6; Ferrell, ed., *Off the Record*, 53–4; idem, ed., *Dear Bess*, 519.

war, the very existence of the bomb assured that it would be used without much thought of the long-range policy or human consequences. In *Day One*, Peter Wyden placed the primary burden for Hiroshima on the atomic scientists who plunged ahead with work on the bomb despite its potential dangers and the threat it posed to postwar peace. He largely absolved policymakers of ultimate responsibility for using the bomb because he believed that they were incapable of understanding the scientific principles or long-term political implications of nuclear weapons. Since Truman and his advisers were unable to control the speed or direction of events, the existence of the bomb guaranteed its use. In *Day of the Bomb*, Dan Kurzman described the developments leading to Hiroshima in a series of personality vignettes that never came together to form a thesis.[12]

Unlike Rhodes, Wyden, and Kurzman, Gar Alperovitz showed no reluctance to deal explicitly with historiographical issues. In an updated edition of *Atomic Diplomacy* published in 1985, he struck back at his critics. He dismissed Rose's work, and although both Sherwin's and Bernstein's conclusions were more to his liking, he still found them objectionable in important respects. Alperovitz contested their emphasis on the weight of Roosevelt's legacy in limiting Truman's options. He argued that the changing situation in Japan gave Truman wide latitude to revise policies he inherited from Roosevelt, and furthermore, that the president realized that the bomb was not necessary to end the war because a number of prominent advisers, including chief of staff William D. Leahy, General Dwight D. Eisenhower, and Undersecretary of the Navy Ralph Bard, told him so. Reaffirming his belief in a "strategy of delay" and in the possibility of ending the war on favorable terms without the bomb, Alperovitz challenged the view that the United States dropped it primarily for military reasons. He insisted that there was no "overriding military necessity" for the bomb and

---

12 Richard Rhodes, *The Making of the Atomic Bomb* (New York, 1987); Peter Wyden, *Day One: Before Hiroshima and After* (New York, 1984); Dan Kurzman, *Day of the Bomb: Countdown to Hiroshima* (New York, 1986). For a review that criticized Rhodes for, among other things, neglecting key sources, embroidering the sources he used, and failing to analyze important issues surrounding the decision to use the bomb, see Barton J. Bernstein, "An Analysis of 'Two Cultures': Writing about the Making and Using of the Atomic Bombs," *Public Historian* 12 (Spring 1990): 83-107.

that Truman and his closest aides knew it. Therefore, in his estimation, only the desire to impress the Soviets and to achieve diplomatic objectives could explain why Truman disdained alternatives to end the war and hastened to use the bomb. In short, after considering the new evidence and interpretations of other scholars, Alperovitz altered his opinions of twenty years earlier very little. In fact, the only changes he said he would make in his first edition would be to place greater stress on Byrnes's role in atomic policy-making and to move material originally located in an appendix into the main body of text.[13]

While Alperovitz was reasserting the correctness of his own position, other scholars were reexamining a number of old issues in light of new evidence and arriving at some fresh conclusions. One such question was whether the bomb was necessary to save large numbers of American lives. Although several writers had addressed this matter by suggesting that the war could have ended and the loss of life been averted without the bomb, new sources indicated that even in the worst case U.S. casualties would have been far fewer than former policymakers asserted after the war. In explaining why the United States had dropped the bomb, Truman, Stimson, and others argued that an invasion of the Japanese islands could have caused half a million American deaths, one million American casualties, or some other appalling figure (the number varied from person to person and time to time). But Rufus E. Miles, Jr., pointed out in an article published in 1985 that during the war, military planners never projected casualty figures that were even close to those cited by Truman and his advisers after the war. Even in the unlikely event than an invasion had been necessary, the pre-surrender estimates did not exceed twenty thousand. Barton J. Bernstein, drawing on newly opened records, found the worst-case prediction to be a loss of forty-six thousand lives, still far short of the policymakers' claims. "The myth of the 500,000 American lives saved," he concluded, "thus seems to have no basis in fact." More recently, John Ray Skates, writing on plans for the

13 Gar Alperovitz, *Atomic Diplomacy: Hiroshima and Potsdam*, rev. ed. (New York, 1985). Barton J. Bernstein argued that Eisenhower did not object to using the bomb against Japan in "Ike and Hiroshima: Did He Oppose It?" *Journal of Strategic Studies* 10 (September 1987): 377–89.

invasion of Japan, offered the same view. "The record," he observed, "does not support the postwar claims of huge Allied casualties to be suffered in the invasion of Japan."[14]

The sparing of forty-six thousand or twenty thousand or many fewer lives might well have provided ample justification for using the bomb, but Truman and other high-level officials did not choose to make a case on those grounds. Indeed, as James G. Hershberg and Bernstein demonstrated, former government authorities consciously and artfully constructed the history of the decision to discourage questions about it. The leader in this effort was James B. Conant, one of the key scientific administrators of the Manhattan Project, who persuaded Stimson to write an article explaining and justifying the use of the bomb as a way of heading off criticism of Truman's action. Stimson's article, which appeared in *Harper's* in 1947, suggested that the atomic attacks had prevented one mil-

14   Rufus E. Miles, Jr., "Hiroshima: The Strange Myth of Half a Million American Lives Saved," *International Security* 10 (Fall 1985): 121–40; Barton J. Bernstein, "A Postwar Myth: 500,000 U.S. Lives Saved," *Bulletin of the Atomic Scientists* 42 (June/July 1986): 38–40; John Ray Skates, *The Invasion of Japan: Alternative to the Bomb* (Columbia, SC, 1994) In brief discussions of the same issue, Martin J. Sherwin and Michael S. Sherry offered support for the view set forth by Miles, Bernstein, and Skates. See Sherwin, *A World Destroyed: Hiroshima and the Origins of the Arms Race*, rev. ed. (New York, 1987); and Sherry, *The Rise of American Air Power: The Creation of Armageddon* (New Haven, 1987).

Edward J. Drea challenged the much lower estimates of Allied casualties in a brief discussion of the issue in his book *MacArthur's ULTRA: Codebreaking and the War against Japan, 1942–1945* (Lawrence, 1992). He based his argument largely on a letter that Truman sent in early 1953 to historians writing an official account of the role of the air force in the Pacific war. Drea suggested that a rapid Japanese buildup of forces on Kyushu so alarmed General Marshall that he told Truman at Potsdam that the invasion of Kyushu and later of Honshu would cost 250,000 to 1,000,000 American casualties. Robert H. Ferrell used this information to support his argument that Truman had received very large casualty projections before the bomb was dropped. In Ferrell's view, Truman "faced the dreadful choice of ordering the army and navy into an invasion of the home islands, with untold numbers of casualties, or ending the war as soon as possible" by using the bomb. See Ferrell, *Harry S. Truman: A Life* (Columbia, MO, 1994). But Truman's claim of hearing estimates of such large numbers from Marshall is very dubious. Bernstein has shown that the meeting at which Marshall supposedly gave the high estimates to Truman almost certainly never took place. The upper end of the casualty projections was a creation of White House staff officials, who wished to bring Truman's estimates into line with those published earlier by Stimson. See Bernstein, "Writing, Righting, or Wronging the Historical Record: President Truman's Letter on His Atomic-Bomb Decision," *Diplomatic History* 16 (Winter 1992): 163–73. To date, no contemporaneous evidence has been found to support estimates of deaths or casualties from an invasion in the range claimed by Stimson, Truman, and others after the war.

lion American casualties – a number that formed the basis for others' claims of U.S. lives saved by the bomb.[15]

Scholars have not provided a single explanation for why former policymakers felt compelled to exaggerate by several orders of magnitude the estimated casualties of an invasion of Japan. Presumably they believed that citing a huge number made the decision to use the bomb appear unassailable or, at a minimum, less vulnerable to the ambiguities that smaller (and more accurate) estimates might have created. Hershberg found that Conant, in addition to his conviction that the bomb had shortened the war, worried about the impact of a loss of public support for nuclear weapons. Only if the American people demonstrated the will to use their atomic arsenal, he reasoned, would the Soviets be amenable to nuclear arms control agreements. Although Conant did not provide the estimates that Stimson cited – the source of the figure of one million casualties is unknown – he was the driving force behind the effort to persuade the public that the use of atomic weapons against Japan had been a sound and proper action.

Hershberg also suggested that Conant's position was influenced by unacknowledged feelings of guilt. "His bristling, his anxiety, and his marshaling of support for the decision to use the bomb reveal an intense personal sensitivity over how history would judge his role in the event," Hershberg submitted, "and a yearning to believe that Hiroshima's destruction was necessary to win both the war *and* the peace." Bernstein speculated that, in a similar manner, Truman felt more ambivalent about dropping the bomb than he ever admitted. This would explain, he argued, not only the need to inflate the number of lives saved by the bomb but also Truman's apparent self-delusion that it had been used on "purely military" targets. Robert L. Messer also addressed the intriguing question of Truman's state of mind regarding the bomb. He suggested that even though the president never acknowledged any feelings of remorse, he harbored a heavy burden of guilt arising from the dis-

15   James G. Hershberg, *James B. Conant: Harvard to Hiroshima and the Making of the Nuclear Age* (New York, 1993); Barton J. Bernstein, "Seizing the Contested Terrain of Early Nuclear History: Stimson, Conant, and Their Allies Explain the Decision to Use the Atomic Bomb," *Diplomatic History* 17 (Winter 1993): 35–72.

crepancy between the mass slaughter of civilians and his own moral convictions.[16]

The observations on the inner conflicts of Truman and other leading American officials added a new dimension to what was always a key, though often unstated, issue in the debate over the bomb: Was its use morally justified? This is, of course, a highly subjective judgment that has usually been implied more than explicitly discussed. If, as the defenders of the Truman administration maintained, the bomb shortened the war and saved lives, the morality of its use is defensible. But if, as many critics suggested, the bomb was not needed to end the war promptly or to save lives, then its morality seems highly questionable.[17] Some writers sidestepped this dichotomy by arguing that war is inherently immoral and that the atomic bombs were no more heinous than the firebombs and napalm that killed tens of thousands of civilians before Hiroshima. The moral desolation of the Pacific war was graphically illustrated by John Dower's *War without Mercy*, which described the atrocities carried out by both sides and reconstructed the cultural context in which the bomb was used. Dower showed that Americans viewed the Japanese as depraved, contemptible, ape-like subhumans, or alternatively, as fanatical, ruthless, and cruel superhumans. Although he said little about the bomb, it seems clear that both images he depicted discouraged open-minded consideration of the moral implications of using it.[18]

The moral aspects of the use of the bomb were addressed more thoroughly and directly in two studies of American strategic bombing policy during World War II. Ronald Schaffer traced the evolution of bombing theory and practice from the precision strikes of the early war to the indiscriminate bombing of cities by the end of the war. The atomic attacks on Hiroshima and Nagasaki were a

16 Hershberg, *James B. Conant*, 279–304 (emphasis in original); Bernstein, "A Postwar Myth," 40, and "Truman at Potsdam," 32; Robert L. Messer, "America's 'Sacred Trust': Truman and the Bomb, 1945–1949" (Paper presented at the annual meeting of the American Historical Association, 1987).

17 For a recent article that departs from the pattern by stating very clearly its argument that the use of the bomb was morally unjustified see Richard H. Minear, "Atomic Holocaust, Nazi Holocaust: Some Reflections," *Diplomatic History* 19 (Spring 1995): 347–65.

18 John W. Dower, *War without Mercy: Race and Power in the Pacific War* (New York, 1986).

logical extension of the rationales developed for terror bombing with conventional weapons. Schaffer found that American leaders and scientists weighed the moral issues involved in the use of the atomic bomb. With the exception of the removal of the ancient city of Kyoto from the target list, however, he submitted that "moral constraints in the hearts and minds of those responsible for the American air war do not seem to have prevented them from employing any of the measures they contemplated using against Japan." Michael S. Sherry agreed that use of nuclear bombs could only be understood in the context of previous U.S. strategic policies. Although the moral aspects of American bombing were not the central theme of his book, as they were with Schaffer's, they were an important and vivid part of it. Sherry suggested that scholars had focused too narrowly on the "sin of atomic bombing," which, "like the sin of the whole war's bombing," resulted from "a slow accretion of large fears, thoughtless assumptions, and incremental decisions."[19]

Assessing the moral implications of the bomb inevitably leads to examining the possible alternatives to it. Several scholars have raised anew the question of why the administration did not pursue, or explore more thoroughly, other options. One was to modify the demand for unconditional surrender and give clear assurances to the Japanese that they could retain the emperor. Sherry contended that the failure to do this was "the most tragic blunder in American surrender policy." Although he acknowledged that such an offer would not have guaranteed an immediate Japanese surrender, he argued that the risks were small and the "moral risks . . . in pursuing an atomic solution . . . were large." Sherry did not view the refusal to soften unconditional surrender and the decision to drop the bomb as an effort to achieve political goals, however. He saw the use of the bomb as an outgrowth of momentum, confu-

---

19 Ronald Schaffer, *Wings of Judgment: American Bombing in World War II* (New York, 1985); Sherry, *Rise of American Air Power*, 301–41, 363. Conrad C. Crane took issue with Schaffer and Sherry by arguing that the United States remained committed to precision bombing throughout the European war. But he agreed that precision bombing in Japan gave way to indiscriminate terror bombing after Curtis LeMay took command of air operations against Japan in early 1945. The atomic bombings were a small step from the "fire raids" against Japanese cities. See Crane, *Bombs, Cities, and Civilians: American Airpower Strategy in World War II* (Lawrence, 1993).

sion, and the "technological fanaticism" that had overtaken American bombing policy.[20]

Martin J. Sherwin criticized the Truman administration even more severely than Sherry and, indeed, more sharply than in his own *A World Destroyed*. He suggested that Truman rejected the idea of modifying the unconditional surrender terms partly for domestic political reasons and partly because "he preferred to use the atomic bomb" to strengthen America's diplomatic position. He further maintained that by electing to wait for the bomb, Truman prolonged the war; it might have ended sooner if the president had moderated the demand for unconditional surrender. Kai Erikson briefly explored another alternative to dropping the bomb on a densely populated city. He examined the question of why the United States did not fire a warning shot by dropping the bomb on a "relatively uninhabited" Japanese target. This would have given enemy leaders a graphic display of what would happen if they did not surrender promptly. The risks of this kind of demonstration were minimal; if it did not work other bombs could still be used on the cities on the target list. Erikson was troubled that neither this nor any other option received serious consideration from American policymakers. He attributed their aversion to any alternative to the bomb to a number of military and political factors, the most important of which was "the wish to make a loud announcement to the Russians."[21]

In a book he published forty years after coauthoring Henry L. Stimson's memoirs, McGeorge Bundy disagreed that the bomb's potential impact on the Soviet Union was a major factor in its use. But he, too, lamented that the highest officials in the Truman administration did not carefully weigh alternatives to the bomb; he acknowledged that Stimson had overstated the extent to which the administration considered other options. In yet another twist on this theme, Bundy suggested that if the United States had admitted respected neutral observers to the successful atomic test shot at Alamogordo, New Mexico, they might have provided a convincing

20 Sherry, *Rise of American Air Power*, 255, 301–56.
21 Martin J. Sherwin, "Hiroshima and Modern Memory," *Nation*, 10 October 1981, 329, 349–53; Kai Erikson, "Of Accidental Judgments and Casual Slaughters," ibid., 3/ 10 August 1985, 80–5.

and effective warning to the Japanese about the power of the bomb. While a number of scholars reopened questions about alternatives to the bomb and faulted the Truman administration for not pursuing them, Akira Iriye argued that the Japanese government shared the blame for needlessly extending the war. He was particularly critical of Japanese leaders for sending peace feelers to the Soviet Union rather than attempting to deal directly with the United States.[22]

Barton Bernstein took issue with those who argued that the war could have ended as soon or even sooner than it did without using the bomb. He suggested that none of the alternatives available to U.S. policymakers – demonstrating the bomb in an isolated location, modifying the unconditional surrender demand, exploring the initiatives of Japanese peace feelers, waiting for Soviet entry into the Asian war, or continuing the naval blockade and intensifying conventional bombing – would have brought the war to a conclusion as rapidly as dropping the bomb. He doubted that any of the alternatives, taken alone, would have been sufficient to force a prompt Japanese surrender. Bernstein concluded that it seems "very likely, though certainly not definite," that a combination of alternatives would have ended the war before the planned invasion of Kyushu on 1 November 1945. Bernstein's disagreement with other scholars over the role of the bomb in determining how soon the war came to a close was necessarily speculative, and the question is unlikely to reach a definitive resolution. But it reopened a historiographical debate that had seemed to be settled, at least among scholars writing on the subject in the 1980s, who had suggested that the bomb was not necessary to end the war as quickly as possible.[23]

Key issues in this resurrected debate, particularly how American policymakers regarded the need for the planned invasion of Kyushu and the likelihood of an imminent Japanese surrender on the eve of Hiroshima, flared into a dispute between Bernstein on

22 McGeorge Bundy, *Danger and Survival: Choices about the Bomb in the First Fifty Years* (New York, 1988); Akira Iriye, *Power and Culture: The Japanese-American War, 1941–1945* (Cambridge, MA, 1981).

23 Barton J. Bernstein, "Understanding the Atomic Bomb and the Japanese Surrender: Missed Opportunities, Little-Known Near Disasters, and Modern Memory," in this volume.

the one hand and Gar Alperovitz and Robert Messer on the other. In an article he published in 1991 on General Marshall's consideration of using tactical nuclear weapons as a part of the assault on Kyushu, Bernstein cautioned that Marshall's thinking "should give sober pause to analysts who conclude that American leaders believed that Japan was very near surrender before Hiroshima, and that these men dropped the bomb primarily to intimidate the Soviets." Alperovitz and Messer responded by insisting that in the minds of key U.S. officials, a Soviet invasion of Manchuria would probably eliminate the need for an American invasion of Japan. They also asserted that Truman's diary and letters indicated that he felt the same way. Bernstein remained unconvinced, and the disagreement reached a historiographical apogee of sorts by hinging in part on the possible placement of a comma in minutes of a meeting. Although the issue was not resolved with the evidence presented, its importance was sharply drawn by the exchange.[24]

One other issue that recent scholarship has revisited is whether or not the United States practiced atomic diplomacy. This is primarily a postwar question, and a discussion of the extent to which the Truman administration used its atomic monopoly for diplomatic purposes after Hiroshima extends far beyond the scope of this essay. But Melvyn P. Leffler suggested that even before the end of

24 Barton J. Bernstein, "Eclipsed by Hiroshima and Nagasaki: Early Thinking about Tactical Nuclear Weapons," *International Security* 15 (Spring 1991): 149–73; Gar Alperovitz and Robert Messer and Barton J. Bernstein, "Correspondence: Marshall, Truman, and the Decision to Use the Bomb," ibid. 16 (Winter 1991–2): 204–21.
  Bernstein's argument received backing from Marc Gallicchio, who also concluded that Marshall's interest in tactical nuclear weapons even after Nagasaki indicated that he did not think that the atomic bombs would necessarily end the war and that an invasion might still be required. See Gallicchio, "After Nagasaki: General Marshall's Plan for Tactical Nuclear Weapons in Japan," *Prologue* 23 (Winter 1991): 396–404. The Alperovitz-Messer view was seconded in Kai Bird's biography of Stimson aide John J. McCloy. Bird maintained that McCloy and other American officials had concluded by the early summer of 1945 that an American invasion of Japan would not be necessary and that the war was virtually over. See Bird, *The Chairman: John J. McCloy, The Making of the American Establishment* (New York, 1992). The Alperovitz-Messer argument also won some indirect support in an article by Robert A. Pape, who contended that the atomic bombs were not decisive in causing the Japanese surrender. Rather, he cited the naval interdiction of Japan and the Soviet attack in Manchuria as the major considerations in persuading Japanese military leaders that they could not effectively resist a U.S. invasion of their homeland. This suggests that the war would have ended just as soon without using the bomb. But Pape did not deal with the perceptions of American leaders, and his article was too derivative and speculative to be conclusive. See Pape, "Why Japan Surrendered," *International Security* 18 (Fall 1993): 154–201.

the war, the possession of the bomb influenced American foreign policy on one important matter. He argued that after learning about the power of the bomb, the administration not only lost interest in Soviet entry into the Asian war but also repudiated the sections of the Yalta agreement dealing with the Far East. "At the time of Japan's surrender," he wrote, "Stalin had more reason to question the American desire to comply with Yalta's Far East provisions than vice versa."[25]

Although recent analyses of the use of the bomb have raised probing questions, the answers they provided have often been tentative and suggestive. They have unsettled the historiography of the subject without redefining it or offering new directions that might clarify outstanding issues. Leon V. Sigal's *Fighting to a Finish*, however, published in 1988, did a little of both. By looking at the decision to drop the bomb from the perspective of bureaucratic politics, Sigal presented answers to some of the questions that had puzzled other scholars. His systematic discussion of bureaucratic factors produced some fresh insights into the use of the bomb.

Sigal suggested that the reason that Japanese leaders did not make direct contact with the United States, a point that Iriye raised, was that bitter factional rivalry prevented it. Army opposition foreclosed direct peace initiatives, so Japanese leaders seeking to end the war were limited to clandestine approaches in Moscow. "It was," Sigal wrote, "Moscow or nowhere for Japan's diplomats." The same kind of bureaucratic forces often, but not always, influenced American actions.

Sigal portrayed top American officials as largely powerless, ineffective, and ill-informed. Truman was too inexperienced and insulated to grasp fully what was going on; his de facto authority was limited to halting the use of the bomb if he chose. But he had no compelling reason to do so. The key decisions on targeting and timing were made not by the president or the secretary of war but by General Leslie R. Groves and other military commanders. Groves, especially, was anxious to justify the effort and the expenditures of the Manhattan Project, and he avoided outlining alterna-

25   Melvyn P. Leffler, "From Accommodation to Containment: The United States and the Far East Provisions of the Yalta Agreements," in *Yalta: Un Mito Che Resiste* [Yalta: A myth that endures], ed. Paola Brunda Olla (Rome, 1989).

tives to Truman that could change existing plans and frustrate his objectives. Thus, the bomb fell more because of bureaucratic imperatives than because of carefully considered questions of national interest. Weighing alternatives to bombing Japanese cities or seeking viable ways to reach Japanese peace advocates never received attentive review by the president or his closest advisers.[26]

Sigal's interpretation offered plausible answers to some important questions. It explained why the Japanese were so circumspect in their peace initiatives, why the United States did not pursue alternatives to the bomb, and why Truman often seemed so confused about issues relating to the bomb. Although much of the information he presented was well known, he offered a new and useful interpretive framework for it. But his interpretation was hardly definitive. It failed to show why Truman and other top policymakers did not act to assert greater control over decisions about the bomb or to overrule their subordinates. The ultimate authority remained at the top; historians still need to sort out what was critical and what was not in the thinking of key officials.

Careful scholarly treatment of the records and manuscripts opened over the past few years has greatly enhanced our understanding of why the Truman administration used atomic weapons against Japan. Experts continue to disagree on some issues, but critical questions have been answered. The consensus among scholars is that the bomb was not needed to avoid an invasion of Japan and to end the war within a relatively short time. It is clear that alternatives to the bomb existed and that Truman and his advisers knew it. Furthermore, most scholars, at least in retrospect, regard an invasion as a remote possibility. Whether the bomb shortened the war and saved lives among those who were fighting in the Pacific is much more difficult to ascertain. Some analysts have argued that the war would have ended just as soon, or even sooner, if American leaders had pursued available alternatives, but this is speculative and a matter of continuing debate. It is certain that the hoary claim that the bomb prevented a half million or more American combat deaths cannot be supported with available evidence. The issue of whether the use of the bomb was justified if it spared

26 Leon V. Sigal, *Fighting to a Finish: The Politics of War Termination in the United States and Japan, 1945* (Ithaca, 1988).

far fewer American lives belongs more in the realm of philosophy than history. But there are tantalizing hints that Truman had some unacknowledged doubts about the morality of his decision.

Since the United States did not drop the bomb to save hundreds of thousands of American lives, as policymakers later claimed, the key question and the source of most of the historiographical debate is why the bomb was used. No scholar of the subject accepts in unadulterated form Alperovitz's argument that political considerations dictated the decision. But nearly all students of the events leading to Hiroshima agree that, in addition to viewing it as the means to end the war quickly, the political implications of the bomb figured in the administration's deliberations. The consensus of the mid-1970s, which held that the bomb was used primarily for military reasons and secondarily for diplomatic ones, continues to prevail. It has been challenged and reassessed in some of its specific points. But the central theme in the consensus that has existed for the past two decades – that U.S. officials always assumed that the bomb would be used and saw no reason not to use it once it became available – remains intact. There were no moral, military, diplomatic, or bureaucratic considerations that carried enough weight to deter dropping the bomb and gaining its projected military and diplomatic benefits.

Since the mid-1970s, when the contention between traditional and revisionist views of why the United States used the bomb was largely resolved, scholarship on the subject has not divided into discrete or discernible schools of interpretation. Within the consensus that currently prevails, there is ample room for disagreement and differing emphases. And not all recent scholarship falls within the bounds of even such a broadly defined consensus. The most prominent dissent appeared in David McCullough's Pulitzer Prize-winning biography of Truman. McCullough's presentation of the decision to use the bomb was a throwback to Stimson's *Harper's* article; he restated the traditional interpretation by arguing that Truman faced a stark choice between dropping the bomb and ordering an invasion. He added that by opting for the bomb the president saved large numbers of American lives, perhaps as many as one million. McCullough rejected the scholarship that took issue with this conclusion and, if his bibliography is a fair guide, simply ignored most of it. His best-selling book was not only a strong reassertion of the rationale advanced by former policymakers but also, in terms of reinforcing popular views of their decision, almost certainly the most influential of recent studies.[27]

From quite a different perspective, Gar Alperovitz also remained outside of the prevailing consensus. In a series of articles he continued to insist that political considerations rather than military needs were the keys to explaining Truman's use of the bomb. The articles presented a preview of what promised to be a major new book, scheduled for publication in mid-1995, in which Alperovitz drew on important new sources to support his position. The appearance of the book seems likely to add new fuel to the historiographical controversy and help prompt careful reexamination of the developments and decisions of the summer of 1945.[28]

As the debate over the decision to drop the bomb continues, several issues merit more attention than they have received. One concerns the meaning of the test explosion of the first nuclear device (it was not, strictly speaking, a bomb) at Alamogordo. The consequences of the Trinity shot in symbolic and scientific terms is clear enough, but its significance for policy is less so. The test was made to prove the design of a weapon fueled with plutonium and detonated by an intricate system of implosion, which was one of two different bombs being built in Los Alamos. The effectiveness of this method was in doubt until the experimental explosion lighted the New Mexico sky. But the atomic scientists were much more certain that the other design, a gun-type method in which one subcritical mass of highly enriched uranium-235 was fired at another, would succeed. Groves told Truman in their first meeting about the Manhattan Project in April 1945 that the uranium bomb would be ready without requiring a test around 1 August, and despite some qualms, scientists remained confident that it would

27 David McCullough, *Truman* (New York, 1992). McCullough later acknowledged that he had misread a memorandum that he cited for casualty estimates of five hundred thousand to one million, but he added that "my own interpretation of events leading to the decision to use the atomic bomb in no way depends on that one sentence [in the cited memorandum]." See *Defense Week*, 11 October 1994, 1.

28 In addition to Alperovitz's publications cited above see his articles in the *Wall Street Journal*, 13 September 1994, and the *Washington Post*, 16 October 1994. For a response to Alperovitz and a preview of a rekindled historiographical debate see an essay by Robert Newman, ibid., 30 November 1994.

work. Their confidence was justified – it was a uranium bomb that destroyed Hiroshima. This suggests that the Trinity test, for all its symbolic meaning, need not have been crucial to policymaking.

If Truman and his advisers realized during the summer of 1945 that the uranium bomb was almost ready and almost certain to work, it is curious that they reacted with so much surprise and elation to the news of the Trinity shot. If they did not understand that they would soon have an atomic bomb no matter what happened at Alamogordo, it suggests that they grasped or remembered little of what they were told about the details of the bomb project. Part of the explanation is that policymakers did not want to rely on the bomb until it definitely had proven to be successful, and they were unwilling to believe that it would make a major difference to them until they were shown what it could do. But they seemed to have little awareness that two types of bombs were being built. Even Stimson, the best-informed and most reflective senior official on matters regarding the bomb, appeared to think in terms of a single weapon that had to be tested at Alamogordo.[29] The issue is not one of transcending importance, but it could help to clarify the significance that Truman and his advisers attached to the bomb and its role in their planning. It might in that way resolve some of the contradictions and apparent confusion in Truman's diary.

The contradictions and confusion in Truman's notes and letters and in other sources have obscured another issue of importance in understanding the decision to use the bomb: Did leading American policymakers regard an invasion of Japan as likely or inevitable without the bomb? Scholars who have studied the end of the Pacific war have certainly not ignored the planning for an invasion. Indeed, many recent publications, including those of Alperovitz, Messer, Skates, Bird, Pape, Sherwin, Miles, and, with conditions, Bernstein, have concluded that the likelihood of an invasion of Japan was small. But the question of what policymakers believed at the time, before authorizing the use of atomic weapons, is more problematic. The debate between Bernstein on the one hand and Alperovitz and Messer on the other pointed out the uncertainties surrounding this issue. How much reliance can scholars place, for

---

29 Sherwin, *A World Destroyed*, 3–6; Henry L. Stimson and McGeorge Bundy, *On Active Service in Peace and War* (New York, 1948), 618, 637.

example, in Truman's diary and letters? Were they random and thoughtless jottings that captured the president's mood more accurately than factual information? Or were they based on reports and assessments that Truman had received from key advisers? If senior officials viewed an invasion as likely, or at least potentially necessary, to end the war, the case for the use of the bomb for military purposes is substantially strengthened, even if the number of lives saved was far less than several hundred thousand. If top American leaders regarded an invasion as unlikely, the political dimensions of the decision take on much greater significance. Even if Truman was confident that Japan was on the verge of surrender in early August 1945, however, it does not necessarily follow that he would have refrained from using the bomb as a means to end the war at the earliest possible moment – for military reasons. The outcome of scholarly investigation and debate on this issue is vital to a full understanding of the complex considerations that led to the atomic bombings.

Another subject that could benefit from further study is the role of scientists in the Manhattan Project. The ideas and activities of the atomic scientists, individually and corporately, have hardly suffered from neglect. Several scholars offered detailed accounts, particularly of the dissenting opinions of some of the Chicago scientists who wanted alternatives to the bomb explored and an approach to the Soviets seriously considered. William Lanouette provided a portrait of, arguably, the most engaging and eccentric of the atomic scientists, Leo Szilard, who was particularly outspoken in presenting his own ideas. The concerns of the scientists had no discernible impact on policy, which has led some scholars to reproach policymakers for failing to heed the warnings of the experts and others to chide the scientists for failing to press their views more effectively.[30]

Richard Rhodes, Peter Wyden, and Joseph Rotblat, a scientist

---

30 William Lanouette with Bela Silard, *Genius in the Shadows: A Biography of Leo Szilard, The Man behind the Bomb* (New York, 1992). Alice Kimball Smith, *A Peril and a Hope: The Scientists' Movement in America, 1945–1947* (Chicago, 1965), portrayed the views of dissenting scientists sympathetically. Brian Loring Villa chided them for waiting too long to try to register their doubts about using the bomb with policymakers. See "A Confusion of Signals: James Franck, the Chicago Scientists, and Early Efforts to Stop the Bomb," *Bulletin of the Atomic Scientists* 31 (December 1975): 36–43.

who left Los Alamos in 1944 after learning that Nazi Germany
had no atomic bomb, critically scrutinized the activities of the
atomic scientists and raised, implicitly and explicitly, a number of
difficult but important questions. What were the motivations of
atomic scientists in building the bomb? Was their quest to prove
their theories about the atom socially and politically irresponsible?
Did they fail to provide moral leadership commensurate with their
scientific leadership? What precisely was the relationship between
the policies being framed in Washington and the process of building the bomb in Los Alamos? What, if any, were the political and
moral obligations of the scientists involved in the bomb project?
Were atomic scientists sedated by an assumption that their spokesmen or political leaders would have the foresight, wisdom, and
power to control atomic energy once it became a reality?[31]

Another topic that deserves further attention is the role of the
Russian bomb project in Soviet-American relations at the close of
the war. David Holloway made a major contribution on this subject in his book *Stalin and the Bomb.* Even with unprecedented
access to individuals who participated in the Soviet atomic program and sources that supplied a wealth of new information, he
regarded his findings as incomplete. Soviet records of potentially
monumental importance remain out of the reach of scholars. Nevertheless, Holloway provided the fullest and richest account of the
Soviet bomb project. He concluded that although Stalin had authorized the effort to build the bomb during the war, he did not
recognize its political implications until after Hiroshima. At that
point he gave the bomb project top priority. Holloway suggested
that, whatever Truman's motives were in dropping the bomb, Stalin viewed it as an anti-Soviet action that seriously distorted the
balance of power. Therefore, attempts to achieve an American-
Soviet agreement on nuclear arms control when only the United
States had the bomb were doomed to failure.[32]

31 Rhodes, *The Making of the Atomic Bomb*; Wyden, *Day One*; and Joseph Rotblat,
    "Leaving the Bomb Project," *Bulletin of the Atomic Scientists* 41 (August 1985): 16–
    19. For other useful discussions of the views of scientists see Martin J. Sherwin, "How
    Well They Meant," Victor F. Weisskopf, "Looking Back on Los Alamos," Robert R.
    Wilson, "Niels Bohr and the Young Scientists," and Rudolf Peierls, "Reflections of a
    British Participant," in ibid., 9–15, 20–9.
32 David Holloway, *Stalin and the Bomb: The Soviet Union and Atomic Energy, 1939–
    1956* (New Haven, 1994).

Walter A. McDougall offered a similar view on the question of whether Roosevelt and Truman could have done more to prevent a nuclear arms race. In a book on the space race, he described the Soviet Union as the original "technocracy," a nation in which technology was "a cold tool of the state." In a brief discussion of the Soviet atomic project, McDougall suggested that the bomb was an inevitable product of the Soviet system. His findings, along with those of Holloway, make clear that the debate over how the use of the bomb affected Soviet-American relations must be carefully and critically evaluated. If the Soviets were immutably committed to developing nuclear weapons, an attempt on the part of the United States to practice atomic diplomacy would have made little or no difference in their determination to build the bomb, though it might have in the urgency with which they proceeded and in their diplomatic posture. McGeorge Bundy added another perspective to this subject by submitting that even though Stalin's decision to build the bomb was irreversible, he was not inalterably opposed to negotiation of atomic issues. But Bundy provided little evidence to support his view that a sincere and unqualified diplomatic approach to the Soviets might have been fruitful, and Holloway took a quite different position. In any event, the issue of atomic diplomacy will remain open until a more complete picture of Soviet atomic policies and progress emerges.[33]

The latest literature on the decision to use the atomic bomb has expanded and enriched our knowledge while at the same time raising new questions. The consensus that emerged in the mid-1970s still prevails, but it has been and surely will continue to be tested and reappraised. The events that led to Hiroshima are so innately interesting, so vital to understanding subsequent developments, so politically and morally ambiguous, and so much a part of popular mythology that it seems certain that they will perpetually occupy the attention of and stir discord among scholars of World War II and the nuclear age.

33   Walter A. McDougall, . . . *The Heavens and the Earth: A Political History of the Space Age* (New York, 1985); Bundy, *Danger and Survival*, 179–82.

3

Understanding the Atomic Bomb and the Japanese Surrender: Missed Opportunities, Little-Known Near Disasters, and Modern Memory

BARTON J. BERNSTEIN

The Allied war against Japan ended on 14 August 1945, following the bombings of Hiroshima and Nagasaki, which were sandwiched around Soviet entry into the Pacific war on the 8th. Tucked away amid these dramatic actions were some important but generally neglected events, virtually lost in modern memory: Japan's offer on the 10th of a conditional surrender with a guarantee of the imperial system; America's intentionally ambiguous reply on the 11th; a resulting sharp split in the Japanese government over whether to continue the war; the emperor's second intervention to push for surrender and peace; and a nearly successful coup in Japan that might have prolonged the war and provoked America's use of a third A-bomb and possibly even more atomic bombs. Because the war ended on the 14th and the third bomb was never used, analysts have generally ignored this important period of 10–14 August. Studies of the A-bomb have often also neglected the heavy conventional bombing of Japan during the spring and summer of 1945, culminating in a thousand-plane attack on the 14th, with some squadrons dropping their deadly cargo after Japan's announced surrender.

In focusing on the atomic bombings, analysts have usually devoted little attention to the related decision, and disputes, about whether and when to invade Japan. In analyzing the use of the A-bombs on Japan, studies have normally dwelled on other contested issues: Why were these weapons used? Were the A-bombs necessary to end the war? Would Japan have surrendered before 1 November 1945 (the date scheduled for the Kyushu invasion) if one or more of the various alternatives had been tried instead of the bomb? Why did Truman not pursue these so-called alternatives instead?

These important questions require an examination of the period well before Hiroshima until slightly after Nagasaki, because the basic decisions about the bomb were made well before 6 August, because the mass conventional bombing during the spring and summer helped define the context for the atomic bombing of cities, because the thinking about the invasion was shaped in that period, and because the little-known events after Nagasaki suggest how easily the war might well have dragged on past 14 August 1945. Had that occurred, Hiroshima and Nagasaki, especially if conjoined to A-bombings of Kokura and even elsewhere, might occupy a different place in modern memory, because the war would not have ended so soon and after only twice dropping the bomb on Japanese cities.

Such informed and useful speculations about how differently the war might have ended in the summer of 1945 do not undercut, or invalidate, conclusions that also move in the opposite direction: that it is *likely, but far from definite*, that a combination of non-nuclear options could have ended the war in the summer without the atomic bombings. Admittedly, the gap between "likely" and "definite" is unfortunately wide enough to suggest a troubling alternative history – of a longer war, more battles, and many dead before Japan surrendered.

But no suggestion that the Pacific war, without the use of the A-bomb, *might* have continued into the autumn or slightly beyond constitutes, necessarily, an ethical justification for the use of that weapon and the killing of over 120,000 and possibly more than 200,000 Japanese, and perhaps over 20,000 Koreans.[1] Put bluntly, this historical analysis of events may influence, but may not control, ethical judgments about the use of the atomic bomb in 1945. It is such judgments, however, that often help define the beliefs

1 The Committee for the Compilation of Materials on Damage Caused by the Atomic Bombs in Hiroshima and Nagasaki, trans. Eisei Ishikawa and David L. Swain, *Hiroshima and Nagasaki: The Physical, Medical, and Social Effects of the Atomic Bombings* (New York, 1981), 359–74, 468–75; the United States Strategic Bombing Survey (USSBS), *The Effects of Atomic Bombs on Hiroshima and Nagasaki* (Washington, 1946), 33.

about Hiroshima, and sometimes Nagasaki, that reside in modern memory.

II

Few events in modern American history have attracted as much attention, and provoked as much dispute, as the use of the atomic bomb. The analysis of the use of that weapon has had a curious, and often polemical, history.[2] One school ("orthodox") stresses that the atomic bombing was necessary, that the bomb saved many American lives (possibly a quarter million or more), and that not using it would have been unconscionable. Another school ("revisionist") argues that the atomic bombing was unnecessary, that American leaders knew that Japan was near defeat and hence near surrender, and that the bomb was used for an ulterior purpose. In this framework, the motive of intimidating the Soviet Union is usually cited as primary, though sometimes analysts define it as secondary but essential, and occasionally historians also stress bureaucratic interests as playing a controlling role in the decision to drop the A-bomb on Japan. By implication, and often by assertion, the revisionists are quite sure that the war against Japan could have been ended without the bomb, that ulterior motives blocked other approaches, and that the use of the bomb was clearly immoral.[3]

Between these two schools, a third has emerged, employing parts of the revisionist and orthodox analyses to conclude in a new synthesis: that the A-bomb was conceived as a legitimate weapon to be used against the enemy; that this assumption under President Franklin D. Roosevelt went largely unexamined and unchallenged; that Truman comfortably inherited this assumption, and that it also fit his inclinations and desires; and that the combat use of the bomb on Japan even came to seem both necessary and desirable. For President Harry S. Truman, the bomb could help end the war

2 Barton J. Bernstein, "The Atomic Bomb and American Foreign Policy, 1941–1945: An Historiographical Controversy," *Peace and Change* 3 (Spring 1974): 1–14; idem, "The Struggle over History: Defining the Hiroshima Narrative," in *Judgment at the Smithsonian*, ed. Philip Nobile (New York, 1995); J. Samuel Walker, "The Decision to Use the Bomb: A Historiographical Update," in this volume.

3 For a recent brief statement of these positions see Gar Alperovitz and Robert Messer, "Marshall, Truman, and the Decision to Drop the Bomb," *International Security* 16 (Winter 1991/92): 204–14.

on American terms, possibly avoid the dreaded invasions, punish the Japanese for Pearl Harbor and their mistreatment of POWs, conform to the desires of the American people, and *also* intimidate the Soviets, perhaps making them tractable in Eastern Europe.

According to this formulation, the atomic bomb might well have been used against Japan on the same days, in the same ways, even if the Bolshevik Revolution had never occurred and the Soviet Union had not existed. But the prospect of intimidating the Soviet Union added another reason, a kind of bonus, or what some would call overdetermination. In turn, the prospects of this bonus may have blocked some policymakers from reconsidering in July or early August the use of the atomic bomb; but there is no reason to conclude that such a reconsideration – had it occurred – would have produced a different policy. In short, the combat use of the A-bomb was, unfortunately, virtually inevitable. Truman's commitment to its use was, basically, the implementation of the assumption that he had inherited.[4]

III

For President Truman and his top advisers in 1945, the use of the atomic bomb was never a question. For them, the important question was how militarily to produce Japan's surrender, and sometimes what kind of surrender was likely. All had come by mid-June 1945, if not somewhat earlier, to endorse the military strategy of invading Kyushu in early November 1945. On 18 June 1945, urged by his united military advisers, Truman had approved full planning for this invasion.[5]

At that 18 June White House meeting, none had even hinted of the earlier army-navy dispute, rooted partly in bureaucratic differences and competing organizational loyalties, about how militarily

4 See Barton J. Bernstein, "Roosevelt, Truman, and the Atomic Bomb, 1941–1945: A Reinterpretation," *Political Science Quarterly* 90 (Spring 1975): 23–69; and Martin J. Sherwin, *A World Destroyed: The Atomic Bomb and the Grand Alliance* (New York, 1975).

5 "Minutes of Meeting held at the White House on Monday, 18 June 1945 at 1530," Records of the Joint Chiefs of Staff, Record Group 218, 336 Japan (2-2-45), National Archives, Washington, DC (hereafter RG 218, with filing information), and also reprinted, with some deletions, in U.S. Department of State, *Foreign Relations of the United States, Conference of Berlin (Potsdam)* (Washington, 1960), 1:903–10.

to produce a surrender. In 1944 and early 1945, Admiral Ernest L. King, the feisty chief of naval operations, had pushed for a siege (blockade-bombing) strategy that he hoped might obviate the need for an invasion. King had not usually opposed an invasion of Japan, but he and his subordinates, by stressing this blockade-bombing strategy and linking it to assaults elsewhere, proposed various plans that would delay the invasion, provide more time for the siege strategy to strangle and pummel Japan, and thus, they hoped, produce a surrender without invasion. To General George C. Marshall, army chief of staff, and his top aides, King's strategy was dangerous and wasteful. It would divert resources, involve unnecessary military campaigns, and delay the desired surrender of Japan. To Marshall and his advisers, the necessary strategy was invasion in late 1945 conducted while both bombing and the blockade also operated against Japan. In Marshall's conception, unlike King's, there was no need for substantial assaults in China, Korea, or elsewhere, after completing the Okinawa campaign, before directing the operation against Kyushu.[6]

By the spring of 1945, Marshall's counsel was triumphing among the military chiefs, and the navy was beginning to endorse his invasion strategy. In late April 1945, various high-level military planning committees, representing both the navy and army, had concluded that the invasion strategy was most likely "to accomplish unconditional surrender or ultimate defeat" of Japan.[7]

Though only about two months in the presidency, Truman knew that he would have to make the decision on how to conduct the war against Japan. Obviously a commitment to an autumn 1945 invasion could always be reversed before the actual attack, but a commitment not to invade, even if changed at a later date, would delay preparation and the invasion itself. Worried by such implica-

6 Department of Defense, *The Entry of the Soviet Union into the War against Japan: Military Plans, 1941–1945* (Washington, 1955), 36–68; Grace Person Hayes, *The History of the Joint Chiefs of Staff in World War II: The War against Japan* (Annapolis, 1982), 603–701; John Ray Skates, *The Invasion of Japan: Alternative to the Bomb* (Columbia, SC, 1994), 18–47; Charles F. Brower, "The Debate over Final Strategy for the Defeat of Japan, 1943–1945," *Joint Perspectives* 2 (Spring 1982): 72–80; and idem, "Sophisticated Strategist: General George A. Lincoln and the Defeat of Japan, 1944–45," *Diplomatic History* 15 (Summer 1991): 321–30.
7 Report by the Joint Staff Planners, "Pacific Strategy," JCS 924/15, 25 April 1945, RG 218, CCS 387 Pacific (1-17-43).

tions, Truman confided to his diary on 17 June 1945, "I have to decide Japanese strategy – shall we invade Japan proper or shall we bomb and blockade? That is my hardest decision to date." And probably it was, in his mind up to then, because the decision involved the likely death of many Americans, the danger of second-guessing at home, and even a public backlash. He added, tellingly, "I'll make it when I have all the facts."[8]

To help him, Admiral William Leahy, chairman of the Joint Chiefs of Staff, informed the military chiefs that the president, at their upcoming White House meeting with him on 18 June, wanted them "to discuss the details of our campaign against Japan" – the number of men and ships involved and estimates of the time required to defeat Japan, as well as the number of "the killed and wounded" in an invasion versus the losses in a siege (blockade-bombing) strategy.[9] Leahy's directive clearly laid out the issues in a way that contrasts, sharply, with the absence of any focused, probing questions among Truman and his top advisers, on the use of the A-bomb in 1945.

In preparation for the 18 June White House meeting, the Joint War Plans Committee, including representatives from both the army and the navy, put together a consensus plan for the Joint Chiefs to present to Truman: Invade Kyushu in November 1945 "for the purpose of further reducing Japanese capabilities by containing and destroying major enemy forces and further intensifying the blockade and air bombardment in order to establish a tactical condition favorable to . . . invasion of the industrial heart of Japan through the Tokyo Plain" in Honshu in about March 1946. Skillfully, the report had never really considered the siege strategy of blockade-bombing *versus* invasion, but, as Marshall had done earlier, the planners had intimately linked these two strategies. The invasion of Kyushu, occurring *during* the conduct of the ongoing siege strategy, would also enhance the further application of that strategy – and prepare the way for a later invasion of Honshu. According to these military planners, the estimated American *fatali-*

---

8 Harry S. Truman Diary, 17 June 1945, Truman Papers, Harry S. Truman Library, Independence, Missouri.
9 Leahy to Joint Chiefs of Staff, 14 June 1945, Department of Defense, *Entry of the Soviet Union,* 76.

ties would range from about twenty-five thousand for the Kyushu campaign to about twenty-one thousand more if the Tokyo Plain assault of March 1946 also became necessary. The total American *casualties* (killed, wounded, or missing) would be about 132,500 (including 105,000 wounded) in the Kyushu operation and about an additional 87,500 (including 65,000 more wounded) in the 1946 operation.[10]

General Douglas MacArthur, when hastily consulted by Marshall shortly before the mid-June White House meeting, provided comforting assessments in line with those by the Joint War Plans Committee. "I believe the operation [the Kyushu invasion]," MacArthur speedily cabled Washington, "provides less hazards of excessive loss than any other that has been suggested and that its decisive effect will eventually save lives by eliminating wasteful operations of nondecisive character."[11] MacArthur, who was eager to lead the invasion, may have given a predictable reply. His words, if crafted by Marshall himself, could not have been more supportive of Marshall's strategy. And so was the counsel from General Henry A. ("Hap") Arnold, commanding general of the army air forces, who was both Marshall's subordinate within the army and an equal member with Marshall and King of the Joint Chiefs. Whether acting partly for bureaucratic reasons and out of loyalty to Marshall or only from sincere judgment, Arnold cabled Marshall, "Continue with our present plan and occupy Kyushu to get additional bases for forty groups of heavy bombers."[12] With King also backing the plan, the high-level military support for the invasion was strong.

At the special 18 June White House meeting, General Marshall, whom Truman greatly respected, presented the united JCS case for the invasion strategy. Other strategies would be costly and not decisive, Marshall asserted, and the invasion of Kyushu, with the blockade-bombing strategy and possibly also Soviet entry or the

10 Joint War Plans Committee, "Details of the Campaign against Japan," JWPC 369/1, 15 June 1945, Records of the Army General Staff, Record Group 319, ABC Japan (3 May 1944), National Archives (hereafter RG 319, with filing information).
11 MacArthur to Marshall, 18 June 1945, RG 319, ABC Japan (3 May 1944). For Admiral Chester Nimitz's casualty estimates of forty-nine thousand in the first thirty days see Skates, *The Invasion of Japan*, 79–80.
12 H. H. Arnold, *Global Mission* (New York, 1949), 567; idem, "Trip to Pacific," 16 June 1945, Arnold Papers, Library of Congress, Washington, DC.

threat of such entry, might well push Japan to surrender without the Honshu invasion and "complete military defeat in the field." In words probably drafted to make Marshall's presentation very forceful, he explained in virtually a lecture to Truman, the former army captain, "It is a grim fact that there is not an easy, bloodless way to victory in war and it is the thankless task of the leaders to maintain their firm outward front which holds the resolution of subordinates. Any irresolution in the leaders may result in costly weakening and indecision in the subordinates."[13] The message to Truman, combining themes of martial values, national sacrifice, and patriotism, was clear and pungent: Be tough and decisive, endorse the Kyushu operation, and be a true leader.

Still new to the presidency, and certainly insecure in the White House, Truman received counsel that few men, and certainly not a newcomer, could have resisted. Because the ongoing siege strategy was linked to the Kyushu operation, Truman never really received a separate assessment of simply the blockade-bombing strategy conducted *without* the Kyushu invasion. Nor apparently, despite his earlier hopes, did he press for separate probing evaluations. Although the precise estimate of American fatalities and casualties may not have been stated at this meeting, the general implication, based upon various sources, was under about 25,000 dead in the Kyushu campaign. It would be bloody, killing possibly about twice the number (13,742) of Americans slain in MacArthur's operations from 1 March 1944 to 1 May 1945, when the dead Japanese, killed at a ratio of 22 to 1, had totaled over 310,000.[14]

Urged on by his Joint Chiefs of Staff and by both Secretary of War Henry L. Stimson and Secretary of the Navy James V. Forrestal, Truman endorsed planning for the Kyushu operation but reserved a decision on the larger 1946 invasion, which might also be necessary. In sanctioning the November plan, the new president had made a major decision. But he and others knew that the A-bomb, to be tested in about a month, might render the dread invasion unnecessary. That was not a firm expectation, but a hope.

13 *FRUS: Potsdam* 1:905.
14 "Minutes of Meeting Held at the White House . . . 18 June 1945"; William Leahy Diary, 18 June 1945, Leahy Papers, Library of Congress; James Forrestal Diary, 18 June 1945, Forrestal Papers, Princeton University Library, Princeton, New Jersey; Henry L. Stimson Diary, 18 June 1945, Yale University Library, New Haven, Connecticut.

In their discussions at this special meeting, the assembled policy-makers had not sharply focused on the A-bomb; perhaps they did not even mention it.[15] The bomb was untested, and there was no question that it would be used. And none saw any reason at the meeting to dwell on its likely impact on the war. That was not the subject of the meeting. The bomb was still a tightly held secret that leaders were often wary of discussing even in top-level sessions, and too little was known about its power, its psychological effects, and the results that it might produce in Japan.

Of those at this White House meeting, only Marshall, Stimson, and probably his assistant secretary, John J. McCloy, knew much about the most recent scientific estimates of the bomb. J. Robert Oppenheimer, the director of the top-secret Los Alamos Laboratory, had recently told Secretary Stimson, in the words of the Interim Committee minutes, "that the visual effect of an atomic bombing would be tremendous. It would be equivalent to about 2,000 to 20,000 tons of TNT. It would be accompanied by a brilliant luminescence that would rise to the height of 10,000 to 20,000 feet. The neutron effect of the explosion would be dangerous to life for a radius of at least two-thirds of a mile." But, in contrast, at that same meeting, Major General Leslie Groves, commanding general of the secret A-bomb project, had warned that the bomb's effect, even if a few were dropped at the same time, "would not be sufficiently distinct from our regular Air Force bombing program."[16] Such counsel did not suggest that the bomb would be *the* decisive weapon in the war, only that it would be a helpful weapon. How helpful was unclear in June, when the bomb was still a prospect, not a reality.

IV

In 1945, American leaders were not seeking to avoid the use of the A-bomb. Its use did not create ethical or political problems for

15 Assistant Secretary of War John J. McCloy later claimed that he had mentioned the A-bomb at this meeting, but his claim seems very dubious in view of the absence of any substantiating evidence in the official minutes and the diaries of Leahy, Forrestal, McCloy, and Stimson. McCloy, *The Challenge to American Foreign Policy* (Cambridge, MA, 1953), 42–3.

16 Interim Committee Minutes, 31 May 1945, paraphrasing various speakers, Records of the Manhattan Engineer District (MED), Record Group 77, Harrison-Bundy Files 100, National Archives (hereafter RG 77, with filing information).

them. Thus, they easily rejected or never considered most of the so-called alternatives to the bomb: (1) a noncombat demonstration as a dramatic warning; (2) modification of the unconditional-surrender demand and an explicit guarantee of the imperial system; (3) pursuit of Japan's peace feelers; (4) a delay of the A-bomb until well after Soviet entry into the war; and (5) reliance (without the A-bomb) on the siege strategy of heavy conventional bombing and a naval blockade. American leaders felt no incentive to pursue these strategies as *alternatives to dropping the bomb on Japan.*

Even by framing a post-Hiroshima analysis in terms of *alternatives* to the use of the A-bomb, there is some risk of distorting history by seeming – though not intending – to imply that American leaders before Hiroshima considered these various approaches, with the single exception of a noncombat demonstration, as alternatives to the bomb. They did not. In examining these so-called alternatives, post-Hiroshima analysts can conclude that these strategies, with various probabilities, *might* have served as alternatives to the bomb by producing a surrender before November 1945. But that is the view from a *post-*, not *pre-*, Hiroshima perspective. In the pre-Hiroshima months, when and if these strategies were considered, and delaying use of the bomb went unconsidered, they were not examined (with the exception of the noncombat demonstration) in terms of avoiding the use of the bomb but sometimes assessed within the context of avoiding the invasion. Even the siege strategy of bombing and blockade, though often linked to the November invasion, raised for policymakers the hope that it might compel a Japanese surrender before the November invasion. Put bluntly, for American leaders, avoiding the dread invasion, even if "only" twenty-five thousand Americans might die in the attack, was a major concern. Avoiding the use of the bomb was never a real concern for policymakers.

After the fact, however, avoiding the use of that weapon is properly an analytical theme for historians who seek to understand, explain, and assess the use of the A-bomb in August 1945. In conducting that historical study, they must be careful not to conflate their morality, that the bomb was a terrible weapon to be avoided, with the beliefs of American leaders before Hiroshima. Such a conflation, though tempting to some analysts, gravely misunderstands Truman and his associates in the pre-Hiroshima world. Such a conflation greatly distorts the past and makes understanding the use of the bomb very difficult, because it leads analysts to search for some hidden ulterior motive that compelled policymakers to overcome their scruples to use the bomb. They did not have such scruples – and there is no need to look for overwhelming hidden motives. Their primary motives were not hidden.

Only had American leaders viewed the bomb as profoundly immoral, or (like the Franck Committee) had they feared the postwar consequences of the bomb's combat use, might they have sought ways not to use it. They did not regard it as profoundly immoral, they were largely inured to mass killing of the enemy, and they also looked forward to the A-bomb's international-political benefits – intimidating the Soviets. American leaders also knew that they might risk a great outcry at home if they did not use the bomb. How could they have justified spending $2 billion on the Manhattan Project, and even diverting scarce wartime resources to that project, and then not using the A-bomb against a hated enemy – especially if the war continued past 1 November 1945 and thousands of Americans died in the invasion? Such lurking domestic-political reasons easily blended into very powerful patriotic motives and easily found additional support in personal and bureaucratic reasons for those American leaders such as Stimson and Marshall, as well as the new president, all of whom bore particular responsibility for the A-bomb project.

Despite these general explanations, there is still need to look closely at *each* of these so-called alternatives and ask two questions: Why were they not pursued *instead* of the bomb? And what might have happened if *one or more* had instead been pursued? Answers to the first question are strictly historical; but answers to the second (what might have happened if?), though greatly influenced by evidence, must necessarily remain somewhat speculative. They rest, in part, on projections of trends, actors' behavior, and events into a future that did not occur.

V

Alternative I: Noncombat Demonstration. This alternative was really only raised on two sets of occasions – at the 31 May 1945

Interim Committee lunch and then in the Franck Committee Report of 11 June, leading to its rejection by the Scientific Advisory Panel on 16 June and by the Interim Committee on 21 June. Each time, this proposal was speedily disposed of because, variously, the bomb might not work, a dud might embolden the Japanese, or Allied POWs might be moved into the demonstration area and be killed by the bomb. Because each of these risks was deeply troubling, and because there was *no strong desire* (and usually no desire) to avoid the combat use of the bomb, the alternative of a noncombat demonstration was easily rejected.[17]

The noncombat demonstration alternative was proposed, and normally judged, in connection with the idea of an advance warning about the bomb. But on two or possibly three occasions, American advisers – General Marshall on 29 May,[18] Undersecretary of the Navy Ralph Bard on 27 June,[19] and maybe Assistant Secretary of War McCloy nine days earlier[20] – proposed a warning without any subsequent demonstration. That tactic, to be accepted, would have required at minimum the support of Secretary of War Stimson, who never expressed any interest in an advance warning. Instead, he thought of the bomb's deadly *use* as a warning to Japan of the increasing destruction that would ensue if Japanese leaders did not surrender.

Even after the dramatic Trinity test of 16 July 1945, when the plutonium bomb was detonated with alarming effects, no policymaker or top-level science adviser reconsidered and suggested a noncombat demonstration. Not even physicist Ernest O. Lawrence, who had raised the possibility on 31 May at lunch, or his colleague,

---

17 On the 31 May meeting see Ernest O. Lawrence to Karl Darrow, 18 August 1945, Lawrence Papers, Bancroft Library, Berkeley, California; and Arthur Holly Compton, *Atomic Quest: A Personal Narratives* (New York, 1956), 238–9. On the fate of the Franck petition see Scientific Advisory Panel (by Oppenheimer) to George Harrison, 16 June 1945, RG 77, Harrison-Bundy Files 76; Oppenheimer, in United States Atomic Energy Commission, *In the Matter of J. Robert Oppenheimer: Transcript of Hearing before Personnel Security Board* (Washington, 1954), 34; and Interim Committee Minutes, 21 June 1945, RG 77, Harrison-Bundy Files 100.

18 McCloy, "Memorandum of Conversation with General Marshall," 29 May 1945, Records of the Secretary of War, Record Group 107, Safe File, National Archives.

19 Bard, "Memorandum on the Use of the S-1 Bomb," 27 June 1945, RG 77, Harrison-Bundy Files 77.

20 For grave doubts about McCloy's later claims about his role in this meeting see Barton J. Bernstein, "Seizing the Contested Terrain of Early Nuclear History: Stimson, Conant, and Their Allies Explain the Decision to Use the Atomic Bomb," *Diplomatic History* 17 (Winter 1993): 62 and note 105.

Arthur H. Compton, who may also have suggested such a possibility, was inclined to urge reconsideration. Perhaps even for these scientists the momentum of the project was so great, and their earlier advice of mid-June against a demonstration seemed so fixed, that they felt blocked, psychologically and bureaucratically, from raising the prospect again. Had they done so, with Truman and his top advisers already at Potsdam and comfortably committed to using the bomb, it is highly unlikely that doubts and possibilities raised by one or two of these scientists, or even by the entire four-man Scientific Advisory Panel, would have provoked any serious reexamination of assumptions, and conclusions, by the policymakers themselves.

At Potsdam, where Truman received the dramatic news of the Trinity test, he wrote in his diary, "We have discovered the most terrible bomb in the history of the world. It may be the fire destruction prophesied in the Euphrates Valley Era, after Noah and his famous Ark." He marveled that "the explosion was visible for more than 200 miles and audible for 40 miles and more." Savoring the bomb's great power, he felt emboldened at the Potsdam Conference and was not seeking to avoid using this new weapon.[21]

In retrospect, given what we now know of the strong opposition among the "militarists" in the Japanese government even after two atomic bombings and Soviet entry, it is difficult to believe that a noncombat demonstration, even if preceded by a warning, would have produced a surrender before 1 November 1945 and the likely invasion of Kyushu. At best, the probabilities seem slight – maybe 5 or 10 percent. And the likelihood is even skimpier of a warning, without such a demonstration, being successful.[22]

VI

Alternative II: Modification of Unconditional Surrender and Guarantee of the Emperor. Some American leaders, most notably Undersecretary of State Joseph Grew and Secretary of War Stimson, pleaded for this strategy – not as an alternative to the A-bomb, but

21 Truman, "Potsdam Diary," 25 July 1945, Truman Library.
22 Such arithmetic estimates should not be taken literally but as *rough* estimates. Because words such as "slight" or "skimpy" or "small" are susceptible to a wide range of interpretation, and misinterpretation, I have chosen the unusual, but useful, tactic of offering arithmetic estimates in some cases in order to minimize misinterpretation.

rather as a way, they hoped, of avoiding the invasion. Grew did not even know of the bomb, and Stimson hoped that a guarantee of the emperor, *together* with the A-bomb and heavy conventional bombing, as well as the blockade, might produce a surrender before 1 November.[23] Grew and Stimson lost on the guarantee because Truman and James F. Byrnes, the new secretary of state, feared a political backlash in America, where Hirohito was likened to Hitler and judged a war criminal, and because Truman and Byrnes feared that such modified surrender terms might also embolden the Japanese to fight on for better terms.[24]

Some analysts have argued that maintenance of the imperial system was the *only* issue blocking a Japanese surrender in late July or early August (before the A-bomb), and that American leaders knew this or should have known it.[25] Such an interpretation of the Japanese position is ill-founded. The Japanese government was badly split both on how and whether to end the war, and even the Japanese "peace" forces were unsure, unsteady, and uncertain.

In June and July, despite divisions within their government, Japanese leaders agreed on the desirability of trying to persuade the Soviets, who had recently announced their intention to end their neutrality pact with Japan, from entering the war on the American side. Japan made vague offers to the Soviets for negotiations, stressed Japan's desire to maintain friendly relations, and promised to send Prince Fumimaro Konoe, a former premier, to Moscow to meet with the Soviets. Wary of Japan's purposes, the Soviet government complained on 18 July, for example, that Japan had not offered specific proposals or explained Prince Konoe's mission. Matching Japanese vagueness and delay with similar tactics, the Soviets easily dragged out the preliminary negotiations.[26] It was a "cat and mouse" game.

23 Joseph Grew to Truman, 28 May 1945, Grew Papers, Houghton Library, Harvard University, Cambridge, Massachusetts; Stimson to Truman, "Proposed Plan for Japan," 2 July 1945, in Stimson Diary, and Stimson Diary, 18 and 19 July 1945, and Stimson to Truman, 20 July 1945, Stimson Papers, Yale University.
24 Cordell Hull in Grew to Byrnes, 16 July 1945, and reply, 17 July 1945, in *FRUS: Potsdam* 2:1267–78.
25 Alperovitz and Messer, "Marshall, Truman, and the Decision to Drop the Bomb," 207–9.
26 Lozovsky to Jacob Malik, 18 July 1945. See also V. M. Molotov to Malik, 8 July 1945, and Malik to Molotov, 13 July 1945, in "Attempts to Tilt the Sand-Glass," *Vestnik* (August 1990): 71–2, called to my attention by David Holloway.

A careful reading of the available Japanese sources (especially the cables between Foreign Minister Shigenori Togo in Tokyo and Ambassador Naotake Sato in Moscow) for late July and early August reveals that the Japanese Foreign Office did not believe that maintenance of the imperial system was the *only* sticking point. In fact, in the weeks before Hiroshima, the Japanese foreign minister was unprepared even to specify peace terms to his own ambassador in Moscow, despite the fact that he was directed to approach the Soviets to serve as intermediaries in peace negotiations. On 27 July, Sato warned Togo, "It is absolutely impossible to cause the Soviet government to make a move with such a noncommittal attitude on our part."[27] The next day, Sato asked some tough questions: Would Japan accept demilitarization and free Korea? On 2 August, Togo informed Sato, "It is difficult to decide on concrete peace conditions here [in Tokyo] all at once. . . . We are exerting ourselves to collect the views of all quarters on the matter of concrete terms." Whether intended or not, that sounded like a strategy of delay, and certainly not a rush toward peace.[28]

And consider Sato's reply of 3 August. He admonished Foreign Minister Togo, "So long as we propose sending a Special Envoy (to Moscow) without at the same time having a concrete plan for ending the war . . . the Russians will politely refuse to receive (him and we are wasting valuable time while Japan is being destroyed)."[29] Despite Sato's admonitions and pleas, the best that the foreign minister would offer, up to the Hiroshima bombing, was the plan of sending an envoy to Moscow who would bear terms. But those terms had not yet been defined.[30]

27 Sato to Togo, 27 and 28 July 1945, *FRUS: Potsdam* 2:1291, 1294–5.
28 Togo to Sato, 2 August 1945, in No. 1225, 2 August 1945, Magic-Diplomatic Summary, Records of the National Security Agency, Magic Files, Record Group 457, National Archives.
29 Sato to Togo, 3 August 1945, in No. 1228, 5 August 1945, Magic-Diplomatic Summary, RG 457.
30 According to the USSBS, Prince Konoe later claimed that "he received direct and secret instructions from the Emperor to secure peace at any price, notwithstanding its severity." USSBS, *Japan's Struggle to End the War* (Washington, 1946), 44. In 1949, Togo obliquely challenged that claim. U.S. Army, Far East Command, Military History Section, "Statements of Japanese on World War II," Modern Military Records Branch, National Archives (hereafter "Statements"), "Statements": Shigenori Togo #50304. Strangely, the survey's summary of Konoe's testimony does not jibe with the key transcript, "Interrogation of Prince Konoye," 9 November 1945, in Records of the USSBS, Record Group 243, National Archives. Most Japanese officials after the war, in

What emerges from these cables, as well as from a larger study of the Japanese government at that time, is a complicated picture: All Japanese leaders wanted to prevent Soviet entry into the war; some leaders wanted a Japanese surrender; all agreed that continuation of the emperor was an essential condition for peace; the Japanese government was divided on the other necessary terms of that peace; some military leaders wanted to hold out for at least three additional terms (no postwar occupation, self-disarmament, and conduct of their own war-criminal trials); these military leaders sometimes spoke of fighting on and thus increasing the toll in lives to secure good terms; and the peace forces were weak, fearful of a military coup, sometimes divided, often compelled to be oblique about their intentions, and never prepared boldly and clearly to push for surrender. The formal leader of the Japanese government, Admiral Baron Kantaro Suzuki, the premier, was often wavering in his quest for peace.[31]

The Japanese army, by withdrawing its representative from the cabinet, could have destroyed any move toward surrender. The militarists wanted honor, which meant far more than just a guarantee of the imperial system. "I was unable to keep the military from insisting," Togo recalled, "that they were not beaten, that they could fight another battle, and that they did not want to end the war until they had staged one last campaign." Even after Soviet entry into the war and the first atomic bombing, as Togo later reported, the army leaders still wanted one more campaign. When Togo "asked whether or not they believed they could ward off an invasion of the homeland, . . . the army chief of staff [General Korechika Anami] replied that, if we were lucky, we could repulse the invaders before they landed, but that all he could say with assurance was that we could destroy the major part of the invading army."[32]

interrogations, usually placed the emperor in the best light – he was responsible for the good, never the bad – and thus there is additional reason to doubt the survey's conclusion. For a far more critical interpretation of Hirohito's actions and influence see Herbert P. Bix, "Japan's Delayed Surrender: A Reinterpretation," in this volume.

31   "Statements" of Togo #50304, Koichi Kido #62131 and #61541, Sumihasa Ikada #54479, and Masao Yoshizumi #54484; *Kido Koich Nikki*, 21 June–9 August 1945, translated copy courtesy of Robert Butow; USSBS, "Interrogation of Premier Baron Suzuki," 26 December 1945, Records of USSBS.

32   "Statements" of Togo #50304.

Given the power of the militarists and their desire, it is *quite unlikely* – but not impossible – that an American guarantee of the imperial system would have produced a Japanese surrender before 1 November on terms acceptable to the United States.[33] Certainly, given American plans for the political reconstruction of Japan and the destruction of Japanese militarism, postwar occupation was essential – even at the price of a prolonged war. Very probably, American concessions on all *four* conditions (the emperor, postwar occupation, self-disarmament, and war trials) could have produced a speedy surrender. But that would not have been the victory that American leaders, as well as much of the public, desired. War is fought for political purposes, and World War II, as historians have come to understand, certainly had its politics.

VII

Alternative III: Pursuit of Japanese Peace Feelers. During the summer, Japanese middle-level diplomats and military attachés in Switzerland and elsewhere in Europe approached intermediaries and American officials to try to move toward a surrender. In June, one Japanese group proposed continuation of the emperor and retention of Korea and Formosa as the main terms for surrender. Allen Dulles, OSS chief in Switzerland, responded that he would not commit the United States but that it was his nation's understanding that the imperial institution would be maintained if Japan surrendered. He had no comment about a deal on Korea and Formosa. Despite Dulles's favorable response about the imperial system, these enterprising Japanese negotiators could not evoke any interest in Tokyo for their venture, and it died.[34]

33 Stimson and McGeorge Bundy, *On Active Service in Peace and War* (New York, 1948), 629; Bernstein, "Seizing the Contested Terrain," 62–5.

34 "Statements" of Yoshikazu Fujimura #64118 and Sadatoshi Tonioka #60951. On Japanese demands see G. Edward Buxton (acting director of OSS) to secretary of state, 4 June 1945, but later Fujimura apparently retreated to request only a guarantee of the emperor. Buxton to secretary of state, 22 June 1945; both items in Records of the Department of State, Record Group 59, 740.00119 P.W. See also other messages in this file indicating the lack of clarity or consistency, or both, in negotiations.

On 10 July, to stifle rumors in America, Acting Secretary of State Joseph Grew declared publicly that there had been some loose Japanese peace feelers. "But in no case," he stressed, "has an appeal been made to this Government, directly or indirectly, by a person who could establish his authority to speak for the Japanese Government.... In no case has this Government [the United States] been presented with a statement purporting to define the basis upon which the Japanese Government would be prepared to conclude peace." He was correct that there had been nothing definite, and he revealed that many American leaders suspected that these peace feelers were designed to weaken America's commitment to the war.[35]

In mid-July, a Captain Nishihara, the Japanese naval counselor in Bern, informed the Navy General Staff in Tokyo that Allen Dulles was interested in a "discussion" about peace. But the navy was wary and passed the matter on to the Foreign Office, which did nothing. "Such [American] schemes as this," the navy cabled Nishihara during the period of the Potsdam Conference, "really indicate what difficulties the enemy is facing." Washington decoded that message and knew that Nishihara had been ordered to withdraw from peace negotiations.[36] During this time, as one Japanese naval officer later recalled, "it was a taboo for ... us to speak out about the problem of peace even if we were considering it deep in [our] heart."[37]

On a few occasions in July, Washington did receive reports that there were peace feelers in Switzerland suggesting that a guarantee of the imperial system was the only sticking point to peace. These peace feelers were, unfortunately, usually directed by Japanese officials through non-American intermediaries, and there was no evidence that these Japanese were acting on authority from their government.[38] In fact, they were not. At best, they had

35 Grew statement of 10 July 1945, in Department of State press release, 10 July 1945, RG 59, 740.00119 P.W.
36 Magic Diplomatic Summary, part II, 28 July 1945.
37 Interrogation of Yoshimasa Suezawa #62051, in U.S. Army, Far East Command, Military History Section, "Interrogations of Japanese Officials in World War II," Modern Military Records Branch, National Archives.
38 Donovan to secretary of state, 16 and 18 July 1945, and Cheston to acting secretary of state, 2 August 1945, *FRUS, 1945* (Washington, 1969), 6:489–94.

loose approval from some peace forces within the sharply divided Japanese government, but the "Magic" intercepts (America's decoding of top-secret Japanese messages) revealed that the government in Tokyo could not agree on specific terms and that the militarists in the government wanted far more than a guarantee of the emperor.[39]

Ironically, these peace feelers, frail and indirect as they were, might have commanded serious interest in Washington, and certainly with Stimson, Forrestal, Marshall, and Grew, if American leaders had not also had access to the official, and bleak, Togo-Sato cables. These cables starkly revealed the weakness of Japan's peace forces and the indecision of Japan's government both before and after the Trinity test of mid-July 1945.

Probably not even Allen Dulles, who would make bolder claims two decades later,[40] was willing in July or early August to argue that a guarantee of the emperor was the *only* issue blocking the peace. At Potsdam, on 20 July, Dulles gave Stimson a report on the peace feelers in Switzerland, leading Stimson to record cryptically in his diary, "[Dulles] told us about something which had recently come to him with regard to Japan."[41] McCloy noted, in his own diary, that Dulles had mentioned what McCloy called "tentative approaches." "I gather that there is something behind it, but just how substantial I do not know," McCloy wrote in his own diary.[42] Apparently neither Stimson nor McCloy, each of whom was hoping for softer American peace terms in order to avoid the costly Kyushu invasion and the possible Honshu operation, took these possibilities very seriously, for there is no evidence that either man acted on them. Given that Stimson wanted softer terms in the forthcoming Potsdam Declaration of 26 July, and that he had earlier proposed an explicit guarantee of the emperor, he would certainly have seized on Dulles's report if it had seemed solid or even especially promising. It could have provided Stimson with the very arguments that he wished to use in his effort to gain the explicit

---

39   See, for example, Sato to Togo, 27 and 28 July 1945, *FRUS: Potsdam* 2:1291, 1294–5.
40   Allen Dulles, *The Secret Surrender* (New York, 1966), 255–6.
41   Stimson Diary, 20 July 1945.
42   John J. McCloy Diary, 20 July 1945, McCloy Papers, Amherst College Library, Amherst, Massachusetts.

guarantee of the imperial institution.[43] And Dulles himself, years later, acknowledged a major problem: The Japanese negotiators had lacked "clear credentials of authority."[44]

About a week after meeting with Stimson and McCloy in Potsdam, Dulles passed on another report on the indirect negotiations in Switzerland. The information that he provided could not have generated optimism for American leaders: Japan's naval officials were wary of trying to act alone; Tokyo was dallying, avoiding any terms, but suggesting that the informal channels in Bern be kept open; and Japanese officials in Bern thought that they might have to push their own government in order to produce real possibilities. Dulles himself called this a "somewhat nebulous stage" in the Bern conversations.[45]

Had the A-bomb not been dropped and had the informal discussions ("back channels") in Switzerland continued for a few more months, while America pummeled Japan from the air and tightened its naval strangulation, perhaps a surrender with a guarantee of the emperor could have been secured before November. But that would have required Japan's powerful militarists to give up their hope for one more battle and sharply cut back their demands for a peace settlement. There is little evidence, only slim hope, that the militarists would have shown such tractability and so redefined honor and necessity unless other events, very painful events, intervened to help, or propel, them to accede to what Emperor Hirohito on 10 August justified as a surrender "to save the nation from destruction."[46]

VIII

Alternative IV: Awaiting Soviet Entry into the War. No top American leader (Truman, Marshall, Byrnes, Stimson, Leahy, Forrestal, King, or Arnold) generally saw Soviet entry into the war as likely

43 Stimson Diary, 20–7 July 1945.
44 Allen Dulles, "Notes for NBC-Television Program on Japanese Surrender Negotiations," 26 March 1965, Allen Dulles Papers, box 142, Seeley G. Mudd Library, Princeton University.
45 Allen Dulles to General John Magruder, 1 August 1945, together with reports of 29 July and 1 August 1945, Dulles Papers, box 21.
46 Quoted from Robert J. C. Butow, *Japan's Decision to Surrender* (Stanford, 1954).

to be decisive *without* the A-bomb, before the scheduled invasion. Some analysts have cited – incorrectly, I think – two sources in order to reach a contrary conclusion: that Soviet entry was foreseen as likely to be decisive *without* the bomb.[47]

Let me discuss these two sources in some detail – the minutes of the top-level White House meeting of 18 June 1945 and Truman's diary entry for 17 July 1945. First, the 18 June minutes. They include a verbatim digest of a key JCS report predicting that Japan *might* surrender "short of complete military defeat . . . when faced by . . . air bombardment and sea blockade, coupled with (2) a landing on Japan . . . , and also *perhaps* coupled with (3) the entry or threat of entry of Russia into the war." By this JCS formulation, Soviet entry *might* also be quite helpful – recall the JCS use of "perhaps." Later, in summarizing this view during the meeting, Marshall offered a more forcefully phrased statement: "the impact of Russian entry on the already hopeless Japanese may well be the decisive action levering them into capitulation at that time or shortly thereafter *if we land* in Japan." Note, again, that the impact of Soviet entry is stressed as important *if* the invasion occurs, not without the invasion. A Soviet invasion alone was not seen as likely to be decisive.[48] On 18 June, American military advisers saw Soviet entry as useful, but not essential. At that meeting, Admiral King stressed that "the Soviets were not indispensable and he did not think we should go as far as to beg them to come in. While the

47 Alperovitz, *Atomic Diplomacy*, 23–5; Robert Messer, "New Evidence on Truman's Decision," *Bulletin of the Atomic Scientists* 41 (August 1985): 54–5; and Alperovitz and Messer, "Marshall, Truman, and the Decision to Drop the Bomb," 205–10.
48 "Minutes of Meeting Held at the White House . . . 18 June 1945," also printed in *FRUS, Potsdam* 1:904–5 (emphasis added). For an earlier view, one placing more weight on the impact of Soviet entry, see the study by Brig. Gen. Lincoln, 4 June 1945, quoted in Ray S. Cline, *Washington Command Post: The Operations Division* (Washington, 1951), 344, in *United States Army in World War II*. This stronger formulation, emphasizing the value of Soviet entry, was revised in mid-June in a digest-paper that Marshall presented at the 18 June White House meeting. See also G.A.L. (Lincoln) to General Norstad, 4 October 1946, George Lincoln Papers, U.S. Military Academy, West Point, New York, called to my attention by Colonel Charles Brower IV. The importance of Soviet entry was also minimized in Joint Staff Planners, "Details of the Campaign against Japan," JCS 1388, 16 June 1945, but stressed more in CCS 643, "Estimate of the Enemy Situation," 6 July 1945, where Soviet entry was assessed as "finally convincing the Japanese of the inevitability of complete defeat" – but this estimate did not promise prompt, or speedy, *surrender*. Department of Defense, *The Entry of the Soviet Union into the War*, 87.

cost of defeating Japan would be greater, there was no question . . . but that we could handle it alone."[49]

There is a second important source on this matter of Soviet entry – Truman's diary entry for 17 July 1945. At Potsdam, on that day, when Stalin promised that Soviet forces would enter the war on 15 August (which, Truman knew, would almost certainly be *after* use of the A-bomb), the president penned in his diary, "Fini Japs when that [Soviet entry] comes about."[50] Some have seized upon this brief note as powerful evidence that Truman believed that Soviet entry, without the A-bomb, would produce an *immediate* or *prompt* Japanese surrender. But if Truman did believe for more than a few hours, if at all, that Soviet entry after the A-bomb would be so decisive so quickly, why did he not then greatly accelerate economic reconversion at home, since he knew that reconversion – with troubling issues of wages, prices, priorities, and possibly jobs – would be a major political problem buffeting his postwar administration? He knew that his domestic economic planners, back in Washington, were assuming that the war would drag on well past mid-August. They were not rushing to get ready, at a break-neck rate, for peace in the next month or so. Yet, Truman did not direct them to accelerate planning greatly for peace.[51]

Truman's phrase about "Fini Japs" has to be construed by looking at his other actions, and thus by placing these arresting words in the larger context of his actions. That phrase, as interpreted in this larger context, meant that Japan might soon be defeated, but "soon" did not mean within days of Soviet entry. And his expectation of "soon" was coupled with his considerable hopes for the powerful impact of the "bomb." "I have some dynamite too," he wrote in his diary on the 17th, right after the Trinity test, and he knew that he could use this "dynamite" (the bomb) in early August – about a week before the Soviets' likely entry into the war.[52]

49 "Minutes of Meeting Held at the White House . . . 18 June 1945."
50 Truman, "Potsdam Diary," 17 July 1945.
51 See, for example, Truman to John Snyder (OWMR director), 8 August 1945, Records of the Office of War Mobilization and Reconversion, Record Group 240, National Archives.
52 Truman, "Potsdam Diary," 17 July 1945.

On 18 July, he went on to write in his diary, "Believe Japs will fold up before Russia comes in. I am sure that they will when Manhattan [the A-bomb] appears over their homeland."[53] Yet, that same day, in a letter to his wife, the president emphasized that he had "gotten what I came for – Stalin goes to war August 15 [and] we'll end the war a year sooner now, and think of the kids who won't be killed!"[54] Actually, despite his euphoric and possibly confusing comments, when they are taken together in context, the evidence is that Truman did not really expect – beyond this brief burst of enthusiasm – that one bomb or two would produce a speedy Japanese surrender. He certainly did nothing, aside from penning this lone diary entry, to indicate that he expected a surrender before 15 August 1945. Like others, he was actually surprised when Japan offered (even with one condition) to surrender on 10 August. Until then, he had assumed – as did General Leslie Groves, Marshall, Stimson, and others – that more than two A-bombs would be dropped before Japan accepted defeat and its government actually surrendered.[55]

The successful Trinity test had the effect, for many American leaders, of minimizing or eliminating the value of Soviet entry into the war. Prime Minister Winston Churchill concluded at Potsdam on 23 July, "It is quite clear that the United States do not at present time desire Russian participation in the war against Japan."[56] Yet, the next day, Churchill and Truman also approved a document by their military chiefs, "Encourage Russian entry into the war against Japan."[57] To Stimson, Soviet entry no longer seemed necessary because in his judgment the primary value of their armed intervention would be to hold up the Japanese army in Manchuria, and that was already being accomplished by the presence of Soviet armies near the border. Thus, in Stimson's formulation, Soviet entry would offer little more than the Soviets had already done in aiding the American effort. Marshall seemed generally to agree,

53 Truman, "Potsdam Diary," 18 July 1945.
54 Truman to Dear Bess, 18 July 1945, Truman Papers.
55 See, for example, the discussions summarized in Stimson Diary, 10 August 1945; Forrestal Diary, 10 August 1945; and Leahy Diary, 10 August 1945; and Marshall to Groves, 10 August 1945 penned note on Groves to Marshall, 10 August 1945, in Marshall Papers, George C. Marshall Library, Lexington, Virginia.
56 Churchill, quoted in John Ehrman, *Grand Strategy* (London, 1956), 5:292.
57 Combined Chiefs of Staff to Truman and Churchill, 24 July 1945, *FRUS: Potsdam* 2:1463.

although he also noted that the Soviets could enter when they wished and thus they could gain various advantages.[58]

But American leaders did not view Soviet entry as a *substitute* for the bomb. Rather, they viewed the bomb as so powerful, and the Soviet presence in Manchuria as so militarily significant, that there was no need for actual Soviet intervention into the war. Thus, it was easy for some American leaders after the Trinity test to try to impede Soviet entry in order to stop the Soviets from grabbing parts of the Asian mainland. In the view of Byrnes, Stimson, Marshall, and presumably other American leaders, this "impeding" strategy would not delay the ending of the war and the surrender of Japan.[59] Nor were most sure that the November invasion could be averted.

In retrospect, we can conclude that Soviet entry on 15 August (without the A-bomb) might well (maybe 20–30 percent probability) have produced a surrender before 1 November.[60] But let me stress that this is a conclusion based on what we now know, not on what American leaders believed at the time. Had they closely, empathetically, and imaginatively read the intercepted and decoded Sato-Togo cables, perhaps American leaders might have anticipated the profound psychological *shock* that Soviet entry into the war produced among Japanese leaders, many of whom were hoping until that fateful day of 8 August 1945 that the Soviets might be entreated to remain outside the Pacific war. To distinguish psychological shock from military significance required subtlety and perhaps the willingness to speculate about the uneasiness

58 Stimson Diary, 23 July 1945.
59 On Byrnes see Forrestal Diary, 28 July 1945; and W. B's (Walter Brown's) Notes, 20 and 24 July 1945, Byrnes Papers, Robert Muldrow Cooper Library, Clemson University, Columbia, South Carolina. On Leahy see Leahy Diary, 24 and 29 July 1945. On Truman, W. B.'s Notes, 3 August 1945. Byrnes tried to follow a strategy of having the Chinese avoid, or delay, concessions to the Soviets partly in order to delay Soviet entry into the war, for the Soviets had made these concessions a condition of their entry. But others were unsure whether Chinese refusal would delay Soviet entry. Leahy Diary, 17 July 1945. For a slightly different view see Leahy Diary, 24 July 1945.
60 Conclusions about the substantial impact of Soviet entry are based upon postwar statements by Japanese officials: See "Interrogation of Konoye," 9 November 1945; "Statements" of Togo #50304 and Sumihasa Ikeda #54479; and interrogation of Admiral Soemu Toyoda, in USSBS, Naval Analysis Division, *Interrogation of Japanese Officials* (Washington, 1947), 2:320. See also Shigenori Togo, *The Cause of Japan*, trans. Fumihoko Togo and Ben Bruce Blakeney (New York, 1956), 315, 16; and Toshizaku Kase, *Journey to the Pacific* (New Haven, 1950), 217.

and vulnerability of the enemy. No American leader – including Stimson, who had argued for a guarantee of the emperor – had the inclination, and perhaps the capacity, in the last weeks of July and the early days of August to engage in such analysis.

In retrospect, we can conclude that American leaders' unwillingness to delay the bomb's use and await Soviet entry, and then, if necessary, to delay the A-bombing for a longer period, may well have been a "missed opportunity." But such a possibility was not adequately understood in late July or early August. And delaying the A-bomb would have seemed a very risky, and unnecessary, gamble – far too risky for men not seeking to avoid its use.

Looking back, Henry Stimson asserted (in words possibly crafted by McGeorge Bundy), that "the dominant fact of 1945 was war, and that therefore, necessarily, the dominant objective was victory. If victory could be speeded by using the bomb, it should be used." Delay would have been both unwise and unconscionable, he assumed. In so publishing his own beliefs, and those of his 1945 associates, Stimson was subscribing to the strong American values of patriotism and of nationalism, values that emphasized the importance of saving American lives and the willingness to slay the enemy.[61]

IX

Alternative V: Bombing and Blockade – The Strategy of Siege without the Atomic Bomb. Probably the most likely way of achieving a Japanese surrender before November 1945 (without the A-bomb) was by continuing the siege strategy of the heavy bombing of Japanese cities – the terror-bombing and the destruction of military and industrial installations – and the strangling naval blockade, including mining operations. During the spring and summer, for American leaders, blockade and bombing had been conceptually and strategically linked in the siege strategy, and they did not argue whether bombing or blockade was more useful or whether one should receive a higher priority. These two parts of the siege strategy were seldom in competition with one another, and thus

61 Stimson and Bundy, *On Active Service*, 649.

there was no reason for sustained argument. Surely, top military leaders before the end of the war had beliefs about whether the bombing or the blockade would be more influential in the ongoing, and even escalating, siege strategy, but they left no clear record of such thinking at that time.[62] Undoubtedly, top navy officials thought more highly of the blockade, and army air force officials rated the bombing more highly. Since bombing and blockade were conjoined in the approved siege strategy, and there was no summertime dissent, there was no need to explore likely differences, rooted in organizational and bureaucratic loyalty, that might divide military leaders in what would have been, during the war, an "academic" enterprise. When possible, they preferred agreement to disagreement. Only after the war, when glory, postwar missions and budgets, and issues of future strategy were at issue, would top military leaders, surveying the closing months of the Pacific war, argue openly, and sometimes strenuously, about whether bombing or blockade contributed most to the defeat of Japan and whether one of these means, alone, could have produced the surrender.[63]

Even before Truman's White House meeting of 18 June with his military advisers, all had assumed that the air force, benefiting from the capture of Okinawa, would soon be significantly intensifying the conventional bombing of Japan. During the spring and summer, such an effort had never been an issue. All of the services formally agreed on its desirability, and army air force leaders, delighted to help end the war and to demonstrate the prowess of bombers, were eager to contribute to the siege strategy. By mid-July, in a report by Arnold that was endorsed by his fellow members of the Joint Chiefs, the American government planned

to achieve the disruption [by bombing] of the Japanese military, industrial, and economic systems. . . . In order to take full advantage of the incendiary attacks . . . , we expect to completely disrupt the Japanese transportation system. We estimate that this can be done with our forces

62 The blockade was greatly assisted in 1945 by B-29 mining operations, and there were some AAF-navy disputes about employing these bombers for that activity. James Cate and Wesley F. Craven, eds., *The Army Air Forces in World War II* (Chicago, 1953), 5:662–73.

63 See, for example, Curtis E. LeMay, with MacKinlay Kantor, *Mission with LeMay: My Story* (Garden City, 1965), 381; Ernest J. King and Walter Muir Whitehill, *Fleet Admiral King: A Naval Record* (New York, 1952), 621.

available in the month prior to the invasion of Japan. Japan, in fact, will become a nation without cities, with her transportation disrupted and will have tremendous difficulty in holding her people together for continued resistance to our terms of unconditional surrender.[64]

Such words did not *promise* that the November 1945 invasion would be unnecessary, or that bombing alone would make the decisive difference. For, all understood that this bombing would occur *within* the context of the ongoing blockade, and that such linked devastation, while adding to the substance of Japan's defeat, did not automatically translate into Japan's surrender. Better than many later analysts, the Joint Chiefs well understood the gap between the conditions for defeat and the production of an actual surrender, because the chiefs knew that enemy leaders did not automatically surrender when defeat was both inevitable and possibly near.

If heavy bombing could contribute to surrender before the planned Kyushu invasion, however, and Arnold and the other Joint Chiefs hoped in mid-July that it would, they were neither assuming nor suggesting that they thought that the A-bomb was unnecessary. For Arnold, as for the other military chiefs before and even shortly after Hiroshima, heavy bombing was not a substitute – but a supplement – to the A-bomb. And the A-bomb was, in turn, for them, a supplement to heavy bombing. In their pre-Hiroshima thinking, conventional heavy bombing may even have seemed a more powerful contributor to ultimate victory than the A-bomb. Unlike Stimson, Truman, and Byrnes, the military chiefs do not seem to have dwelled, after Trinity and before Hiroshima, on the atomic bomb's great power in the war. Probably the chiefs, as is often true of military leaders, were more conservative in their thinking about this new technology.

64 "Report on Army Air Operations in the War against Japan," JCS 1421, 16 July 1945, RG 218, file CCS 381 Japan (6-16-45), box 291, and also partly excerpted in Cline, *Washington Command Post*, 346. Alperovitz, "More on Atomic Diplomacy," *Bulletin of the Atomic Scientists* 41 (December 1985): 36, reaches the strained conclusion that Arnold *promised* that "the war could *easily* be ended by September or October" (emphasis added). For dubious, oblique support from a questionable book, based possibly on some postwar interviews with air force officers, see Fletcher Knebel and Charles W. Bailey II, *No High Ground* (New York, 1960), 111. Partial support for Knebel and Bailey's statement is available in Herman Wolk to General Ira Eaker, 19 October 1974, and reply, 22 October 1975, courtesy of Herman Wolk.

After the war ended, Admiral Leahy argued that Japan could have been defeated, and propelled to surrender, before 1 November 1945 and the use of the A-bomb. He had deep bureaucratic incentives to offer such judgments in his own memoirs.[65] He may have been right; he may have been wrong. But it is worth emphasizing that none of the American chiefs ever explicitly stated, let alone argued, this case *before* Hiroshima. Until then, not even Leahy, who, alone among the group, probably ethically disliked the use of the A-bomb, had ever said that it should not be used. None had ever promised Truman, or even told one another, that heavy conventional bombing or a naval blockade, or both, would *definitely* produce Japan's surrender before 1 November 1945 and thus obviate the Kyushu invasion.[66] All wanted to avoid that terrible invasion — with possibly thirty-one thousand casualties in the first thirty days and maybe as many as twenty-five thousand killed in the battles for Kyushu — and certainly the large invasion of about 1 March 1946.

Indeed, Arnold actually expected that the November invasion would be necessary in order to gain air bases on Kyushu to bomb other parts of Japan. In mid-June, he had so informed the other Joint Chiefs of his analysis, and he had even sent a deputy to the 18 June White House meeting to present this argument.[67] In mid-July, when crafting a report endorsed by his fellow chiefs, Arnold had stressed, again, that the Kyushu operation had great value for the continued bombing of Japan. The establishment of air bases in Kyushu, Arnold explained, would mean that "the full destructive power of the air force will be brought against the remaining elements of the Japanese war machine."[68]

Amid the strangling naval blockade, and without the A-bomb, perhaps the heavy bombing of Japanese cities in August, September, and October 1945 would have forced Japan to surrender before

---

65 William D. Leahy, *I Was There: The Personal Story of the Chief of Staff to Presidents Roosevelt and Truman Based on His Notes and Diaries Made at the Time* (New York, 1950), 440–1. There is no available evidence, in Leahy's papers and diaries or in any other source, that he had ever given such advice *before* Hiroshima.
66 For a different, virtually opposite, view see Alperovitz, *Atomic Diplomacy*, esp. 285.
67 Arnold, "Trip to the Pacific," 16 June 1945; "Minutes of Meeting Held at the White House . . . 18 June 1945."
68 Arnold in "Report on Army Air Operations in the War against Japan," JCS 1421, 16 July 1945.

November. For months before Hiroshima, the air force had been pounding many of Japan's cities. By mid-July, already, more than half the built-up areas of Tokyo and Kobe, and at least a fifth of the built-up areas of Osaka, Yokohama, and Nagoya, among others, had been destroyed. By early August, over sixty cities had been heavily bombed, probably about six hundred thousand had been killed and another million injured, and over eight million had been evacuated from the cities. Indeed, only because of Washington's special order were a few cities – Hiroshima, Kokura, Nagasaki, and Niigata – largely spared from conventional bombing and reserved for the atomic bomb. By the summer, both Japanese production and morale had fallen, and fear often disrupted life. Japan was near defeat.[69]

But the question remains, to be asked even after nearly a half-century, whether Japan's military leaders would have been willing to surrender, or whether they would have insisted on fighting at Kyushu and perhaps at Honshu, too? The movement from recognizing defeat to offering surrender can be jagged, and the process can be filled with self-deception, the quest for glory, and the faith in hope. Surrender, for many leaders, can be the most devastating failure – an event to be resisted at great cost to self and others.

In 1946, the United States Strategic Bombing Survey concluded (in an often-quoted sentence), "it is the Survey's opinion that certainly prior to 31 December 1945, and in all probability prior to 1 November 1945, Japan would have surrendered even if the atomic bombs had not been dropped, even if Russia had not entered the war, and even if no invasion had been planned or contemplated." Those who have relied heavily on this report have usually overlooked its slight hedge ("in all probability") and also some very disconcerting contrary evidence.[70]

After the war, some Japanese leaders testified on this issue. Prince Fumimaro Konoe told the Bombing Survey, in answering an

69 USSBS, *The Effects of Strategic Bombing on Japanese Morale* (Washington, 1947), 33–40; idem, *Summary Report (Pacific War)* (Washington, 1946), 23–4.
70 Chairman's Office, USSBS, *Japan's Struggle to End the War*, 45. The strongest support for this conclusion from a high-level Japanese leader came from Koichi Kido, Privy Seal, in his interrogation of 10 November 1945 by the survey, but he was also very eager to please his questioners and seemed rather slippery. "Interrogation of Kido," Records of the USSBS.

explicit question, that, if the atomic bomb had not been dropped, "the war probably . . . would have lasted all this year [1945]."[71] Admiral Baron Kantaro Suzuki, Japan's premier during the empire's last days, though never directly confronting the question, gave similar testimony to American interrogators after the war. He stressed the Japanese military's plans, and hopes, for a last battle. "The Supreme War Council [The Big Six]," he told the survey, "had proceeded with the one plan of fighting a decisive battle at the landing point and was making every possible preparation to meet such a landing. They proceeded with that plan until the atomic bomb was dropped."[72] After the survey's published 1946 report, former Foreign Minister Togo informed American questioners that the bomb had made a powerful difference. On the 7th, more than a day before Soviet entry, Togo met with the emperor, who (in Togo's later words) "indicated clearly that the enemy's new weapon made it impossible to go on fighting [and he] told me to try to end the war immediately." In Togo's recollection of events, the bomb had propelled the emperor to push more ardently for peace.[73]

After the war, Admiral King publicly argued that a naval blockade would have produced a Japanese surrender, and thus implied that the atomic bombing had been unnecessary. But he did not claim success by 1 November, only an ultimate triumph. A loyal navy man, he questioned after the war – as have few analysts – whether in the spring and summer the army should have insisted upon an invasion. He chose not to admit that he had never argued against the Kyushu invasion in front of Truman and that he had actually seemed to endorse the operation itself, not just planning for it.[74]

Had American leaders been willing to risk prolonging the war, there is no question that a naval blockade, as King later wrote, "would *in the course of time*, have starved the Japanese into sub-

71 "Interrogation of Konoye," 9 November 1945.
72 "Interrogation of Suzuki," 26 December 1945.
73 "Statement" of Togo #50304. Togo, *Cause of Japan*, 315–16, places this meeting on the 8th and is less emphatic about the emperor's wishes.
74 King and Whitehill, *Admiral King*, 621. On the 18 June meeting see "Minutes of Meeting Held at the White House . . . 18 June 1945"; Leahy Diary, 18 June 1945; Stimson Diary, 18 June 1945; Forrestal Diary, 18 June 1945.

mission through lack of oil, rice, medicine, and other materials."[75]
By mid-1945, largely because of American naval operations, Japan's merchant fleet had been reduced to about 10 percent of its prewar size, its oil supplies cut to under 3 percent of the prewar peak, most imports of foodstuffs, oil, and other materials blocked, and Japan's economy was in shambles. Food supplies had perilously dwindled, with sharp cuts in food rations in 1944 and again in 1945. The 1945 rice crop had been a disaster, and imports were virtually impossible.[76] In June 1945, a then-secret Japanese analysis for the cabinet warned, "The food situation has grown worse and a crisis will be reached at the end of this year. The people will have to get along on an absolute minimum of rice and salt required for subsistence."[77]

That bleak and rather accurate estimate was, of course, not available to American leaders. During the last months of war, Marshall's plans for the invasion, endorsed by Truman and his other military advisers, had easily triumphed. None ever argued in the summer for a prolonged blockade and no invasion in late 1945 or even early 1946. Truman, despite his uneasiness in mid-June 1945 about the invasion plan, was easily diverted from seriously considering postponement of the invasion and trying to "starve out" the Japanese in order to save American lives. Had he received different counsel from his military advisers, or had they split in June 1945 as they had at times in 1944, the president might have dwelled on the siege strategy of blockade and bombing without invasion. Still, such a strategy would have easily included for him, and for his advisers, the use of the atomic bomb.

The siege strategy (without the A-bomb) might have produced the desired Japanese surrender by 1 November. The probabilities are not very high (maybe 25–30 percent), because the crucial problems, in this counterfactual history, are whether the peace forces would have pushed ardently for surrender, whether the emperor would have intervened if his government had been divided, whether the militarists would have yielded to his sense of necessity, and whether

75   King and Whitehill, *Admiral King*, 621 (emphasis added).
76   Jerome B. Cohen, *Japan's Economy in War and Reconstruction* (Minneapolis, 1949), 104–5, 109, 144, 368–70.
77   "Survey of National Resources as of 1–10 June 1945," in *Japan's Struggle to End the War*, appendix, vii–viii.

the government would have accepted defeat and moved to surrender. That process would have involved many contingencies and have required the Japanese government to deal directly with the United States.

X

Single and Multiple Alternatives. There is good reason to have serious doubts that any *single* "alternative" – a noncombat demonstration, guaranteeing the emperor, pursuing peace feelers, awaiting Soviet entry, or continuing heavy conventional bombing and the blockade – would *alone* have produced surrender before November without the use of the A-bomb. But it does seem very likely, though certainly not definite, that a synergistic combination of guaranteeing the emperor, awaiting Soviet entry, and continuing the siege strategy would have ended the war in time to avoid the November invasion. And quite possibly Soviet entry amid the strangling blockade and the heavy bombing of cities could have accomplished that goal without dropping the atomic bomb.

There was, then, more probably than not, a missed opportunity to end the war without the A-bomb and without the November invasion. And it is virtually definite, had the Kyushu invasion occurred with these other strategies, and without the A-bomb, that Japan would have surrendered well before the March 1946 invasion. Such conclusions, though emerging from the uneasy realm of counterfactual history, do place in question the contention that the atomic bomb was necessary. These conclusions challenge that concept of "necessity" and require that its meanings be carefully spelled out, that the implied costs be carefully expressed and analyzed, and that scholars and laypeople, in discussing these issues, carefully distinguish between what now seems known, what was known or believed before Hiroshima, and whether the pre-Hiroshima processes of decision making and analysis were adequate, on ethical and international-political grounds, to the important actions being taken.

To dwell upon the process of decision making alone would be unduly mechanistic, but it is certainly important to recognize that the A-bomb decision, contrary to some contentions, was not "carefully considered" and that the movement toward the November invasion, despite Truman's desires, was not fully and critically examined in his presence. He never sought "carefully" to consider the use of the A-bomb, nor was there any need for him to hold a meeting with advisers on whether it should be used, because he and they all assumed that it would be used.[78] The process that he followed implemented that assumption. The question of the invasion was far more troubling to him. Had Japan not surrendered by the summer or early autumn, probably Truman would have returned to another session with his military advisers to discuss the necessity for the November invasion. At such a meeting, perhaps they would have served him better than they did in mid-June, at the special White House session, where they smoothed over earlier differences and thus presented the siege strategy with the Kyushu invasion of November as the only reasonable strategy.

XI

On 9 August 1945, three days after the Hiroshima bomb, in implementing the orders to use bombs "as made ready,"[79] the air force dropped the second atomic bomb, killing about thirty-five to eighty thousand at Nagasaki. This bomb was almost definitely unnecessary. Without that bombing, Japan would have surrendered – very probably on the 10th. Amid the continuing blockade and the heavy conventional bombing, the powerful hammerlike blows of the Hiroshima weapon on the 6th and Soviet entry on the 8th had emboldened the peace forces in the Japanese government to try to end the war with only the single condition of the guarantee of the emperor. The day before the Nagasaki bombing, the emperor had agreed to intervene in deliberations, if necessary, to end the war with that one condition.[80] "We must put an end to the war as speedily as possi-

---

78 Henry L. Stimson, "The Decision to Use the Atomic Bomb," *Harper's Magazine* 194 (February 1947): 98–101; Bernstein, "Seizing the Contested Terrain," 45–72. For great doubts about whether such a meeting was held see Barton J. Bernstein, "Ike and Hiroshima: Did He Oppose It?" *Journal of Strategic Studies* 10 (September 1987): 378–9.

79 General Thomas Handy to General Carl Spaatz, 25 July 1945, RG 77, Harrison-Bundy Files 64.

80 Barton J. Bernstein, "Doomsday II," *New York Times Magazine*, 27 July 1975, 7, 21ff.; Sherwin, *World Destroyed*, 233–6.

ble," he had instructed the Lord Privy Seal Koichi Kido.[81] Undoubtedly, Hirohito would have intervened without the Nagasaki bombing to plead, successfully, for Japan's surrender.

Indeed, according to some later reports, the emperor would have intervened without both the second bomb and Soviet entry. Undoubtedly, that Soviet action on the 8th made it easier for the emperor to break precedent and try to shape policy, and certainly the Soviet attack smashed many lingering hopes in the cabinet that had allowed the peace forces to dawdle until the 8th and 9th.[82]

In Washington, because no one had foreseen such an early Japanese surrender, no one had suggested delaying before using a second atomic bomb. Even after the Hiroshima bomb, top officials in Washington were unsure how long the war might continue and thus whether to risk cutting back military procurement contracts.[83] On the 8th, Secretary of the Navy Forrestal, apparently expecting that the November invasion would occur, worried about which American commander would be chosen for "the final operations against Japan in the Pacific."[84] That same day, Truman, having just returned from Potsdam, directed a key official to have a reconversion plan by the *end* of August.[85] On the 9th, recording his own uncertainty, Stimson wrote in his diary, "the bomb and the entrance of the Russians into the war will certainly have an effect on hastening the victory. But just how much that effect is on how long and how many men we will have to keep to accomplish that victory, it is impossible to determine."[86]

In the Pacific, because bad weather had been forecast for a few days after the 9th, scientists had rushed to prepare the plutonium

81 "Statements" of Kido #61541 and #61476.
82 For evidence, often *within* the assumed context of the bombing and blockade, about the decisive impact of the first A-bomb on the emperor and others see "Statements" of Kido #61541 and #61476 and Togo #50304; Togo, *Cause of Japan*, 313–14; "Interrogation of Suzuki"; and Far East Command, G-2 Historical Section, "Interrogation of Hisatsune Sakomizu," 3 May 1949, Modern Military Records Branch, National Archives. Some others mentioned *both* the first A-bomb and Soviet entry in such a way that it is hard to assess their sense of the comparative impact of each event. See, for example, "Interrogation of Konoye"; Toyoda in USSBS, *Interrogation*, II, 320; Kase, *Journey*, 320; and "Statements" of Ikeda #45479.
83 Robert P. Patterson (undersecretary of war) to George Harrison, 2 August 1945, and Harrison to Patterson, 8 August 1945, RG 77, Harrison-Bundy Files 8.
84 Forrestal to Truman, 8 August 1945, Forrestal Diary.
85 Truman to John Snyder, 8 August 1945, OWMR Records.
86 Stimson Diary, 9 August 1945.

weapon for prompt dropping on a Japanese city. The bomb's use was automatic – not because some wanted to test this kind of bomb on a city but because no one had seen any reason to delay it. No one had foreseen the great psychological impact of the first bomb on Japan, and there was no available evidence, beyond the inner circles of Japan's government, that the peace forces had been galvanized toward action even before the Nagasaki bomb.[87]

But even the two bombs, sandwiched around Soviet entry into the war, did not alter the expressed positions of leading militarists in the Japanese government – General Korechika Anami, the minister of war (army); General Yoshijiro Umezu, army chief of staff; and Admiral Soemu Toyoda, navy chief of staff. All three still wanted to hold out for maintenance of the imperial system and three other conditions (no postwar occupation, self-disarmament, and conduct of their own war trials). They were, as historian Robert Butow remarked, "true samurai."[88]

War Minister Anami, the most powerful of the three militarists, continued to look forward to a last battle unless America yielded and granted all four conditions. An associate later characterized Anami's beliefs: "Although Japan's victory in the decisive battle of the homeland is not certain, there is still some possibility. Therefore, the battle should be fought on the homeland at least once with a resolution to seek a way out of a desperate situation."[89]

Only after the emperor broke precedent and pleaded in the early hours of the 10th for peace with the single condition of a guarantee of the imperial system did Anami and the other two military leaders accept the cabinet majority's position.[90] Without Hirohito's crucial intercession, the militarists would probably not have yielded. The war would have dragged on – perhaps even into the bloody battle, scheduled by America to begin in November, that Anami, in his quest for honor, desired for himself, for the army that he loved, and for the polity that he cherished.

87   Bernstein, "Doomsday II"; Sherwin, *World Destroyed*, 233–6.
88   "Statements" of Togo #50304 and Toyoda #61340 and #57670; Butow, *Japan's Decision to Surrender*, 160–1, who also notes some occasional relaxation of the condition of no occupation to allow postwar occupation of all of Japan except Tokyo.
89   "Statements" of Masao Yoshizumi #54484 (source of quotation) and stronger statement in #59277.
90   On Anami see "Statements" of Yoshizumi #54484 and #59277; Makato Tsukamato #59466; Saburo Hayashi #61436; and Seimo Sakonji #58226.

Truman's administration was unprepared for Japan's peace offer on 10 August. Policymakers had not expected such a speedy response, nor had they even hoped for it. So little did Stimson anticipate that anything significant was likely to happen that week that he was actually leaving for a much-needed vacation when Japan's message arrived. He dashed to the White House to join the important discussion on whether the air force should continue its conventional bombing and use more atomic bombs.[91]

That day, Truman sharply redefined his policy on the atomic bomb. No longer would its use be automatic. He actually wanted to avoid dropping another one. As he told his cabinet (in Henry Wallace's words): "The thought of wiping out another 100,000 people was too horrible. He didn't like the idea of killing 'all those kids.' " For the first time, Truman admitted that the A-bombs had killed many innocent noncombatants.[92] But Truman chose to continue the heavy conventional bombing of Japanese cities, which would kill thousands of others.

Unlike Stimson,[93] who had earlier agonized about the mass bombing of cities, Truman neither before nor after Hiroshima and Nagasaki seemed worried about such mass killings by conventional means. But before the Hiroshima bombing, in what can only be interpreted as self-deception, he had managed not to know that the A-bombs would slay many noncombatants. At Potsdam, the president, after a meeting with Stimson, had written in his diary that they had agreed that the bomb would be used "so that military objectives and soldiers and sailors are the target and not women and children. Even if the Japs are savages, ruthless, merciless and fanatic, we as the leader of the world for the common welfare [are not]. The target will be a purely military one." After discussing the A-bomb with Stimson, President Truman, unless engaging in a form of self-deception, could *not* have believed his own diary words.[94]

91 Stimson Diary, 10 August 1945. His diary of 9 August did mention hopes for a surrender before the use of the third bomb, which could have been used in about ten days, but his diary for 10 August indicates how sincerely surprised he was by Japan's decision at that time.
92 Henry A. Wallace Diary, 10 August 1945, Wallace Papers, University of Iowa, Iowa City.
93 Stimson Diary, 6 June and 5 March 1945; Barton J. Bernstein, "An Analysis of 'Two Cultures': Writing about the Making and the Using of the Atomic Bombs," *Public Historian* 12 (Spring 1990): 96–9.
94 Truman, "Potsdam Diary," 25 July 1945.

Briefly facing the reality of the A-bomb's great destruction, including the killing of noncombatants, Truman was still unwilling to accede, fully and unequivocally, to the single Japanese condition – even though agreement would end the war promptly and, as Stimson stressed, thus block Soviet claims for any role in the postwar occupation of Japan. Byrnes, earlier so worried about the Soviets grabbing territory on the Asian mainland, was now willing to risk prolonging the war in order to avoid granting the imperial system. The administration's guarantee of the emperor, Byrnes warned, could mean the "crucifixion of the President" at home. Byrnes believed that Americans would not tolerate Hirohito and the throne. The secretary of state was willing to place domestic politics above his own anti-Soviet concerns. For him, international considerations were secondary.[95]

The dispute on the 10th at the White House ended in an uneasy compromise, a kind of middle way between Byrnes and Stimson. Advisers worked out an intentionally ambiguous response that neither accepted nor rejected Japan's single condition.[96] That reply briefly split the fragile peace coalition in Japan, briefly pushed the premier into the militarists' camp, emboldened the militarists to fight on, propelled them again to insist upon their other three conditions, and required the emperor to intervene once more.[97]

Before Hirohito's intervention, some high-ranking military men below the cabinet level ardently pleaded for continuing the war. Vice Chief of the Naval Staff Onishi, planner of the kamikaze attacks, argued, "we would never be defeated if we were prepared to sacrifice 20,000,000 lives in a 'special attack' effort."[98] Such suicidal contentions, linking national honor and eternal glory, em-

95   On the meeting see Stimson Diary, 10 August 1945; Leahy Diary, 10 August 1945; Forrestal Diary, 10 August 1945; and Byrnes quoted in W. B.'s Notes, 10 August 1945. For Truman's earlier political fears about modifying the unconditional surrender demand see "Minutes of Meeting Held at the White House . . . 18 June 1945." These events are treated in Barton J. Bernstein, "The Perils and Politics of Surrender: Ending the War with Japan and Avoiding the Third Atomic Bomb," *Pacific Historical Review* 46 (February 1977): 1–12.

96   The U.S. reply is reprinted in Butow, *Japan's Decision to Surrender*, 245.

97   Bernstein, "Perils and Politics of Surrender," 17–23.

98   Onishi is paraphrased in "Statements" of Togo #50304. For a slightly different version see Butow, *Japan's Decision to Surrender*, 205. For sentiments similar to Onishi's see "Interrogation of Lt. Gen Kawabe" (deputy chief, Imperial General Headquarters), Records of the USSBS.

phasized to Umezu, Toyoda, and Anami the dangerous passions among their underlings and the perils of seeking a surrender in Japan in mid-August.

Even after Hirohito's dramatic intervention on the 14th for peace, some Japanese militarists almost staged a successful coup. Had they succeeded, President Truman, with a third A-bomb that could be at Tinian and ready for use in about a week, would have soon faced a painful decision – whether to use the bomb, as Americans would have expected, or whether instead to rely upon conventional warfare and hope that the November invasion would not be necessary. Most likely, Truman would have chosen to use the third atomic bomb.[99]

Truman never had to face that decision because two Japanese leaders, War Minister Anami and Chief of Staff Umezu, intervened to block the coup and thus maintained the government. The more powerful of the two was Anami. Loyal to the emperor, General Anami acceded to Hirohito's tearful plea for peace through surrender. But had Anami chosen instead to resign from the cabinet, it would have fallen and the speedy peace would have been lost. Anami stayed in the cabinet and deftly prevented a coup by calling on the army to be loyal to him, to its sense of honor, and to the emperor. Had he instead supported the coup and joined it, he would have taken powerful sections of the army with him. He was the keystone in the fragile arch that could lead to a prompt peace or a prolonged war.[100] Had Anami chosen differently, analysts might well be discussing the use of the third atomic bomb, the extension of the war, and perhaps even the November invasion of Kyushu.

Concern with the use of the two A-bombs requires return to an important but generally neglected theme: Truman on the 10th had felt a moral distinction between the atomic bomb and heavy conventional bombing. Though feeling moral revulsion about the future use of the A-bomb, he remained willing to bomb Japanese cities with high explosives and incendiaries. Perhaps at least

99   Mr. Balfour to Foreign Office, 14 August 1945, F.O. 800/461, Public Record Office, Kew, United Kingdom.
100 Bernstein, "Perils and Politics of Surrender," 18–22; Butow, *Japan's Decision to Surrender*, 196–209.

twenty thousand died in those conventional attacks during the last week of the Pacific war. Some, indeed, even died on 14 August, when American bombers, in their largest attack of the Pacific war, pummeled Japan, sometimes dropping their deadly cargo even after Japan had publicly accepted Washington's terms for surrender.[101]

XII

World War II was virtually total war. All the major powers had killed noncombatants intentionally. That policy repudiated the older morality that soldiers should seek to spare noncombatants. In the 1930s, when much of the civilized world had been horrified by the killings of noncombatants in Shanghai and Guernica, Roosevelt had deplored the barbarism. But by 1945, after the deadly bombings of Hamburg and Dresden, Americans welcomed the bombings, and mass killings, of Tokyo, Yokohoma, Nagoya, . . . Hiroshima, and Nagasaki. The older morality had crumbled in the crucible of what had become virtually total war. Undoubtedly, the impersonality of bombing – the distance between the crew and the victims – made such killing easier. To bayonet civilians could still seem barbarous; to kill them from the air came to seem easy, necessary, and desirable. Technology made such warfare possible; it did not compel these decisions.

The older morality crumbled in the crucible of what became virtually total war. Almost any weapon (gas and biological warfare were usually exceptions) was generally used.[102] General Marshall wanted to cross the moral threshold and employ gas against Japanese soldiers.[103] And according to one official's postwar recollections, there was also a plan to use biological warfare – not the bacterial form but the chemical mode – to destroy the Japanese rice crop in the early autumn to starve the Japanese into submis-

---

101 *New York Times*, 15 August 1945; Bernstein, "Perils and Politics of Surrender," 16–17.
102 Barton J. Bernstein, "America's Biological Warfare Program in the Second World War," *Journal of Strategic Studies* 11 (September 1988): 292–317; idem, "Why We Didn't Use Poison Gas in World War II," *American Heritage* 36 (August–September 1985): 40–5.
103 McCloy, "Memorandum of Conversation with General Marshall," 29 May 1945.

sion. Perhaps only Japan's earlier surrender prevented that kind of assault upon Japan.[104]

In the emerging conception of nearly total war, the enemy was not simply soldiers but noncombatants. They worked in the factories, ran the economy, maintained the civic life, constituted much of the nation, and were the core of national cohesion. Kill them, and production would tumble, the national fabric would rip, armies would soon feel homeless, and the government might surrender.

Stimson, sometimes in moral agony, presided as secretary of war over this transformed morality. It profoundly troubled him, he often chose not to recognize it, and he even told Truman in June that he wanted to be sure that he held the air force to precision bombing partly because, "I did not want to have the United States get the reputation of outdoing Hitler in atrocities."[105] Stimson's second reason, undercutting his first, was, as he told Truman, "I was a little fearful that before we could get ready the Air Force might have Japan so thoroughly bombed out that the new weapon would not have a fair background to show its strength."[106] Just six days before his conversation with Truman, Stimson had prescribed, with the concurrence of the Interim Committee, "that the most desirable target [for the A-bomb] would be a vital war plant employing a large number of workers and closely surrounded by workers' houses." Stripped of the euphemisms that these official minutes used, the meaning is clear: Workers and their families would also be the targets of the bomb, whose deadly effects "would be dangerous to life for a radius of at least two-thirds of a mile."[107]

Before Hiroshima, although none of Truman's advisers ever opposed the use of the A-bomb on Japan, one man, and only one, did object to the targeting of this new weapon on noncombatants. He was General George C. Marshall, the very leader who was willing to cross the moral threshold to employ gas against enemy soldiers, but reluctant to further cross the moral threshold after the conventional

104 Robert Lovett oral history (1960), Oral History Office, Columbia University, New York City.
105 Stimson Diary, 6 June 1945.
106 Stimson Diary, 6 June 1945.
107 Interim Committee, 31 May 1945, paraphrasing Stimson on targeting and Oppenheimer on dangers.

bombing of noncombatants to use the A-bomb on them. Older martial values, in his case, came to the fore in his quest to protect noncombatants from the atomic bomb. On 29 May 1945, two days before the Interim Committee decision and eight days before Stimson's conversation with Truman, Marshall had urged, unsuccessfully, that the new weapon "might first be used against straight military objectives such as a large naval installation and then if no complete result was derived from the effect of that, he thought we ought to designate a number of large manufacturing areas from which the people would be warned to leave." In that unsuccessful conversation with Stimson, General Marshall had stressed that he feared that the United States would otherwise have to bear the "opprobrium which might follow from an ill-considered employment of such force."[108]

Rebuffed by Stimson on the 29th, Marshall apparently never again raised these issues with the secretary, Truman, or anyone else. Loyal to both men, Marshall, in the aftermath of war, never disclosed that he had held, as previously expressed, such strong doubts. Understanding the need to legitimize decisions and to shape national memory, he was always unwilling to mention the moral objections that he had briefly stated, but perhaps deeply felt, in the period before Hiroshima.

XIII

World War II was a terribly bloody war. It killed many millions and maimed many more. It helped transform morality. It ushered in the atomic age. It dramatized the dark side of human capacity and prompted some to redefine "human nature." In America, the war – with its barbarism – was a helpful midwife in the shift in liberal sensibility from the optimistic rationality of John Dewey to the emphasis on the pessimistic irrationality of Reinhold Niebuhr. For some, the names of Buchenwald, Dachau, and Auschwitz would be joined, perhaps uneasily, to Dresden, Hamburg, and Tokyo, and occasionally also to Hiroshima and Nagasaki. They

108 McCloy, "Memorandum of Conversation with General Marshall," 29 May 1945, paraphrasing Marshall, who later approved this memorandum of his discussion with Stimson.

were not moral equivalents, because intentional genocide and intentional mass killing of some noncombatants were not morally
identical, but all were powerful testimonials to the fact of massive
deaths organized by nation-states, implemented by modern warriors, and endorsed by their civilian populations.

Ultimately, to understand, to rue, and even to deplore the use of
the A-bomb are separable, and not necessarily linked, judgments.
To fail to understand the reasons for the bombings of Hiroshima
and Nagasaki is regrettable. To judge those actions by a set of
ethical standards usually abandoned in World War II and sometimes revived in later years is appropriate. But to ascribe those
moral standards to the leaders and citizens of the United States, or
the other major powers, during World War II is to distort the
history of that terrible war and to misinterpret the important decisions made in it.

4

Japan's Delayed Surrender: A Reinterpretation

HERBERT P. BIX

The saying goes that hindsight is always twenty/twenty, and when the look backward is of one's own life, and one tries to be honest, maybe twenty/twenty can be reached. But not always. Usually we see instead not quite what we really did, or why we really did it, or what the real consequences were.

When the retrospective view is wide, societal rather than personal, of events that for years have been disguised or covered over, when the view is of history and the eyes are those of the historian, the twenty/twenty truism can seem irrelevant. Past events, of course, are refracted through the mind of the person who records them, shaped by the values that person seeks to realize in the present and future. Inevitably, they are slippery and fogged. So it is with battles and war, and the images and memories they leave behind. So it was with the events of 1945.

The Problem in the Sources

For the past half-century, Western interpretations of the ending of the Pacific war have centered on the atomic bombings of Hiroshima and Nagasaki, while slighting not only the military context in which American leaders operated but also the Japanese context. When we look at the Japanese context, we see the heavy responsibility of Japan's leaders in prolonging the war, and we also see that Emperor Hirohito played a pivotal role at every stage of the process that led to Japan's delayed surrender.

These interpretations reveal the strong influence of four sources:

Joseph C. Grew and his views on "unconditional surrender"; Hisatsune Sakomizu's (and later Kainan Shimomura's) firsthand accounts of the emperor's actions in the days before the surrender; the U.S. Strategic Bombing Survey study, entitled *Japan's Struggle To End The War*, which built on Sakomizu and the statements of the principal defendants at the Tokyo War Crimes Trials; and Robert J. C. Butow's classic work, *Japan's Decision to Surrender*, which brilliantly synthesized the available materials at the time he wrote. Many other excellent books and articles have since advanced the debate, identifying controversial issues and giving shape to later explanations of Japan's surrender, both orthodox and revisionist.[1] But these four specific works set the original interpretive parameters of the discussion.

Former Ambassador to Japan Joseph C. Grew, America's most famous official spokesman on Japan during the 1930s and early 1940s, criticized Truman's insistence on implementing Roosevelt's "unconditional surrender" goal. Grew saw Emperor Hirohito as the "queen bee in a hive . . . surrounded by the attentions of the hive" and the man who held the key to Japan's surrender.[2] At various times, before and during the war, he described the emperor as a "puppet" of the militarists, a constitutionalist, and a pacifist. Grew had enormous confidence in the influence upon policy of those whom he termed the "moderates" around the Japanese throne. At the very center of these moderates, Grew placed the emperor. As the final collapse of the Japanese empire approached in the spring of 1945, Grew was willing to allow these individuals

1 Noteworthy in this regard are the writings of Barton J. Bernstein, especially his "The Atomic Bomb and American Foreign Policy, 1941–1945: An Historiographical Controversy," *Peace and Change* 2 (Spring 1974): 1–16; idem, *The Atomic Bomb: The Critical Issues* (Boston, 1976); idem, "Roosevelt, Truman, and the Atomic Bomb, 1941–1945: A Reinterpretation," *Political Science Quarterly* 90 (Spring 1975): 23–69; idem, "The Perils and Politics of Surrender: Ending the War with Japan and Avoiding the Third Atomic Bomb," *Pacific Historical Review* 46 (February 1977): 1–27; and idem, "Marshall, Truman, and the Decision to Drop the Bomb," *International Security* 16 (Winter 1991/92): 214–21. Leon V. Sigal, *Fighting to a Finish: The Politics of War Termination in the United States and Japan, 1945* (Ithaca, 1988), also contains useful suggestions for deepening the analysis of war termination.
2 The "queen bee" analogy comes from Grew's speech to a U.S. Senate committee hearing on 12 December 1944. See Masanori Nakamura, *The Japanese Monarchy: Ambassador Joseph Grew and the Making of the "Symbol Emperor System," 1931–1991* (Armonk, NY, 1992), 66.

"to determine for themselves the nature of their future political structure."[3]

In his memoirs, published in 1952, long after President Harry S. Truman and Secretary of State James M. Byrnes had rejected his efforts to include in the Potsdam draft declaration a clause guaranteeing the position of the imperial house, Grew wrote that,

The main point at issue historically is whether, if immediately following the terrific devastation of Tokyo by our B-29s in May, 1945, "the President had made a public categorical statement that surrender would not mean the elimination of the present dynasty if the Japanese people desired its retention, the surrender of Japan could have been hastened. . . . From statements made by a number of the moderate former Japanese leaders to responsible Americans after the American occupation, it is quite clear that the civilian advisers to the Emperor were working toward surrender long before the Potsdam Proclamation, even indeed before my talk with the President on May 28, for they knew then that Japan was a defeated nation. The stumbling block that they had to overcome was the complete dominance of the Japanese Army over the Government. . . . The Emperor needed all the support he could get, and . . . if such a categorical statement about the dynasty had been issued in May, 1945, the surrender-minded elements in the Government might well have been afforded . . . a valid reason and the necessary strength to come to an early clear-cut decision. . . . Prime Minister [Kantaro] Suzuki . . . was surrender-minded even before May, 1945, if only it were made clear that surrender would not involve the downfall of the dynasty.[4]

Grew was impressed by the views of the emperor's civilian advisers, their pro-Anglo-American stance in diplomacy at the start of the 1930s, and their professed support for party cabinets earlier. Yet Grew never understood the dynamics of Japanese politics during his tenure as ambassador (1932–42), and thus could not grasp how such moderate gentlemen of high lineage, some of whom he likened to the Saltonstalls, the Sedgwicks, and the Peabodys he had known from his days in Boston, gradually narrowed their distance from the military during the course of Japan's protracted war in

3   Joseph C. Grew, *Turbulent Era: A Diplomatic Record of Forty Years, 1904–1945* (Boston, 1952), 1435. Grew endorsed the Truman administration's decision to retain the emperor for postwar purposes, but even he never imagined that Hirohito would be able to absolve himself of war guilt and not step down.
4   Grew, *Turbulent Era*, 1425–6.

China. Nor did he perceive how one faction of the moderates, centered on Emperor Hirohito and his chief adviser, Lord Keeper of the Privy Seal Koichi Kido, had eventually entered into a loose alliance with the military that made Pearl Harbor possible. For Grew it was always the military acting on their own. Nonetheless, Grew was correct in identifying the moderates as central to the surrender process, and thereby in alerting us to the fact that how we define and understand the moderates around the throne largely determines how we evaluate wartime and early postwar Japanese history.[5]

Hisatsune Sakomizu was the chief cabinet secretary in the cabinet of Kantaro Suzuki (7 April–15 August 1945), and the son-in-law of the "senior statesman" Keisuke Okada. He attended the 9–10 August imperial conference and drafted notes of that meeting that revealed how Japan's leaders were brought to accept the Potsdam Declaration, and the emperor's role in the process. Sakomizu argued that the key figures who had struggled all along to overcome the military and stop the fighting were Emperor Hirohito, Prime Minister Suzuki, and Lord Keeper of the Privy Seal Kido.

In his testimony to American interrogators and in his later writings, however, Sakomizu obscured the emperor's responsibility for the long delay in moving to accept the Potsdam terms.[6] He also exaggerated the hegemony of the military in the policymaking, projecting a misleading image of an imperial court oppressed by the military.

5 See Yutaka Yoshida, *Showa tenno no shusenshi* [A history of the Showa emperor in the war termination process] (Tokyo, 1992), 228–9. Yoshida notes that "without the tacit recognition and approval of the moderates after the fact, or without their support and cooperation, the line pushed by the military could not have become national policy."

6 Sakomizu published "Kofukuji no shinso" [The trust about the surrender], based on his deposition of December 1945, in *Jiyu kokumin* (February 1946). In his later account of the event – *Kikanjuka no shusho kantei: 2.26 jiken kara shusen made* [The prime minister's official mansion under the gun: from the February 26, 1936, uprising to the end of the war] (Tokyo, 1964) – the emperor is portrayed as a deus ex machina, external to the action until the very last stage. The tone of Sakomizu's chapter on the 9–10 August imperial conference may be gathered from his opening words (253): "Writing this today, I fear that readers might think how foolish the Japanese government at that time was. Viewed providentially, however, Japan was groping in absurd directions with its eyes covered. Feelings of deep regret, of shame at our incompetence, and past credulous naivete – these inexpressible emotions almost bring tears to my eyes. But Japan's domestic situation was not so simple. . . . Prime Minister Suzuki's only wish was to maintain the unity of the race whether by continuing the war or ending it."

It may further be observed that Sakomizu, in the spirit and pattern of faithful subordinates in all bureaucracies, made his superior, Kantaro Suzuki, look more peace-minded and less flawed than he probably really was. He did this by presenting the distinctive Japanese cultural practice of *haragei*, whereby two parties to a negotiation advanced their respective goals by nonverbal, very subtle, mutual deception. Thus, Sakomizu rationalized and obscured the genuine opportunism, vacillation, and professional incompetence of Suzuki and other members of the wartime government as they shifted from a policy of war to one of surrender.[7]

Japan's Struggle To End The War was a short report issued in July 1946 by the U.S. Strategic Bombing Survey to press the Army Air Force's "claim to credit for winning the war against Japan."[8] Centered on a simple chronology of events, from the fall of Hideki Togo to Japan's capitulation, it acknowledged the roles of the rival military services but concluded that air power had largely "determined the timing of Japan's surrender and obviated any need for invasion." For, "in all probability prior to 1 November 1945, Japan would have surrendered even if the atomic bombs had not been dropped, even if Russia had not entered the war, and even if no invasion had been planned or contemplated."[9]

Tucked into *Japan's Struggle* is the notion of a remote emperor finally brought into a delicately balanced decision-making process at the last moment. The atomic bombing of Hiroshima, it asserted, "contribut[ed] to a situation which permitted the Prime Minister to bring the Emperor overtly and directly into a position where his decision for immediate acceptance of the Potsdam Declaration could be used" to break a 3–3 split among the members of the Supreme War Leadership Council.

Japan's Struggle drew directly on the testimony of Sakomizu, Suzuki, and Kido, augmented by the impressions of the "senior statesmen" (*jushin*) and other principal defendants in the Tokyo War Crimes Trials. Based on the views of men whose sole, overrid-

7 Nobumasa Tanaka, *Dokyumento Showa tenno, dai go kan, haisen (ge)* (Tokyo, 1988), 476.
8 John Ray Skates, *The Invasion of Japan: Alternative to the Bomb* (Columbia, SC, 1994), 251.
9 U.S. Strategic Bombing Survey, *Japan's Struggle To End The War* (Washington, July 1946), 12–13.

ing objective was to "preserve the national polity [*kokutai*]," defend the emperor, and obfuscate their own failures of leadership and judgment, *Japan's Struggle* translated the official Japanese version of the emperor's role in ending the war into the official American version.

Building on testimony about the emperor by Sakomizu, Suzuki, and Kido; the Strategic Bombing Survey reports, unpublished interrogations compiled by the Military History Section of General Douglas MacArthur's headquarters, the records of the International Military Tribunal for the Far East, the diaries of Koichi Kido, and many other primary sources, Robert J. C. Butow authored *Japan's Decision to Surrender*, a work of exceptionally clear focus that set the standard for all subsequent discussion.[10]

Unfortunately, however, Butow failed to scrutinize his Japanese sources for unintended suggestions that the emperor's role in events had been other than they asserted. As a consequence, Butow misdescribed Hirohito as "nothing more than a convenient emblem to be brandished at the proper moment – a mere symbol behind whom the civilian and military elite selfishly and independently gambled for the stakes of power."[11] In short, Butow accepted the myth of the emperor as a standard European-style monarch, constitutionally bound to obey the decisions of his advisers and unable to declare his own will except when his ministers deadlocked.

The notion that the emperor became a decision arbiter only at the very last moment of defeat is undermined by documented historical facts that have accumulated for the past forty years. Throughout the war, Hirohito's influence continued to grow. He settled interservice disputes over the allocation of scarce war resources. He intervened frequently and directly in ongoing combat operations as well as in planning by the imperial general headquarters. If he was indeed strong enough to surrender his empire at the end, that was because he had been equally strong enough to have surrendered earlier. His loss of ability to judge the war situation

10 Kainan Shimomura's account of the ending of the war was originally written at Kantaro Suzuki's request in 1947 and published the following year under the title *Shusenki* [Notes on the termination of the war]. A revised and expanded version, entitled *Shusen hishi* [Secret history of the termination of the war] appeared three years later in 1950, and has since been reprinted.

11 Robert J. C. Butow, *Japan's Decision to Surrender* (Stanford, 1954), 228–9.

coolly and objectively during the first half of 1945, and, above all, his (and Kido's) vacillation after having ordered the start of peace maneuvers in June 1945, has to figure prominently in any realistic reassessment of how the war ended.

In February 1945, before Japan's cities had been reduced to rubble, the emperor canvassed the opinions of his seven "senior statesmen" concerning the war outlook. They were Kiichiro Hiranuma, Koki Hirota, Reijiro Wakatsuki, Nobuaki Makino, Keisuke Okada, Fumimaro Konoe, and Hideki Tojo. The meetings, though interrupted by air raids, revealed a general consensus to go on with the struggle.

Prince Fumimaro Konoe, however, did not concur.[12] A descendant of the famous Fujiwara family of court nobles who for centuries had regularly intermarried with imperial princesses and during the Heian period (794–1185) had ruled Japan, he distinctly was not awed by the "emotional and reverent haze" that surrounded the emperor.[13] Konoe's memorial, presented on the 14th, pleaded with the emperor to sue quickly for peace before a Communist revolution occurred that would make preservation of the *kokutai* impossible.[14] Hirohito rejected Konoe's recommendation, saying that to conclude the war would be "very difficult unless we make one more military gain." Konoe allegedly replied, "is that possible? It must happen soon. If we have to wait much longer, . . . [a victory] will be meaningless."[15] Emperor Hirohito, however, stuck

12 Teiji Yabe, a Tokyo Imperial University scholar and ideologue who served as Konoe's political adviser, observed after the war that Konoe's private audience with the emperor in February was the first he had been allowed to have in nearly three years. Yabe also noted that, "Until around the time of the fall of Saipan, Kido had absolute faith in Tojo, and what anyone told Kido was immediately passed on to Tojo." See Teiji Yabe, "Koshitsu no chi nagareru Konoe Fumimaro," in *Bungei shunju, tokushugo: tenno hakusho* (October 1956), 190.

13 The words are those of the Strategic Bombing Survey report, *Japan's Struggle To End The War*, 2.

14 For a translation and insightful analysis of the entire Konoe Memorial see John W. Dower, *Empire and Aftermath: Yoshida Shigeru and the Japanese Experience, 1874–1954* (Cambridge, MA, 1979), 260–4.

15 Hisanori Fujita, *Jijucho no kaiso* (Tokyo, 1987), 66–7; Akira Yamada and Atsushi Koketsu, 180, citing from the 1978 Chuo Koronsha version of *Hosokawa nikki*.

    After the war, in an effort to give the emperor a pacifist image, MacArthur's personal secretary, Brigadier General Bonner Fellers, claimed in public addresses and in an article written for *Foreign Service* magazine, published by the Veterans of Foreign Wars, that "Emperor Hirohito's struggle to surrender" began in February 1945, when he resolved on a peace maneuver through the mediation of the Soviet Union. This

to his position, optimistically imagining that the war situation could be restored by fighting and winning one last decisive battle. He did not budge even after his military intelligence forecasters warned him, on 15 February, that the Soviet Union was likely to abrogate its neutrality pact with Japan by the spring and come into the war at any time thereafter if it judged Japan's power to have weakened.[16] Nor did he change his mind when Tojo conceded, at his audience on 26 February, that there was a "fifty-fifty" chance of the Soviet Union rising against Japan militarily. The emperor's war-mindedness made the battle of Okinawa both inevitable and needlessly costly. Ultimately, he also shares with Japan's other war leaders responsibility for dooming Hiroshima and Nagasaki to destruction.

Toward a Reinterpretation

In March and April 1946, replying to questions arising in the course of American preparation for the Tokyo War Crimes Trials that were to convene in May, five imperial household officials presented questions to Hirohito, and the resulting text – his dictated answers – was then partially amended and circulated among higher echelons of General MacArthur's staff. Soon afterward, the "monologue" disappeared. A version finally reappeared and was published after Hirohito's death in 1989. It shows him strongly defending General Hideki Tojo, who had served as both prime minister and war minister during the first thirty-two months of the Pacific war. It also reveals the emperor to have been an active commander-in-chief of the armed forces, yet a very hu-

article, reprinted in the Japanese edition of *Reader's Digest* (September 1947), concluded (23): "Was Hirohito always a pacifist who had been made a tool of the fanatic militarists without means of fighting back? I left Japan convinced that he was. As titular leader of Japan, of course, the Emperor cannot but share technically the war guilt of his leaders. Yet that does not lessen the high drama of a figurehead Emperor who dared face down his own fanatic militarists, usurp their power, and compel them by sheer strength of will to surrender a defeated country to a superior enemy." Like his superior, General MacArthur, Fellers probably had this view of the emperor before he even arrived in Japan.

16 See *Haisen no kiroku: sanbo honbu shozo, Meiji hyakunen-shi sosho, dai 38 kan* [Records of the defeat: Archives of the General Staff, the Meiji Centennial History Collection, Vol, 38] (Tokyo, 1967), 230–1.

man one who lays blame for Japan's failures on everyone but himself.[17]

Other recent important contributions to understanding the ending of the war include *Dokyumento Showa tenno, dai go kan, haisen ge* [A documented history of the Showa Emperor, Volume 5: defeat] (1989), which is part of an excellent eight-volume political history by journalist and historian Nobumasa Tanaka. It has shed new light on the emperor's activist role throughout the war, the surrender, and the occupation. Two other notable achievements of Japanese scholarship are Akira Yamada and Atushi Koketsu, *Ososugita seidan: Showa tenno no senso shido to senso sekinin* [The imperial decision that came too late: The Showa Emperor's war leadership and war responsibility] (1991), and Yutaka Yoshida, *Showa tenno no shusenshi* [A history of the Showa Emperor in the war termination process] (1992).

Drawing from these and other Japanese-language sources, the following discussion briefly interprets "unconditional surrender" as the wartime goal of the anti-fascist alliance. It then reexamines several key moments leading to "the imperial decision that came too late" to save Hiroshima and Nagasaki. These were: (a) the Tojo cabinet's resignation (18 July 1944); (b) the Koiso cabinet's plan for eliciting Soviet assistance in closing the war and the emperor's involvement in preparations for staging one last decisive campaign; (c) the Suzuki cabinet's vague, futile efforts to negotiate an end to the war through the Soviet Union; (d) the period between the Suzuki cabinet's rejection of the Potsdam Declaration on 28 July 1945 and the bombing of Hiroshima on 6 August; and, finally, (e) the Japanese government's debates over surrendering with "one condition versus four conditions." Even the briefest review of these five topics will reveal many other reasons for the delayed surrender beyond American policymakers' desire to practice atomic diplomacy, or realize ulterior objectives vis-à-vis the Soviet Union.

---

17 For discussion and analysis see Herbert P. Bix, "Emperor Hirohito's War," *History Today* 41 (December 1991): 12–19; and idem, "The Showa Emperor's 'Monologue' and the Problem of War Responsibility," *Journal of Japanese Studies* 18 (Summer 1992): 295–363.

Unconditional Surrender, the Potsdam Declaration, and the Bomb

In seeking to maintain a high degree of patriotic fervor and international cooperation in the fight against the Axis, President Franklin D. Roosevelt and Prime Minister Winston S. Churchill relied, among other things, on abstract war slogans and the goal of unconditional surrender. Their policy of no negotiated termination of the war never aimed at just smashing the fascist states. Its true objective was the military occupation and postwar reform – always the two together – of those states so that the philosophies of fascism and militarism could be uprooted and their societies democratized.

Roosevelt did say, at Casablanca in January 1943, that the Allies would punish the leaders of the fascist regimes but not destroy their peoples. But until they had won total victory over the Axis, he and Churchill steadfastly resisted pressures to clarify the meaning of their formula. Needing Soviet military might, yet keenly aware of Stalin's distrust of them for not having opened a second front in Europe to relieve the hard-pressed Red Army, Roosevelt and Churchill had ample reason for displaying an uncompromising attitude toward the enemy states.[18] Alliance imperatives, in short, strengthened their resolve to eschew any formal contractual offers made by the aggressor states of Germany, Japan, and Italy and to retain a free hand to occupy and reform them after toppling their governments and destroying their military power. Thus, the unconditional surrender formula, which aimed at exercising state power and carrying out reforms in the post-surrender period, was a precondition for building a new world order.[19]

After the German army signed unconditional surrender documents with the Allied forces on 7 May 1945, and the Third Reich, in the words of William L. Shirer, "simply ceased to exist," Japan

---

18 Daizaburo Yui, "Beikoku no sengo sekai koso to Ajia" [The American conception of the postwar world and Asia] in *Senryo kaikaku no kokusai hikaku: Nihon, Ajia, Yoroppa,* ed. Daizaburo Yui, Masanori Nakamura, and Narahiko Toyoshita (Tokyo, 1994), 12–13.

19 Kentaro Awaya, "Nihon haisen wa jokentsuki kofuku ka" [Was Japan's defeat surrender with conditions attached to it?], in *Nihon kindaishi no kyozo to jitsuzo 4: kofuku – "Showa" no shuen,* ed. Akira Fujiwara et al. (Tokyo, 1989), 14–20.

alone remained in the war.[20] At that point, with the battle of
Okinawa still raging, newly installed President Truman declared
on 8 May that Japan's surrender would not mean the "extermina-
tion or enslavement of the Japanese people." Because his remark
left the unconditional surrender goal unaltered, Joseph Grew,
leader of the "Japan faction" within the State Department, pressed
the president to make public a clear definition of the term so as to
persuade the Japanese to surrender. Immediately, Grew met fierce
opposition from his colleagues in the State Department – the
"China crowd" – who argued that to keep the emperor was to
compromise on the very essence of Japanese fascism.[21] They –
Dean Acheson, Archibald MacLeish, and James Byrnes – certainly
did not want to interpret the supreme war goal more leniently for
Japan than had been the case with Germany and, by so doing,
leave an unwanted impression, at home and abroad, of "appease-
ment." These disagreements clearly highlighted the interrelation-
ship, during the spring and summer of 1945, between wartime
goals and postwar policies.

The Potsdam Declaration was issued on 26 July 1945 in the
form of an ultimatum aimed at hastening Japan's surrender.[22] The
Japanese government was informed that if it fulfilled certain unilat-
eral obligations ("our terms"), which the victorious powers would
impose *after* the Japanese government had proclaimed "the unconditional surrender of all Japanese armed forces" and furnished
"proper and adequate assurance of their good faith in such action," Japan would *then* be allowed to retain its peace industries
and resume participation in world trade on the basis of the principle of equal access to raw materials. "The alternative for Japan,"
the declaration concluded, "is prompt and utter destruction." Article 12 stated, "The occupying forces of the Allies shall be with-
drawn from Japan as soon as these objectives have been accomplished and there has been established in accordance with the

20 William L. Shirer, *The Rise and Fall of the Third Reich* (New York, 1990), 1139.
    Italian partisans summarily executed Mussolini on 28 April, and the war in Italy ended
    on 2 May. Hitler committed suicide on 30 April.
21 Nakamura, *The Japanese Monarchy*, 70–7.
22 The declaration was largely the work of Secretary of War Henry L. Stimson and his
    aides, but Secretary of State James Byrnes polished it and influenced the timing of its
    release.

freely expressed will of the Japanese people a peacefully inclined and responsible government." Deleted from this article was the phrase that Grew advised was necessary: "this may include a constitutional monarchy under the present dynasty." Consequently, the status of the emperor was not guaranteed, and the policy of unconditional surrender remained intact.

The rest of the story can be even more briefly summarized. The Japanese government received the declaration on July 27 and showed no intention of immediately accepting it. On the contrary, the Suzuki cabinet first ordered the tightly controlled press to publish the Domei News Service's edited version (with surrender terms 1 through 4 deleted) and to minimize the significance of the declaration by not commenting on it.[23] Next, on 28 July, at the urging of Army Minister Korechika Anami, Chief of the Naval General Staff Soemu Toyoda, and others, Prime Minister Suzuki made Japan's rejection explicit by formally declaring, at an afternoon press conference, that the Potsdam Declaration was no more than a "rehash" (*yakinaoshi*) of the Cairo Declaration and that he intended to "ignore" it (*mokusatsu*). If Hirohito, who read the newspapers daily, was displeased or even very concerned about the impression of intransigence that Suzuki and his cabinet were conveying to the world, we have no record of it. Kido probably would have mentioned any conversation he had with the emperor on the subject in his detailed diary, but did not.[24]

Also on 28 July, when an allegedly moderate "senior statesman," Navy Minister Mitsumasa Yonai, was asked by his secretary, Rear Admiral Sokichi Takagi, why the prime minister had been allowed to make such an absurd statement, Yonai replied: "If one is first to issue a statement, he is always at a disadvan-

23 The deleted surrender terms were as follows: (1) "WE . . . agree that Japan shall be given an opportunity to end this war. (2) The prodigious land, sea and air forces of the United States, the British Empire and of China . . . are poised to strike the final blows upon Japan. . . . (3) The result of the futile and senseless German resistance . . . stands forth in awful clarity as an example to the people of Japan. . . . The full application of our military power, backed by our resolve, *will* mean the inevitable and complete destruction of the Japanese homeland. (4) The time has come for Japan to decide whether she will continue to be controlled by those self-willed militaristic advisers whose unintelligent calculations have brought the Empire of Japan to the threshold of annihilation, or whether she will follow the path of reason."
24 Tanaka, *Dokyumento Showa tenno, dai go kan*, 430–2.

tage. Churchill has fallen, America is beginning to be isolated. The government therefore will ignore it. There is no need to rush."[25]

"No need to rush" directly contravened Article 5 of the Potsdam Declaration ("We shall brook no delay") and was a position that further strengthened the contemporary Western analysis that, as of 28 July, the Japanese, following the leadership of their emperor, had neither reversed their decision, nor loosened their will to fight to the finish, while making overtures for peace on a separate track.[26] Suzuki's intention was not misunderstood.

The Americans now accelerated their preparations for the use of atomic bombs and for an invasion of southern Kyushu (Operation Olympic), scheduled to begin on 1 November. On 6 August a single B-29 destroyed much of the undefended city of Hiroshima, immediately killing an estimated 100,000 to 140,000 people and taking the lives (over the next five years) of perhaps another one hundred thousand.[27] Two days later, citing as a pretext Japan's rejection of the Potsdam Declaration, the Soviet Union declared war on Japan.[28] On 9 August, the United States dropped the second atomic bomb on Nagasaki, immediately killing approximately thirty-five to forty thousand people and injuring more than sixty thousand.[29] That same day, in a nationwide radio report on the

25 Jo Minomatsu, ed., Takagi Sokichi copy, *Kaigun taisho Yonai Mitsumasa oboegaki* [Memoirs of Admiral Yonai Mitsumasa] (Tokyo, 1978), 143–4, as cited in Tanaka, *Dokyumento Showa tenno, dai go kan*, 434. Churchill did indeed lose the British general election of 5 July 1945. A Labour party Cabinet headed by Clement Attlee replaced his Conservative-dominated coalition government on the 27th.

26 Truman notes in his memoirs, "On July 28 Radio Tokyo announced that the Japanese government would continue to fight. There was no formal reply to the joint ultimatum of the United States, the United Kingdom, and China. There was no alternative now. The bomb was scheduled to be dropped after August 3 unless Japan surrendered before that day." Harry S. Truman, *Memoirs*, Vol. 1, *Year of Decisions* (Garden City, NY, 1955), 421.

27 Tanaka, *Dokyumento Showa tenno, dai go kan*, 449.

28 The Soviet declaration of war stated: "Japan remains the only great power after the defeat and surrender of Hitlerian Germany which still insists on continuing the war, and has rejected the demand for the unconditional surrender of its armed forces, put forth on July 26 by the three nations: the United States of America, Britain, and China." Source: Nihon Jyanarizumu Kenkyukai, ed., *Showa "hatsugen" no kiroku* [A record of public statements of the Showa era] (Tokyo, 1989), 94. Needless to say, Stalin did not need Suzuki's *mokusatsu* statement or the Yalta agreement to enter the war against defeated Japan. He would have done so in any case.

29 Tanaka, *Dokyumento Showa tenno, dai go kan*, 475. Also see for higher figures, Committee for the Compilation of Materials on Damage Caused by the Atomic

Potsdam Conference, President Truman gave full expression to the vengeful mood of most Americans:

Having found the bomb we have used it. We have used it against those who attacked us without warning at Pearl Harbor, against those who have starved and beaten and executed American prisoners of war, against those who have abandoned all pretense of obeying international laws of warfare. We have used it in order to shorten the agony of war, in order to save the lives of thousands and thousands of young Americans.[30]

Meanwhile, in Tokyo, during the interval between the Potsdam Declaration and the 6 August atomic bombing of Hiroshima, the emperor himself said and did nothing about accepting the Potsdam terms, though he did make clear to Kido (on 31 July) that the imperial regalia had to be defended at all costs.[31] Kido also did nothing because (as he said later at Sugamo Prison on 17 April 1950) he thought "it would be best if we could unite the country by negotiations which would save our honor ... [and] maybe we could do that through the good offices of the Soviet Union."[32] Prime Minister Suzuki, after his initial rejection of the Potsdam ultimatum, also saw no need to do anything further. When his Cabinet Advisory Council, reflecting the views of the nation's leading businessmen, on 30 July recommended acceptance of the Potsdam Declaration terms, Suzuki told the head of the Cabinet Intelligence Bureau and Advisory Council member, Shimomura Kainan, that

For the enemy side to say something like that means that circumstances have arisen that force them also to end the war. That is why they are talking about unconditional surrender. Precisely at a time like this, if we

Bombs, *Hiroshima and Nagasaki: The Physical, Medical, and Social Effects of the Atomic Bombings*, trans. Ishikawa Eisei and David L. Swain (New York, 1981), 114. The entire picture of human damage wrought by the atomic bombs is difficult to grasp even today.

30 Cyril Clemens, ed., *Truman Speaks* (1946; reprint, New York, 1969), 69.
31 Koichi Kido, *Kido Koichi nikki, gekan* [Koichi Kido diary, vol. 2] (Tokyo, 1966), 1221. Earlier, on 25 July, Hirohito told Kido that the three regalia had to be protected in order to maintain the imperial house and the *kokutai*. The imperial regalia consisted of three sacred objects – a mirror, curved jewel, and sword – symbolizing the legitimacy of the emperor's rule. Here we see the emperor acting in accordance with his commitment to his imperial ancestors and his imperial "house" (*ie*) rather than in a way appropriate to saving the lives of the Japanese people.
32 Tanaka, *Dokyumento Showa tenno, dai go kan*, 440–1, citing Koichi Kido, *Kido nikki, Tokyo saiban-ki* [Koichi Kido diary: The Tokyo trials period] (Tokyo, 1980).

hold firm, then they will yield before we do. Just because they broadcast their Declaration, it is not necessary to stop fighting. You advisers may ask me to reconsider, but I don't think there is any need to stop [the war].[33]

So for ten days the Potsdam Declaration was "ignored." The bombs were dropped, and Soviet forces invaded along a wide front from northern Manchuria to Korea. Then, Foreign Minister Shigenori Togo (no dove) persuaded the emperor that the declaration in itself really signified *conditional* surrender, not unconditional, though he probably had his own doubts about that interpretation. With that sticking point out of the way, Hirohito, strongly assisted by Kido, took the gamble and authorized Togo to notify the world that Japan would accept the Allied terms with only one condition, "that the said declaration does not comprise any demand which prejudices the prerogatives of His Majesty as a Sovereign Ruler." The next day, 11 August, Secretary of State Byrnes replied ambiguously to this first surrender communication by alluding to the subordination of the emperor's authority to the Supreme Commander of the Allied Powers. He did not clearly answer the Japanese on the emperor's status, but he did hint at the possibility that the emperor's position might be guaranteed after surrender.

At that point, another dispute erupted among the leaders in Tokyo, forcing the emperor to rule once again, on 14 August, in favor of acceptance. Afterward, he went before a microphone and recorded his capitulation announcement, which was broadcast to the Japanese nation at noon on 15 August. By then, the main concern of the moderates had already shifted to divorcing the emperor from both his actual conduct of the war and the unrealistic thinking and failed policies that had brought Japan to defeat.

Why did Japan's top leaders delay for ten days before finally "bowing to the inevitable" and surrendering without negotiation? If Grew and the critics of unconditional surrender had had their way in May, June, or even July and had cut a deal on the issue of guaran-

33 Tanaka, *Dokyumento Showa tenno, dai go kan*, 443, citing Kantaro Suzuki denki hensan iinkai ed., *Suzuki Kantaro den* [The life of Kantaro Suzuki] (1960), 372.

teeing the dynasty, would Japan's leaders then have surrendered immediately? Or was there not more to this issue than meets the eye? What, in other words, did the Suzuki government and the "moderates" around the throne (the court group) really mean by their insistence on preserving "the prerogatives of the emperor to rule the state"? A short review of turning points and episodes leading directly to the capitulation will help to answer these questions.

(A) Tojo's Resignation

From early 1943 until 18 July 1944, a small group of court officials and "senior statesmen" worked covertly to force Tojo out of office. These men never doubted that the emperor, who had allowed Tojo to build up dictatorial power, could dismiss his prime minister with support from his immediate staff. Indeed, they regarded the emperor as the main obstacle in their path to peace.[34]

Koichi Kido, the quintessential backstage man, was once as great an admirer of Tojo as the emperor. Kido played the key role in Tojo's downfall, yet during the tenure of Tojo's successor, General Kuniaki Koiso (July 1944–April 1945), Kido continued to support the prowar faction of the army, as did the emperor. Tojo's dismissal, in other words, did not connote an intention on the part of either the emperor or Kido to end the war. The emperor's view of the war situation certainly became less sanguine after Tojo's fall, but both he and Kido remained unwilling to consider an early peace effort. The same was true of many senior statesmen who participated in "peace maneuvers" around Prince Konoe.[35]

Politically, however, Hirohito's dismissal of Tojo signaled a pro-

34 Morisada Hosokawa, Konoe's secretary, was deeply involved in discussions to overthrow the Tojo cabinet. His diary entry of 15 February 1944 reported on a meeting he had just attended, called at the request of some middle-echelon navy officers to consider the worsening crisis. "I told them that I thought the only way to break the deadlock was a coup d'etat. However, I hesitate to do it – and it is hard for me to say this – because Tojo is so trusted at Court that if a coup were to be carried out, it would bring about an even worse result. This is why I hesitate to carry it out. The Emperor trusts Tojo because no one tells him the truth about anything. The newspapers, Marquis Kido, and the cabinet ministers only tell him about government reports." These lines suggest that the main obstacle to the Tojo cabinet's removal was Emperor Hirohito's trust in Tojo.

35 Yamada and Koketsu, *Ososugita seidan*, 132–3; Sigal, *Fighting to a Finish*, 31.

found shift. In the autumn of 1941, at the time of the decision to broaden the war by attacking Pearl Harbor, the emperor's chief political adviser, Koichi Kido, was instrumental in forming a loose alliance between the court group and some senior statesmen, on the one hand, and the prowar forces composed of the military elite, "renovationist bureaucrats," and top leaders of the business world on the other.[36] Ambassador Grew had never imagined such a grouping. As for Prince Konoe, who had headed the previous cabinet, he stepped down from office, becoming an opponent of war with the United States and Britain (though not, of course, publicly so).[37] Now, almost three years later, Tojo's 1944 resignation brought Konoe and the men around him, representing elites from all the key areas of Japanese life, back to the political stage. Unenchanted by the mystique of the throne, and possessed of a realistic insight into Japan's predicament, Konoe took the initiative in trying to break out of the hopeless war situation.

(B) Koiso's Failure and the Emperor's Participation

The cabinet of Tojo's successor, Prime Minister Kuniaki Koiso – a virtual unknown when the emperor chose him – lasted for only eight months (July 1944–April 1945). During that time the war situation grew increasingly desperate. The Supreme War Leadership Council, established on 5 August 1944, thereupon launched new diplomatic initiatives aimed at getting the Nationalist government in Chungking to perceive Japan's "sincerity" and also plotted its first vague overtures to the Soviet Union. The latter plan, sponsored by the Foreign Ministry, ostensibly sought Soviet help in bringing about reconciliation between the Chinese Communists and Chiang Kai-shek's Nationalists. Japan could then conclude peace with the new regime in China and be in a better position to wage the "War of Greater East Asia." In return, Japan would endeavor to promote restoration of relations (that is, peace) between its Nazi ally, the Third German Reich, and the Soviet Union.[38] And why? So that Japan's crumbling hegemony in East

36 Yamada and Koketsu, *Ososugita seidan*, 148.
37 Yoshida, *Showa tenno no shusenshi*, 14.
38 Yamada and Koketsu, *Ososugita seidan*, 167–8.

Asia might be stabilized. This first Soviet-centered peace plan amounted to little and ended in nothing.

During the first half of 1945, American armed forces sank most of the Japanese navy, cut through the Japanese inner defense perimeter, reconquered the Philippines, and moved steadily closer to the Japanese heartland. Until the very end of this period, the emperor was not thinking of shifting policy and abandoning the war. He was preoccupied with the conduct of reckless defensive battles being fought in order to set the stage for eventually seeking an honorable way out of the war. From January through July, he attended numerous flag bestowal ceremonies at court for regiments being reorganized or newly activated for the homeland defense, reviewed plans for battles being waged on various Pacific fronts, and involved himself fully in planning for the repulse of the expected American invasion of the home islands.

The emperor's military aide, Kaizo Yoshihashi, reports in his memoir (published in 1965) that on New Year's Day, 1945, with the capital under enemy air attack, the emperor and empress were pleased to check out the special last-meal rations being provided to the departing members of the suicide units. Thereafter the emperor continued to show gratitude for these "special attack forces."[39] The suicidal sacrifice of loyal subjects in battles that they had no hope of winning was rapidly becoming Japan's short-cut way of preserving the *kokutai*.

On 9 January 1945, the United States began retaking Luzon and by 3 March had occupied Manila, though the fighting in the Philippines continued until virtually the end of the war. Six days later, B-

---

39   Kaizo Yoshihashi, "Jiju bukan toshite mita shusen no toshi no kiroku" [Record of the last year of the war as seen by a military aide] in *Gunji shigaku*, No. 2 (August 1965), 96–7. Yoshihashi notes (97) that, "around that time [January 1945], because of the ferocity of the war, we asked the emperor to receive formal reports on important military affairs even on Saturday and Sunday. On that particular day I reported on the battle situation in the Philippines in the vicinity of Lingayen Gulf. When I was reporting on the commander's expression of gratitude to the suicide attack of one of the special pilots, the emperor suddenly stood up and silently made a deep bow. I was pointing at the map and His Majesty's hair touched my head, causing me to feel as though an electric current had run through my body. On a later occasion, I reported about a corporal who had made a suicide attack on a B-29 in the sky over Nagoya, and the emperor did the same thing: stood up and bowed deeply. Both times only the emperor and I were in the room. For each individual who died for the country, but especially for the special attack forces, he showed sympathy and gratitude from the bottom of his heart."

29s launched the first night incendiary air raid over Tokyo, turning large portions of the capital into ash and burning to death an estimated eighty thousand people. Nine days later, on 18 March, the emperor inspected the capital by car. Military aide Yoshihashi, who accompanied him in a separate vehicle, later commented that,

The victims, who had been digging through the rubble with empty expressions on their faces, watched the imperial motorcade pass by with reproachful expressions. Although we did not make the usual prior announcement, I felt that they should have known that his was a "blessed visitation" (*gyoko*), because three to four maroon automobiles bearing the chrysanthemum crest were going by. Were they grudgeful to the emperor because they had lost their relatives, their houses and belongings? Or were they in a state of utter lethargy and bewilderment (*kyodatsu*)? I sympathized with how His Majesty must have felt upon approaching these unfortunate victims.[40]

Yoshihashi's observation of "exhaustion and bewilderment" on the part of the people is worth noting. By March, factory production had started to fall; absenteeism was on the increase; so too were instances of lese majesty – always of keen concern for the Imperial Household Ministry. Over the next five months, from April to August, members of the militarized imperial family as well as the senior statesmen would speak of a crisis of the *kokutai*. The threat from within that Konoe had warned the emperor of in February seemed more and more palpable. Yet until the very end, most Japanese people, especially those living in rural areas, remained steadfast in their resolve to obey their leaders and to work and sacrifice for the victory that they were constantly told was coming.

(C) "Ketsu-Go" and the Potsdam Declaration

On 1 April 1945, the battle of Okinawa began, and lasted until mid-June, by which time an estimated 94,000 to 120,000 Japanese combatants and 150,000 to 170,000 noncombatants had died. American loses were put at approximately 12,500 killed and over 33,000 wounded.[41] Five days into the battle, on 5 April, the em-

40 Ibid., 97–8.
41 Keiichi Eguchi, *Jugonen senso shoshi* [A short history of the fifteen-year war] (Tokyo, 1991), 237; Yamada and Koketsu, *Ososugita seidan*, 183–4.

peror chose his former grand chamberlain and trusted adviser, retired Admiral Kantaro Suzuki, to lead a new government that would carry out the emperor's will. Neither the emperor nor Suzuki was then thinking of making any sort of policy change that might lead to the conclusion of the war.[42] It was only *after* the battle of Okinawa had been fought and horribly lost, and large portions of Japan's largest and medium-sized cities had been leveled by American incendiary air attacks, that the emperor indicated his desire for peace and official maneuvers looking to end the war got under way.

In the diary of Koichi Kido, the first clear indication that the emperor would be asked to think seriously of peace appears on 8 June 1945, when Kido prepared his own "Draft Plan for Controlling the Crisis Situation" (*Jikyoku shushu no taisaku shian*). That moment was a true turning point in the surrender process. It occurred after the imperial palace had been inadvertently bombed (25 May), all hope of saving Okinawa had been lost, and on the day that the Supreme War Leadership Council adopted the "Basic Policy for the Future Direction of the War."[43] Kido's "plan," a nebulous one, called for seeking the Soviet Union's assistance as a go-between so that Japan could obtain more leverage in negotiating with its enemies. By drafting it, Kido indicated that he had ended his long honeymoon relationship with the military hardliners. A few weeks later, on 22 June, the emperor himself finally informed the Supreme War Leadership Council directly of his desire to commence maneuvers to end the war.

In early July, after Soviet Ambassador Jacob Malik had broken off his inconclusive talks in Japan with former prime minister Koki Hirota, Hirohito, for the first time, showed a keen interest in expediting direct negotiations with the Soviet Union by dispatching a special envoy to Moscow. But neither the emperor nor the Suzuki government ever devised a concrete plan on the basis of which the Soviets could mediate an end to hostilities, assuming the Soviets were ever interested in doing so, which they were not.

---

42 Yamada and Koketsu, *Ososugita seidan*, 193.
43 See *Kido Koichi nikki, gekan*, 1208–9; Shinobu Oe, *Gozen kaigi: Showa tenno jugokai no seidan* [Imperial conferences: The Showa emperor's fifteen sacred decisions] (Tokyo, 1991), 235.

Negotiation with the Soviets to guarantee the emperor's position and the future of the monarchy, and the search for peace to end the killing and suffering never came together in the Japanese approach to war termination.[44]

American unwillingness to compromise on the policy of unconditional surrender also needs to be assessed in light of the tremendous sacrifices that the emperor kept imposing on his people, at home and abroad, in preparation for turning the home islands into a battlefield. From 8 April 1945 until its capitulation, the Suzuki government's chief war policy was "Ketsu-Go," a plan for the defense of the homeland.[45] Its defining characteristic was heavy reliance on suicide tactics. This involved using massive numbers of kamikaze "special attack" planes, human torpedoes (*kaiten*), "crash-boats" (*renraku-tei*), and suicide charges by specially trained ground units. While preparations for operation "Ketsu" went forward, a special session of the Imperial Diet, passed, on 9 June, a "Wartime Emergency Measures Law" and five other measures designed to mobilize the entire nation for that last battle.

The same day, the emperor issued another imperial rescript in connection with his convocation of the Diet, ordering the nation to "smash the inordinate ambitions of the enemy nations" and "achieve the goals of the war." If any possibility had ever existed of enlisting public opinion in support of ending the war, the emperor's rescript ordering total resistance to the enemy helped put an end to it.[46] Concurrently, the controlled press waged a daily Die-for-the-Emperor campaign, a campaign to promote gratitude for the Imperial Benevolence, and, from about mid-July onward, a campaign to "protect the *kokutai*."[47]

Pressed by imperial edicts to continue their preparations for the final homeland battle and to think only of victory, the Japanese people complied as best they could. During late July and August,

44 Yamada and Koketsu, *Ososugita seidan*, 204–6.
45 Skates, *The Invasion of Japan*, 102. An English translation of the Ketsu-Go plan can be found in *Reports of General MacArthur: Japanese Operations in the Southwest Pacific Area, Volume II, Part II* (Washington, 1966), 601–7.
46 Yamada and Koketsu, *Ososugita seidan*, 196. For the text of the 9 June 1945 rescript see Senda Kako, *Tenno to chokugo to Showashi* [The emperor, imperial rescripts, and Showa history] (Tokyo, 1983), 389.
47 For discussion of these press campaigns see Sozo Matsuura, *Tenno to masu komi* [The emperor and the mass media] (Tokyo, 1975), 3–14.

when the nation's prefectural governors, police chiefs, and officers of the "special higher policy" submitted to the Home Ministry reports on the rapidly deteriorating spirit of the nation, there was not (according to historian Kentaro Awaya) a single reference in their nearly two thousand pages of reports (entitled *Chian joho*) to any popular intention to accept the terms of the Potsdam Declaration.[48] Even immediately after the dropping of the atomic bombs and the Soviet declaration of war, people generally clung to the hope of a final victory, and thus the belief that their "divine land" was indestructible. Mobilized in the service of death, the collective memory of the "divine winds" (kamikaze) that would save Japan helped to maintain the will to fight on.[49]

American intelligence analysts, meanwhile, watched all these main island preparations and saw how the Japanese people had fought and died on Okinawa. When political leaders in Washington said that the Japanese were likely to fight to the death rather than surrender unconditionally, they were not exaggerating what the Japanese government itself was saying.

(D) Overtures to Moscow and Prince Konoe's Role

The conventional treatment of the Emperor Hirohito's role in ending the war presents Japan's request for Soviet mediation (the Koki Hirota-Jacob Malik talks) and the secret messages that Foreign Minister Shigenori Togo sent (in June, July, and early August) to Ambassador Naotake Sato in Moscow as serious attempts to quit the war and surrender. Yet the participants in these peace overtures perceived them as a tactic that would merely delay the inevitable capitulation.

In his "monologue," the emperor said of these Soviet negotiations that,

48 Kentaro Awaya and Takamine Kawashima, "Gyokuon hoso wa teki no Boryaku da" [The broadcast of the emperor's voice is an enemy trick] in *This Is Yomiuri* (November 1994), 47. The *Chian joho*, published in seven volumes by Nihon Tosho Senta in Tokyo in late 1994, is an invaluable source for understanding Japanese opinion at the time of the ending of the war.

49 Twice in the late thirteenth century, the "winds of the gods" decimated invading Mongul armadas off the shores of Kyushu. By taking the name "kamikaze," the pilots who attacked Allied ships came to incarnate one of the most powerful memories in Japanese history.

We chose the Soviet Union to mediate peace for two reasons. All other countries had little power. Therefore, even if we had asked those countries to mediate, we feared they would be pressured by the British and Americans, and we would have to surrender unconditionally. By comparison, the Soviet Union had both the power and the obligation that came from having concluded a neutrality treat.

Since we did not think the Soviet Union was a trustworthy country, it was first necessary to sound them out. Consequently, we decided to go ahead with Hirota-Malik talks [3–4, 24, and 29 June], in which we said that if they allowed us to import oil, we would not mind giving them both southern Karafuto and Manchuria.

However, even when it came to the beginning of July, there was no answer from the Soviet Union. For our part, we had to decide this matter prior to the Potsdam Conference. . . . For that reason, I consulted Suzuki and decided to cancel the Hirota-Malik talks and negotiate directly with the Soviets.[50]

Leaving aside the fact that it was Malik, not the emperor, who effectively ended the talks, Hirohito, in early July, did indeed become more concerned about negotiating an end to the war. Around that time, he and Kido pushed for secret direct negotiations with the Soviets by sending Prince Konoe to Moscow as the emperor's special envoy. Concurrently, former foreign minister Hachiro Arita, in a memorial to the throne of 9 July, pointed out to the emperor, "There is almost no chance of our bringing Chungking, Yenan, and the Soviets to our side, or of using them to improve our position. . . . [I]f we try to do this, we will merely be wasting precious time in a situation where every minute counts." Judge the big picture coolly and rationally, pleaded Arita in his audience with the emperor, for "merely to call for absolute victory will produce nothing." In order to make "the divine land . . . imperishable," we must "bear the unbearable."[51]

More important, ever since 8 June the Japanese ambassador in

50 Hidenari Terasaki and Mariko Terasaki Miller, eds., *Showa tenno dokuhakuroku – Tersaski Hidenari, goyogakari nikki* [The Showa emperor's monologue and the diary of Hidenari Terasaki] (Tokyo, 1991), 120–1.

51 Arita concluded his memorial with the words: "Your Majesty confronts this crisis with his inherent wisdom. I humbly ask Your Majesty to view the trend of the war and resolutely act to save the imperial nation at its critical moment. I am respectfully reporting this with utter trepidation and awe." Source: Gaimusho, hen, *Shusen shiroku 3* [Historical records of the ending of the war, volume 3], 208.

Moscow, Naotake Sato, had been telling Togo that it was unimaginable that the Soviets would ever help Japan.[52] On 13 July, Sato warned Togo that just because "we are overawed by the fact that the dispatch of a special envoy is the Imperial wish," it would not mean anything to the Soviets, and would only cause trouble for the Imperial Household, "if the Japanese Government's proposal brought by him is limited to an enumeration of previous abstractions, lacking in concreteness."[53] On 20 July – one day after Sato had notified Tokyo that the Soviets had indeed refused to accept the special envoy "on the grounds that the mission is not specific" – (just as he had been saying they would do all along), the ambassador sent his most emotional telegram yet to Togo, summing up his feelings about the whole situation. Sato (like Arita on 9 July, and Prince Konoe ever since February) urged immediate surrender because the state was on the verge of being destroyed. "[T]his matter of protecting the national polity [*kokutai*]," Sato emphasized, could be considered as "one of a domestic nature and therefore excluded from the terms of a peace treaty."[54] In other words, there was no need for Japan to insist on securing a foreign guarantee of its monarchy: The *kokutai* could be saved without delaying surrender and rehabilitated later when Japan once again became independent.

Nevertheless, because the emperor was adamant on precisely this point, Togo persisted, telling Sato that Japan could not indicate its peace plan in advance and that he should concentrate on learning Soviet intentions and getting them to accept Prince Konoe as the emperor's special peace envoy. On 2 August, a week after the Potsdam Declaration was issued, Togo sent another message to Sato responding to the ambassador's earlier criticism of sending Konoe to Moscow. In the telegram, Togo stated,

Right now the urgent matter for us is to have the Soviet Union agree to receive our envoy. The emperor too is deeply concerned with the development of this issue. The prime minister and the military leaders are also

52 Sato to Togo, 8 June 1945, in Gaimusho, hen, *Shusen shiroku 3*, 191.
53 Sato to Togo, 13 July 1945, in U.S. Department of State, *Foreign Relations of the United States, The Conference of Berlin (The Potsdam Conference), 1945* (Washington, 1960), 1:881.
54 Sato no. 1227 to Togo, 19 July 1945, and Sato no. 1228 to Togo, 20 July 1945, in ibid. 2:1251 and 1256. For the Japanese original see Gaimusho, hen, *Shusen shiroku 3* (Tokyo, 1977), 199.

placing their hopes on this one matter. Consequently, although you might have your own opinion, understand this situation and somehow stimulate the Soviet side to accept our special envoy.[55]

After receiving Tojo's message, Sato cabled the Foreign Ministry on 4 August again urging acceptance of the Potsdam Declaration.[56]

Neither Sato nor retired foreign ministers Mamoru Shigemitsu or Hachiro Arita ever believed the war could be ended through the good offices of the Soviet Union. Foreign Minister Togo himself doubted it. But, in compliance with the emperor's wishes, Togo persisted even after 4 August. As Nobumasa Tanaka noted, Togo would not agree to direct negotiations with the Allied powers even when the president of the Cabinet Intelligence Bureau, Kainan Shimomura, visited his private residence on 4 August and pleaded with him that, "It is not enough to have dealings only with the Soviet Union. There is no hope if we continue like this. Somehow, by backdoor channels, we must negotiate with the United States, Britain, and China."[57]

Togo sent his last message to Sato, still asking him to discover the attitude of the Soviet side, on 7 August. But by then Stalin already knew about the atomic bombing of Hiroshima. (Caught off guard by the news of the American destruction of an entire Japanese city, he decided to enter the war on 9 August, a week earlier than previously scheduled, or a week earlier than President Truman had anticipated.[58] By dropping the atomic bomb on Hiroshima, Truman inadvertently deepened the Soviet dictator's suspicion of the United States and contributed to the later onset of the Cold War.)

Since the Foreign Ministry's messages to Moscow were intercepted and decoded by U.S. intelligence and probably read, at least in part, by Truman, it has been argued that the president could –

55 Tanaka, *Dokyumento Showa tenno, dai go kan*, 439, citing Gaimusho, hen, *Shusen shiroku* (Tokyo, 1952), 524–5.
56 Tanaka, *Dokyumento Showa tenno, dai go kan*, 440.
57 Ibid., 444.
58 Ibid., 461–2. In his memoirs, Truman claims not to have been surprised by the Soviet decision. On the initial Soviet reaction to Hiroshima see David Holloway, *Stalin and the Bomb: The Soviet Union and Atomic Energy, 1939–1956* (New Haven, 1994), 127–9; and the review of Holloway by Vladislav Zubok in *Science* 266 (21 October 1994): 466–8.

and should – have backed away at least somewhat on the unconditional surrender formula. But the messages clearly were always too tentative and vague to constitute a serious attempt at negotiating an end to the war.[59]

Even the letter that the Foreign Ministry had already prepared for Konoe's projected (but unrealized) secret mission as the emperor's special envoy is reported to have aimed mainly at obtaining a Soviet guarantee of the future of the throne and its current occupant.[60] Preservation of the *kokutai* was the single condition for peace. Furthermore, the "emperor's letter" reportedly implied that the war had been generated spontaneously, and that insofar as the United States and Britain insisted on unconditional surrender, they, not Japan, were the main obstacles to peace.[61]

Unable to decide to end the war unless the future of the throne and its occupant were absolutely guaranteed, the Suzuki cabinet and the Supreme War Leadership Council never framed a peace maneuver from the viewpoint of saving the Japanese people from further destruction.[62] They waited, instead, until their foreign ene-

59 Historians of the A-bomb decision generally conclude that Truman knew of the contents of the intercepted and decoded Japanese "peace feelers," and that Secretary of the Navy James Forrestal and Army chief of staff General George C. Marshall were also informed of the cables. But it is equally important to understand that these cables were not evidence of the Japanese government's commitment to surrender unconditionally, because there was no such commitment prior to Hiroshima and the Soviet entry into the war. Elliptical statements in Truman's diaries that the emperor was "asking for peace" should not be misunderstood. What the emperor and Kido were promoting up to that time was the preservation of the emperor's power and his imperial "house," both matters of profound political and cultural significance to all the ruling elites. On U.S. knowledge see, for example, Walter Millis, ed., *The Forrestal Diaries* (New York, 1951), 74–7; Robert Ferrell, ed., *Off the Record: The Private Papers of Harry S. Truman* (New York, 1980), 53–4; and Truman, *Year of Decisions*, 396.

60 Yamada and Koketsu, *Ososugita seidan*, 212–13. The "emperor's letter" that Konoe was to have carried to Moscow was apparently quite short. The full text of it seems not to have been printed, though a precis of it can be found in Gaimusho, hen, *Shusen shiroku 3*, 160–1.

61 Yamada and Koketsu, *Ososugita seidan*, 212.

62 The "Essentials of Peace Negotiations" (*wahei kosho no yoryo*), a document that Konoe and his advisers drafted after Konoe had accepted his mission to Moscow, is another example of ruling elite thinking about surrender terms. Yoshida Yutaka points out that the "Essentials" stipulated the preservation of the emperor system as the absolute minimum condition for peace, but showed a willingness to concede, for a fixed period of time, all overseas territories and complete disarmament. More significant, a detailed "interpretation" attached to the "Essential" noted, with respect to the "interpretation of the *kokutai*," that "the main aim is to secure the imperial line and carry out politics by the emperor. In the worst case scenario, however, the transfer of the throne to a successor might be unavoidable." "Some revision of regulations means

mies had created a situation that gave them a face-saving excuse to surrender in order to prevent the *kokutai* from being destroyed by antiwar, antimilitary pressure originating from the Japanese people themselves. The bomb, followed by the Soviet declaration of war, gave them the signs they needed. This is why (as Nobumasa Tanaka pointed out) Mitsumasa Yonai could say to Sokichi Takagi, on 12 August, that

I think the term is perhaps inappropriate, but the atomic bombs and the Soviet entry into the war are, in a sense, gifts from the gods [*tenyu*, also "heaven sent blessings"]. This way we don't have to say that we have quit the war because of domestic circumstances. Why I have long been advocating control of the crisis of the country is neither for fear of an enemy attack nor because of the atomic bombs and the Soviet entry into the war. The main reason is my anxiety over the domestic situation. So, it is rather fortunate that now we can control matters without revealing the domestic situation.[63]

Similar reasons of political expediency also account for why Konoe called Soviet participation in the war "a godsend for controlling the army." An internal power struggle was going on, making it immaterial to the players if one hundred thousand or two hundred thousand people died as long as they could get their desired outcome: an end to the war that left the monarchy intact, available to control the forces of discontent that defeat would inevitably unleash. In the final scene of the war drama, as in earlier ones, the Japanese "moderates" found it easier to bow to outside forces than to act positively on their own to end the war.

(E) One Condition vs. Four Conditions

The twin psychological shocks of the first atomic bomb and the Soviet entry into the war, coupled with Kido's and the emperor's concern over growing popular criticism of the throne and its occu-

that, in an unavoidable situation, it will extend to the revision of the constitution and undemocratic laws." Significantly, even Konoe did not dare to seek the emperor's approval of his attached "Interpretation." Source: Yoshida, *Showa tenno no shusenshi*, 23–4.

63 On Yonai and Takagi see Yoshida, *Showa tenno no shusenshi*, 27. For the full statement quoted here see Sokichi Takagi, *Takagi kaigun shosho oboegaki* [Memoirs of Rear Admiral Takagi] (Tokyo, 1979), 351, cited in Tanaka, *Dokyumento Showa tenno, dai go kan*, 475.

pant, and the possibility that, sooner or later, the people would react violently against their leaders if they allowed the war to go on much longer – these factors finally caused Hirohito to accept, in principle, the terms of the Potsdam Declaration.[64]

At meetings of the Supreme War Leadership Council on 9 August, War Minister Korechika Anami and Chief of Staff Yoshijiro Umezu, representing the army, Yonai, representing the navy, and Togo, representing the Foreign Ministry, debated not whether to surrender but whether to try to surrender with conditions – one condition (preservation of the *kokutai*), or four.

The army (and in some accounts, initially the navy, represented by Yonai) insisted on four.[65] These were preservation of the *kokutai*, assumption by the imperial headquarters of responsibility for disarmament and demobilization, no occupation, and the delegation to the Japanese government of the punishment of war criminals.[66] The self-serving desire of the army to have autonomous war

64 Kido's diary around the time of capitulation shows him meeting frequently with the chief of the Home Ministry's Police Bureau and the superintendent-general of the Metropolitan Police, while also collecting the latest information about the worsening domestic situation directly from the commander of the Military Police. In addition, Rear Admiral Sokichi Takagi recalled after the war that on 12 July 1945, when Prince Konoe told Hirohito, "The situation today has reached the point where people hold a grudge against the imperial house," the emperor "agreed completely." Sources: Yoshida, *Showa tenno no shusenshi*, 29–30, citing Takagi, *Takagi kaigun shosho oboegaki*. Also see Shigeru Hayashi et al., eds., *Nihon shusenshi jokan, hachi gatsu jugonichi no kudeta hoka* [History of the termination of the war] (Tokyo, 1962), 196–210; Tanaka, *Dokyumento Showa tenno, dai go kan*, 460; and John W. Dower, "Sensational Rumors, Seditious Graffiti, and the Nightmares of the Thought Police," in John W. Dower, *Japan in War and Peace: Selected Essays* (New York, 1993), 101–54.

65 In his dictated statement to Atsushi Oi of GHQ's Historical Section on 28 November 1949, Togo said, "I cannot recall that Minister of the Navy Yonai introduced all the four conditions" and went on to accuse Anami, Umezu, and Toyoda of adding three conditions to the single one that he, Togo, had proposed. But other officials interrogated in the follow-up interviews stated otherwise.

66 According to Nobumasa Tanaka's reconstruction, based on the memoirs of Seomu Toyoda and Shigenori Togo, General Umezu stated the case for self-disarmament as follows: "Up to now the Japanese military has not permitted open surrender. The word 'surrender' is not in the Japanese military lexicon. In military education, if you lose your weapons, you fight with your bare hands. When your hands are no longer any good, you fight with your legs. When you can no longer use your hands and legs, you bite with your teeth. Finally, when you can no longer fight, you bite off your tongue and commit suicide. That is what we have been teaching. I do not think that it will go smoothly to order such an army to abandon its weapons and surrender. Our army and the allied army will designate the place and time in each theater of operations. We ourselves will collect the weapons in those designated places and the units also will gather there to hand over their weapons. Only afterwards will we act according to

crimes trials was predicated on their belief that the Allies would use such trials to indict the military on political grounds. Hence, they wanted to preempt the work of any international tribunal by conducting their own trials – exactly as the Germans had done after World War I.[67]

Supporting the military's views were three civilian members of the Suzuki cabinet: Justice Minister Hiromasa Matsuzaka, Home Minister Toji Yasui, and Minister of Health Tadahiko Okada.[68] Foreign Minister Togo alone held that the sole condition to be insisted on was preservation of the *kokutai*.

Nobumasa Tanaka believes there is no evidence to show that the emperor and Kido initially sided with Togo and opposed the four conditions of the senior military leaders. The more likely inference is that they still sympathized with the military die-hards, who preferred to continue the suicidal war rather than surrender unconditionally. This may account for why Konoe had Morisada Hosokawa urge Prince Takamatsu to press Hirohito (his elder brother) to accept the Potsdam terms, and why Konoe also enlisted the help of Mamoru Shigemitsu in persuading Kido to change his stand. At the urging of Takamatsu and Shigemitsu, Kido did indeed shift to the Foreign Ministry's position.

As Yutaka Yoshida pointed out, however, credit for ending the war must also be given to the younger generation of bureaucrats who assisted the court leaders: Kido's secretary, Yasumasa Matsudaira; Suzuki's secretary, Hisatsune Sakomizu; Togo's and Shigemitsu's secretary, Toshikazu Kase; and the assistant to Navy Minister Mitsumasa Yonai, Rear Admiral Sokichi Takagi. Not only were these men instrumental in pressing the emperor's top aides to accept the Potsdam terms. They also played a major role

their instructions. That is what we should request of them." Source: Tanaka, *Dokyumento Showa tenno, dai go kan*, 479–80. In fact, the Japanese military had already begun to disintegrate from within when Anami made his statement.

67 Kentaro Awaya, "Tokyo saiban ni miru sengo shori" [Postwar management as seen in the Tokyo trials] in Kentaro Awaya et al., *Senso sekinin, sengo sekinin: Nihon to Doitsu wa do chigau ka* [War responsibility, postwar responsibility: How Germany and Japan differ] (Tokyo, 1994), 79–80.

68 Tanaka, *Dokyumento Showa tenno, dai go kan*, 493–4. See also Togo's dictated statements to investigators from the Historical Section of GHQ in the follow-up interviews of 17 May 1949 and 17 August 1950. In *U.S. Army Statements of Japanese Officials on World War II* (n.p., 1949–50), Volume 4, Microfilm Shelf No. 51256, National Archives, Washington, DC.

behind the scenes, after the surrender, in shielding the emperor from the terrible consequences of defeat.[69] The desire to protect the emperor would thereafter limit and distort how the surrender process was depicted. Yasumasa Matsudaira even managed to get the false official version of the emperor's role in the war inserted into *The Reports of General MacArthur*. His essay ("The Japanese Emperor and the War") appears as the "Appendix" to "Volume II – Part 2" of the *Reports*, which MacArthur's staff group printed in Tokyo in 1950, under the general editorship of Major General Charles A. Willoughby.[70]

The crafting of historical memory of how the war ended began in Tokyo in the early morning hours of 9–10 August, when the emperor, who had joined the "peace camp" belatedly in June, and thereafter vacillated, formally accepted the Potsdam Declaration, in a speech to his ministers scripted for him by Kido and delivered in his characteristic high-pitched voice. Sakomizu, who knew beforehand that the forty-four-year-old emperor was going to give a speech that night, had come to the meeting prepared to document it. He wrote up the emperor's words in smooth, businesslike language. A brief precis of the speech may also be found in Kido's diary entry of 10 August. Many months later, in his "monologue," the emperor himself recounted what was most relevant to understanding the motivation for his *seidan* on the night of 9–10 August.

The [Supreme War Leadership] Council continued meeting until after 2 A.M. on August 10, but failed to reach agreement. Suzuki made his decision and expressed his wish that I should decide between the two opinions.

Six people, apart from Prime Minister Suzuki, were present at the meeting: Hiranuma, Yonai, Anami, Togo, Umezu and Toyoda.

Although everybody agreed to attach the condition of preserving the *kokutai*, three – Anami, Toyoda and Umezu – insisted on adding three further conditions: not to carry out an occupation with the aim of secur-

---

69 Yoshida, *Showa tenno no shusenshi*, 31.
70 See *Reports of General MacArthur: Japanese Operations in the Southwest Pacific Area, Volume II – Part 2* (Washington, 1966), 763–71. According to General Harold K. Johnson's "Foreword" to this four-volume history, "While he lived, General MacArthur was unwilling to approve the reproduction and dissemination of the *Reports*, because he believed they needed further editing and correction of some inaccuracies." One of the more conspicuous inaccuracies is Matsudaira's essay. 'For Matsudaira's role in the Japanese campaign to protect the emperor see Bix, "The Showa Emperor's 'Monologue,' " 322–34, 358.

ing specific surrender terms, and to leave disarmament and the punishment of war criminals to us. Not only that, they insisted that negotiation on these matters was still possible at the present stage of the war. But four people – Suzuki, Hiranuma, Yonai and Togo – argued against them, saying there was no room to negotiate.

I thought, then, that it was impossible to continue the war. From the Chief of the Army General Staff I had heard that the defenses of Cape Inubo and Kujukuri coastal plain were still not ready. Also, according to the Army Minister, the materials needed to complete the armaments for the divisions which would fight the final battle in the Kanto region could not be delivered until September.

How could the capital be defended under such conditions?

How was a battle even possible? It was beyond my comprehension.

I told them that I supported the Foreign Ministry's proposal. . . . The main motive behind my decision at that time was that if we let matters stand and did not act, the Japanese race would perish and I would be unable to protect my subjects [*sekishi*=literally, infants, children]. Second, Kido agreed with me on the matter of defending the *kokutai*. If the enemy landed near Ise Bay, both Ise and Atsuta shrines would immediately come under their control. There would be no time to transfer the sacred treasures [regalia] of the imperial family and no hope of protecting them. Under these circumstances, protection of the *kokutai* would be difficult. For these reasons, I thought at the time that I must make peace even at the sacrifice of myself.[71]

Four features of this speech deserve comment. First, the emperor says that he had been told by his army minister that the capital could not be defended. But ever since June he had known that continuation of the war was impossible. Why had he waited so long before making a policy decision to surrender? Second, the emperor already knew, before Hiroshima was bombed (6 August), that his cabinet was divided on accepting the Potsdam terms; he also knew that only he could unify government affairs and military command. Why, then, had he waited until the evening of the 9th – that is, until after yet another act of tremendous outside pressure had been applied – to call the Supreme War Leadership Council into session?[72] Third, the emperor expresses his fear of the extinc-

71 Terasaki and Miller, eds., *Showa tenno dokuhakuroku – Terasaki Hidenari, goyogakari nikki*, 125–6.
72 Tanaka, *Dokyumento Showa tenno, dai go kan*, 472.

tion of the Japanese race, hereby laying the greatest weight of all on his duty as an individual to his imperial ancestors. If the people ("my loyal subjects") are all wiped out, he will not be able to fulfill the main mission of his life, which was to bequeath the throne to his imperial descendants.[73] Fourth, the emperor uses the phrase "Even at the sacrifice of myself" — and repeats it on several occasions thereafter — in order to convey the impression of a sacrificial spirit. But what, one might ask, did those words mean when measured against the scores of millions who, by that time, had died in his war?

Once the emperor had made his "sacred decision" (*seidan*), a cabinet conference deliberated on Togo's one condition. At the suggestion of Privy Council President Kiichiro Hiranuma, they agreed to reformulate their acceptance to read: "with the understanding that the said declaration does not comprise any demand which prejudices the prerogatives of His Majesty as a Sovereign Ruler [*tenno no kokka toji no taiken*]."

This was an affirmation that the emperor's rights of sovereignty antedated the constitution and were determined by the gods in antiquity, just as the preamble to the Meiji Constitution stated.[74] The Japanese government, in other words, was still fighting to maintain the *kokutai*; and despite all that had happened, it was asking the Allies to guarantee the emperor's political power to rule the state on the theocratic premises of state Shinto.[75] It was not constitutional monarchy that the Suzuki cabinet was seeking to have the Allies assure, but monarchy based on the principle of oracular sovereignty. In the final analysis, the *kokutai* meant to them, in their extreme moment of crisis, the orthodox Shinto-National Learning view of the state and the retention of real, substantial political power in the hands of the emperor, so that he and the "moderates" might go on using it to control the people.[76]

If Grew and the Japan crowd had gotten their way, and the principle of unconditional surrender had been contravened, it is highly unlikely that Japan's post-surrender leaders, now the "mod-

---

73 Ibid., 504. In Sakomizu's memorandum, the emperor's words are: "My duty is to bequeath to posterity Japan, the country I inherited from my ancestors."
74 Tanaka, *Dokyumento Showa tenno, dai go kan*, 506.
75 Ibid., 507.
76 Kisaburo Yokota, *Tennosei* [The emperor system] (Tokyo, 1949), 183–4.

erates" around the throne, would ever have discarded the Meiji Constitution and democratized their political institutions.

Conclusion

The preceding analysis of war termination in Japan during 1945 shows that never at any time did the Japanese military exercise complete dominance over the political process. As the losing war dragged on after the fall of the Tojo cabinet, the senior leaders of the army and navy became increasingly beholden for their positions of power to the court and the moderates around the throne.

More important, the analysis underscores the active role of the Showa Emperor Hirohito in supporting the actions carried out in his name. When he is properly restored in the overall picture as supreme generalissimo, it becomes possible to draw the following conclusions: neither (a) American unwillingness to make a firm, timely statement assuring continuation of the throne, as Grew had argued for, nor (b) the last-minute anti-Soviet strategic stance of Truman and Byrnes, who probably wanted use of the atomic bomb rather than diplomatic negotiation, are sufficient, in and of themselves, to account for use of the bomb, or for Japan's delay in ending the suicidal conflict. Rather, Emperor Hirohito's reluctance to face the fait accompli of defeat, and then to act, positively and energetically, to end hostilities, plus certain official acts and policies of his government, are what mainly prolonged the war, though they were not sufficient cause for use of the bomb. In the last analysis, what counted on the one hand, was not only the transcendent influence of the throne, but the power, authority, and unique personality of its occupant, and on the other, the power, determination, and unique character of Harry Truman.

From the very start of the war, the emperor was a major protagonist of the events going on around him. Before the battle of Okinawa he had constantly pressed for *a* decisive victory. Afterward, he accepted the need for an early peace, but vacillated, steering Japan toward continued warfare rather than toward direct negotiations with the Allies. When the final crisis was fully upon him, the only option left was surrender without negotiation. Again, it was not so much the Allied policy of unconditional surrender that prolonged the Pacific war, as it was the unrealistic and incompetent actions of Japan's highest leaders.

Blinded by their preoccupation with the fate of the imperial house, those leaders let pass every opportunity to end the lost war until it was too late. Hirohito and his inner war cabinet – the Supreme War Leadership Council – could have looked reality in the face and acted, decisively, to sue for peace during February, when Prince Konoe made his report and military intelligence officers altered them to the likelihood of the Soviet Union entering the war against Japan by mid-summer.

Their second opportunity missed came in June, when the showdown-battle of Okinawa had been lost, when government analyses indicated that the war could soon no longer be waged, and when General Umezu unveiled for the emperor the bleak results of his personal survey of the situation in China.[77] Considering that Foreign Minister Molotov had earlier notified Tokyo (on 5 April) that the Japan-Soviet Neutrality Pact would not be extended, and that the Germans had surrendered unconditionally (on 7 May), this certainly would have been an opportune moment for them to have opened direct negotiations with the United States and Britain.

Their third opportunity missed was 27–28 July, when the Potsdam Declaration arrived and the Suzuki cabinet, after careful deliberation, twice publicly rejected it.

Last was the interval between their receipt of the declaration and the bombing of Hiroshima, when the emperor and Kido waited for a response from Moscow – a response that Sato and many others repeatedly stated would never come.

The Japanese "peace" overtures to the Soviets, which followed Germany's capitulation to the Allies, were vague, feeble, and counterproductive, in effect of no importance at all. Those maneuvers certainly did not constitute a serious attempt to negotiate an end to the war. Togo himself conceded as much when he said, on 17

---

77 In his "monologue" the emperor says, "Umezu returned from Manchuria the day after the [imperial] conference [of 8 June]. According to his report, even with all our forces in China we could only resist eight American divisions. If, therefore, the United States landed ten divisions in China, there was absolutely no chance of winning. It was the first time that Umezu ever complained like this." Source: *Showa tenno dokuhakuroku, Terasaki Hidenari, goyogakari nikki*, 116–17.

August 1950, that "although I asked the Soviet Union to act as peace mediator, I was unable to advise her of our peace conditions in any concrete form."[78]

Would Japan's leaders have surrendered promptly if the Truman administration had clarified the status of the emperor prior to the cataclysmic double shocks of the atomic bomb and Soviet entry into the war? Probably not, though they were likely to have surrendered in order to prevent the *kokutai* from being destroyed from within.

The emperor's staging of the *seidan* on the night of 9–10 August, his repeat of it on the morning of the 14th, and finally, the dramatic radio reenactment of the *seidan* on a national scale (with the whole nation participating) at noon on the 15th – these events reinforced the emperor's charisma while preparing him for his public role in the new drama that was about to begin in the postwar period. The emperor's rescript ending the war was a shocking act, a bolt from the blue, which caught the Japanese people totally unprepared and literally staggered them. To ensure popular understanding of his message, the radio announcer Shinken Wada reread the entire rescript in ordinary language. A cabinet announcement followed, condemning the United States for use of the atomic bombs in violation of international law, and the Soviet Union for declaring war against Japan. Thereupon, Wada made this commentary on the news:

We people who invited a situation where we had no choice but to lay down our arms, were unable to live up to the great benevolence of the emperor, but he did not even scold us. On the contrary, he said that whatever might happen to himself, "I can no longer bear to see the people die in war." In the face of such great benevolence and love, who could not reflect on his own disloyalty.[79]

Wada ended by reiterating the imperial message, "Since the situation has developed this way, the nation will unite and, believing in the indestructibility of the divine land, put all of its energies into rebuilding for the future."

78   Togo statement of 17 August 1950, p. 4, in U.S. Army Statements of Japanese Officials on World War II, Vol. 4, Microfilm Shelf No. 51256.
79   Yoshida, *Showa tenno no shusenshi*, 33, citing Akiko Takeyama, *Gyokuon hoso* [The broadcast of the emperor's voice] (Tokyo, 1989), 128.

In the weeks and months that followed, while vast amounts of secret materials pertaining to Japanese war crimes and the war responsibility of the nation's highest leaders went up in smoke, the media and the cabinet of Prince Naruhiko Higashikuni, which succeeded Suzuki's on 17 August, represented the emperor to the nation as the benevolent sage who had ended the war. The surrender broadcast "ritual" confirmed his inherent power to create a radically new situation in which the Japanese people could return to peaceful economic pursuits, ever mindful that their emperor had saved them, and the rest of the world, from further destruction by atomic bombs.[80]

Meanwhile, the very naming of this event had impeded a deeper understanding of it. For Hirohito's *seidan*, or "sacred decision," denoted not only his act of ending the war, but the preexisting (post-1868) imperial narrative into which it was fitted. In short, the events of 9–10, 14, and 15 August automatically partook of a framework of meaning that protected the emperor's actions from criticism. Yet seldom have writers in English commented on the multiple (political and memorializing) functions that the last *seidan*(s) have served.

Ironically, when Emperor Hirohito first toured Hiroshima after the war, over seventy thousand well-wishing citizens cheered, and the brass band of the Hiroshima Railway Bureau played the national anthem as his motorcade crossed Aioi Bridge at the epicenter of the atomic explosion.[81] As he stood on the roof of the city hall and looked out over the rapid reconstruction that had taken place since the bomb was dropped, there was no *visible* expression of popular resentment against him.

80 The notion of the surrender as a broadcast "ritual" comes from Takeyama, *Gyokuon hoso*, 71.
81 On the Hiroshima visit see Masao Suzuki, *Showa tenno no gojunko* [The Showa emperor's local tours] (Tokyo, 1992), 210–13.

5

The Bombed: Hiroshimas and Nagasakis in Japanese Memory

JOHN W. DOWER

Mieko Hara, who was a youngster in Hiroshima when the city was bombed, later wrote of herself that "the Mieko of today is completely different from the Mieko of the past."[1] Most *hibakusha* experienced this fracturing of identity, and for Japan as a whole the very meaning of time was altered by the atomic bombings of 6 and 9 August 1945.

Such a profound sense of disjuncture was, of course, not peculiar to Japan. For much of the world, the holocaust in Europe and the nuclear genocide of Hiroshima/Nagasaki signified the closure of "modernity" as it had been known and dreamed about until then and the advent of a new world of terrible and awesome potentialities. In Japan, however, the situation was unique in two ways. Only the Japanese actually had experienced nuclear destruction. And in the years immediately following, only they were not allowed to publicly engage the nature and meaning of this new world. Beginning in mid-September 1945, U.S. authorities in occupied Japan censored virtually all discussion of the bombs.

Such censorship reflected both the general U.S. policy of secrecy concerning nuclear matters and, on a different plane, the broad agenda of media control pursued as part of U.S. occupation policy in defeated Japan. Where Hiroshima and Nagasaki specifically were concerned, the rationale for censorship within Japan was essentially twofold. American occupation authorities feared that unrestricted discussion of the effects of the bombs

---

1 Mieko Hara, untitled memoir in *Children of Hiroshima*, ed. Publishing Committee for "Children of Hiroshima" (Tokyo, 1980), 244–6, quoted in John Whittier Treat, *Writing Ground Zero: Japanese Literature and the Atomic Bomb* (forthcoming, Chicago).

might incite "public unrest" against them (the most elastic and all-encompassing rationale of censors everywhere). More specifically, statements by Japanese politicians and the print media early in September conveyed the impression that the Allied policy of publicizing Japanese war atrocities and conducting war-crimes trials might confront a Japanese countercampaign that called attention to the Allies' own atrocious policies, most graphically exemplified by the nuclear destruction of the two essentially civilian targets.[2]

Such a hypothetical countercampaign was plausible. Mamoru Shigemitsu, a once and future prime minister (and future convicted war criminal in the interim), authored an early internal memorandum explicitly proposing that the Japanese use the atomic bombs as counterpropaganda to Allied accusations of Japanese war crimes. Ichiro Hatoyama, an ambitious conservative politician who aspired to the premiership (the occupation-period purge disrupted his timetable, but he did serve as prime minister from the end of 1954 to 1956), rashly voiced similar opinions in public.[3] In the opening weeks of occupation, the Domei news agency and leading newspapers, such as the *Asahi*, also naively attempted to balance the record of war behavior in this manner. With the advantage of hindsight, however, it can be said that the censorship of Japanese discussion of the bombs and their human consequences

2　The first occupation forces did not arrive in Japan until the very end of August; the formal surrender ceremony took place on 2 September; and the occupation headquarters in Tokyo did not become effectively operational until early September. Formal occupation censorship generally is dated from 19 September 1945, when a press code was announced. Beginning 5 October, prepublication censorship was imposed on major newspapers and periodicals. For general accounts concerning nuclear-related censorship see Sozo Matsuura, *Senryoka no Genron Danatsu* [Suppression of speech under the occupation] (Tokyo, 1969), esp. 167–212; Committee for the Compilation of Materials on Damage Caused by the Atomic Bombs in Hiroshima and Nagasaki, comp., *Hiroshima and Nagasaki: The Physical, Medical, and Social Effects of the Atomic Bombings*, trans. Ishikawa Eisei and David L. Swain (New York, 1981), 5, 503–13, 564, 585 (hereafter this basic source, originally published in Japanese in 1979, is cited as *Hiroshima and Nagasaki*); Monica Braw, *The Atomic Bomb Suppressed: American Censorship in Occupied Japan* (Armonk, NY, 1991); and Glenn D. Hook, "Censorship and Reportage of Atomic Damage and Casualties in Hiroshima and Nagasaki," *Bulletin of Concerned Asian Scholars* 23 (January–March 1991): 13–25.

3　Hatoyama's statement appeared in *Asahi Shimbun*, 15 September 1945. His account of this incident and enduring contempt for the "recklessness" and hypocrisy exemplified in the U.S. use of the atomic bombs and punishment of him for criticizing this emerges clearly in his memoirs: *Hatoyama Ichiro Kaikoroku* [Ichiro Hatoyama memoirs] (Tokyo, 1957), 49–51.

was misguided, perhaps counterproductive, certainly disdainful of the needs of the survivors themselves.

Between 6 and 9 August, when the bombs were dropped, and mid-September, when censorship was imposed by the U.S. occupation force, Japanese responses to the new weapon actually were varied and provocative. Until the American victors established their presence in defeated Japan, of course, the media was censored by Japan's own imperial government. Thus, the historian faces a biased public record both before and after the occupation commenced. Still, it is possible to re-create a kaleidoscope of responses beyond the overwhelming sense of horror and shock experienced by those who suffered the bombings directly, and apart from the political notion of playing Allied atrocities against Japanese ones.

Initially, rage was one such response. In Hiroshima immediately after the bombing, for example, survivors came upon uninjured American POWs (they had been confined in underground cells) and beat them to death.[4] In a makeshift Hiroshima medical facility, the rumor spread that Japan had retaliated by bombing the United States with its own secret weapon, causing comparable atrocious death and suffering – and the Japanese survivors, it was reported, were pleased. The government and media naturally condemned the new weapon as evidence of the enemy's barbaric and demonic nature. Early in September, before occupation censorship was imposed, the *Asahi* ran a vivid article about the hatred of Americans visible in the eyes of Hiroshima survivors. Later, in one of the countless unnoticed individual tragedies of the occupation period, a Nisei soldier affiliated with the U.S. force visited relatives in Hiroshima, where his parents came from, and was so shattered by their hostility to him as an American "murderer" that he committed suicide soon afterward in his quarters in Tokyo.[5]

4 On American POWs in Hiroshima see "Nijusannin no Beiheri Horyo mo Bakushi Shite Ita" [Twenty-three American POWs also killed by bombing] *Shukan Yomiuri*, 13 August 1978, 28–31; Barton J. Bernstein, "Unraveling a Mystery: American POWs Killed at Hiroshima," *Foreign Service Journal* 56 (October 1979): 17ff; and Robert Karl Manoff, "American Victims of Hiroshima," *New York Times Magazine*, 2 December 1984, 67ff. This became the theme of a 1971 mural by the painters Iri and Toshi Maruki, who are discussed below. See John W. Dower and John Junkerman, eds., *The Hiroshima Murals: The Art of Iri Maruki and Toshi Maruki* (Tokyo, 1985), 21, 78–81.
5 *Asahi Shimbun*, 7 September 1945; Grant Goodman, *Amerika no Nihon – Gannen, 1945–1946* [America's Japan – the first year, 1945–1946] (Tokyo, 1986), 120–3.

Perhaps surprisingly, however, at least at first glance, hatred against the Americans did not become a dominant sentiment in the weeks, months, and years that followed. The destructiveness of the bombs was so awesome that many Japanese initially regarded them – much like the calamitous losing war itself – almost as if they were a natural disaster. Then, as the man-made nature of the disaster sunk in, what riveted attention was the realization that science and technology suddenly had leapt to hitherto unimagined levels. Such attitudes soon became conspicuous even in the two bombed cities themselves (although the Americans took care to assign British and Australian forces to oversee local occupation administration in Hiroshima). Certainly they were prevalent throughout defeated Japan as a whole, where rage dissipated quickly in the face of the urgent challenges of recovery – and indeed, simple daily survival.

The Japanese identified the new weapon as a nuclear bomb within a matter of days. Their own scientists had investigated the possibility of developing such weapons after Pearl Harbor and had concluded that doing so was technically feasible but practically impossible for many decades to come.[6] Yoshio Nishina, an eminent physicist who had studied with Niels Bohr and supervised some of the wartime research on the military application of nuclear fission, was sent to Hiroshima right after the attack and immediately recognized that these long-term projections had been naïve. (Nishina died of cancer in 1951, and it is popularly believed that his illness resulted from his exposure to residual radiation in Hiroshima.)

By 15 August, when Japan capitulated, it was widely known throughout the country that a weapon of entirely new dimensions had devastated the two cities. The emperor himself, in his careful, self-serving address of this date announcing acceptance of the Potsdam Declaration, took care to emphasize this. "The enemy has for the first time used cruel bombs to kill and maim extremely large numbers of the innocent," Hirohito informed his subjects, "and the heavy casualties are beyond measure; if the war were continued, it would lead not only to the downfall of our nation but also

6 Japan's research on the possibility of making nuclear weapons is described in "'NI' and 'F': Japan's Wartime Atomic Bomb Research," in John W. Dower, *Japan in War and Peace: Selected Essays* (New York, 1993), 55–100.

to the destruction of all human civilization."[7] Japan's capitulation, in the official imperial rendering, thus became a magnanimous act that saved humanity itself from possible annihilation.

By the time the first contingent of U.S. occupation forces actually arrived in Japan at the very end of August, popular responses to the defeat and unconditional surrender had begun to assume complex configurations politically. The bombs quickly became a symbol of America's material might and scientific prowess – and this symbol was all the more stunning because it contrasted so sharply with Japan's relative material backwardness. While the Americans had been perfecting nuclear weapons, Japan's militaristic government had been exhorting the emperor's loyal subjects to take up bamboo spears and fight to the bitter end to defend the homeland. A year after the surrender, Etsuro Kato, a famous cartoonist, perfectly captured this dichotomy in the opening pages of a little book of illustrations chronicling the first year of occupation. An exhausted Japanese man and woman lay on the ground on 15 August, fire buckets discarded beside them, contemplating the absurdity of pitting bamboo spears and little pails against atomic bombs.[8]

Kato's juxtaposition of atomic bombs against bamboo spears captured a widespread and politically explosive sentiment. In sum, it amounts to this: Japan's ideologues and military spokesmen had deceived the people and led the country into a hopeless war against a vastly superior United States. Personally, they obviously were fools (thus, there was not much popular Japanese hand-wringing about the showcase Tokyo war-crimes trials). More generally, one clearly could not trust military appeals or military solutions in the future (thus, the "no-war clause" of the new 1947 Japanese constitution, originally drafted by the Americans, found strong support among ordinary Japanese).[9]

The popular antimilitary sentiment that has influenced so much

7 *Hiroshima and Nagasaki*, 496.
8 Etsuro Kato, *Okurareta Kakumei* [The revolution that was given to us] (Tokyo, 1946). A copy of this fascinating booklet, which is now almost impossible to find in Japan, is in the Gordon Prange Collection in McKeldin Library, University of Maryland, College Park.
9 The great majority of Japanese at the time exonerated the emperor from such criticism. Post-surrender propaganda by the Japanese elites, parroted by U.S. occupation authorities, strongly emphasized that the emperor too had been misled by the military.

of postwar Japanese politics has its genesis in such visceral feelings. The "fifteen-year war" in general was devastating for Japan. Close to three million Japanese soldiers, sailors, and civilians were killed between the Manchurian Incident of 1931 and Japan's surrender in 1945, and a total of sixty-six cities, including Hiroshima and Nagasaki, were bombed. In the end, misery and humiliation were the only conspicuous legacies of the so-called holy war.[10] The atomic bombs quickly came to exemplify this tragic absurdity.

In these various ways, a complex symbolic field already had begun to resonate around the bomb by the time the victorious Americans arrived. The horror of a war brought home with unimagined destructiveness was one aspect of this, Japan's own backwardness another, the immense potentiality of science yet another. This Japanese did not place a negative construction on "science" in this context, but on the contrary singled out deficiency in science and technology as an obvious explanation for their defeat and an immediately accessible means by which the country could be rebuilt.

Scarcely a day passed between Japan's capitulation and the imposition of censorship by the Americans in mid-September that did not see a statement by the government or press about the urgent necessity of promoting science. On 16 August, in his first broadcast after being named prime minister, Prince Naruhiko Higashikuni declared that "science and technology" had been Japan's biggest shortcoming in the war. A day later, the outgoing minister of education thanked school children for their wartime efforts and urged them to dedicate themselves to elevating Japan's "science power and spiritual power" to the highest possible levels. On 19 August, the press reported that under the new minister of education, Tamon Maeda, the postwar school system would place "emphasis on basic science." "We lost to the enemy's science," the *Asahi* declared bluntly in a 20 August article, going on to observe that "this was made clear by a single bomb dropped on Hiroshima." The article was head-

10 From the historian's perspective, we now can identify many ways in which Japan's fifteen-year mobilization for war created positive technological, technocratic, and institutional legacies for the postwar state, but these certainly were not apparent in the immediate post-surrender years. See "The Useful War" in Dower, *Japan in War and Peace*, 9–32.

lined "Toward a Country Built on Science."[11] In the years that followed, improving science education remained one of the country's foremost priorities.

In Japan, as elsewhere, the bomb thus became Janus: simultaneously a symbol of the terror of nuclear war and the promise of science. More than in other countries, however, the peculiar circumstances of the nuclear bombings, unconditional surrender, and, later, the new pacifist constitution created a postwar milieu in which "building a nation of science" almost invariably was coupled with an emotional emphasis on "peace" maintained through nonmilitary pursuits. Economically, the long-term consequences of this development were spectacular. Japan's emergence as an economic superpower by the 1980s resulted in considerable part from the fact that, after the surrender, the vast majority of talented Japanese scientists, businessmen, and bureaucrats devoted themselves to promoting *civilian* applications of science. Unlike the United States, where many scientists and engineers found the sweetest problems and most lucrative funding in weapons-related research, in Japan such work carried a social stigma.[12]

11 The quotations come from the *Asahi Shimbun* in the period immediately following capitulation, but such sentiments were ubiquitous.
12 The social stigma attached to weapons-related research was reinforced by institutional constraints. In the early reformist phase of the occupation, the imperial military establishment was eliminated. Although constitutional prohibition of the maintenance of military forces under the new "no war" charter was violated after the Korean War broke out and Japan began to rearm (beginning in July 1950), the constitutional restraint did remain strong enough to prevent the creation of an institutionalized militarism comparable to the Pentagon and military-academic-industrial complex in the United States. Preservation of bureaucratic turf helped to perpetuate this situation over the decades, for primary responsibility for budgetary allotments resided in the hands of the Ministry of Finance, which remained largely committed to civilian-oriented policies. There is still no defense ministry per se in Japan. At the same time, public opinion, while tolerating incremental remilitarization, remained opposed to constitutional revision and the more blatant sort of all-out militarization this might permit. There is no question that the "no war" constitution is an anomaly in the 1990s, when Japan does in fact have a large military budget, has become a major producer of "dual use" technologies, and has sent "peace keeping forces" abroad under UN auspices in response to immense U.S. pressure. Nonetheless, the persistence of popular opposition to constitutional revision for almost half a century to date has conspicuously influenced the nature and balance of Japan's economic and political policies in nonmilitary directions; and the most effective arguments against such revision consistently have played upon memories of Japan's "victimization" in World War II, of which Hiroshima always will remain the prime symbol. Contemporary political struggles over who will control the memory of war (as seen in the Ministry of Education's notorious efforts to produce sanitized textbook coverage of this topic) are intimately tied to these issues of constitutional revision and whether or not

The immediate sanguine linkage between the tragedy of Hiroshima/Nagasaki and the promise of a "country built on science" had ramifications beyond just the material promotion of science and technology. Science itself became equated with the development of more "rational" modes of thinking in general. The disastrous folly of the lost war, that is, was attributed to a weakness in critical thought and "conceptual ability" throughout Japanese society. From this perspective, it was only a short but momentous step to linking the promotion of science to promotion of democracy in postwar Japan, on the grounds that scientific progress was possible only in a "rational" environment that encouraged genuinely free inquiry and expression. In this manner, a seemingly technological response to defeat contained within itself a political logic that contributed greatly to support for casting off the shackles of the imperial state and instituting progressive reforms.[13]

At the same time, the trauma of nuclear devastation and unconditional surrender also reinforced an abiding sense of Japan's peculiar vulnerability and victimization. As the bombs came to symbolize the tragic absurdity of war, the recent war itself became perceived as fundamentally a Japanese tragedy. Hiroshima and Nagasaki became icons of Japanese suffering – perverse national treasures, of a sort, capable of fixating Japanese memory of the war on what had happened to Japan and simultaneously blotting out recollection of the Japanese victimization of others. Remembering Hiroshima and Nagasaki, that is, easily became a way of forgetting Nanjing, Bataan, the Burma-Siam railway, Manila, and the countless Japanese atrocities these and other place names signified to non-Japanese.

"Victim consciousness" (*higaisha ishiki*) is a popular euphe-

---

Japan should become a more "normal" state with a bona-fide military. In this contest, Japanese liberals and leftists commonly are able to make more effective neonationalistic use of the bombs than their conservative and right-wing opponents. To encourage popular support for constitutional revision and more "normal" militarization, the latter must perforce downplay the horrors of the old war – not only the suffering of the imperial forces caused to others but also the horrors brought home.

13 For good early examples of this political logic equating "science" with a more "rational" democratic society generally see *Asahi Shimbun*, 22 August 1945; and Yoshio Toyoshima's comments in the September–October 1945 issue of *Bungei*, quoted in Shugo Honda, *Monogatari: Sengo Bungaku Shi* [The story of postwar literary history] (1966; reprint, Tokyo, 1992), 1:13.

mism in postwar and contemporary Japan, and the bombs occupy a central place in this consciousness. From this perspective, it can be observed that nuclear victimization spawned new forms of nationalism in postwar Japan – a neonationalism that coexists in complex ways with antimilitarism and even the "one-country pacifism" long espoused by many individuals and groups associated with the political Left.

II

Such considerations leave out the fate of the nuclear victims themselves; and, in fact, most Americans and Japanese at the time were happy to ignore these victims. Official U.S. reports about the two stricken cities tended to emphasize physical damage and minimize human loss and suffering. Prescient early journalistic accounts about the horrible consequences of radiation sickness were repudiated or repressed by occupation authorities. Japanese film footage was confiscated. Accounts of fatalities were conservative.

The U.S. policy of prohibiting open reporting from Hiroshima and Nagasaki was made clear at an early date, in a celebrated incident involving the Australian journalist Wilfred Burchett. Burchett made his way to Hiroshima early in September and succeeded in dispatching a graphic description of victims of an "atomic plague" to the London *Daily Express*. This was the first Western account of the fatal effects of radiation, and occupation officials immediately mounted an attack on what Burchett had reported. He was temporarily stripped of his press accreditation, and his camera, containing film with yet undeveloped Hiroshima exposures, mysteriously "disappeared." A comparable early account by an American journalist in Nagasaki never cleared General Douglas MacArthur's press headquarters, and reports to the outside world thereafter were carefully controlled through complacent, officially approved mouthpieces, such as William Laurence, the science editor of the *New York Times*.[14] Some eleven thousand feet of movie film shot in the two

14 See Wilfred Burchett, *Shadows of Hiroshima* (London, 1983), esp. chaps. 1–3. Burchett's story, essentially as published in the *Daily Express*, is reproduced on 34–7. The counterpart scoop from Nagasaki, squelched by occupation headquarters, was by George Weller of the *Chicago Daily News* and totaled some twenty-five thousand words. Ibid., 44–5.

cities between August and December by a thirty-two man Japanese camera crew was confiscated by U.S. authorities in February 1946 and not returned to Japan until two decades later, in 1966.[15]

Accurate estimates of atomic bomb fatalities also have been difficult to come by over the years. In June 1946, the prestigious U.S. Strategic Bombing Survey placed the number of deaths at approximately seventy to eighty thousand individuals in Hiroshima and thirty-five to forty thousand in Nagasaki. An honest estimate at the time, these figures have been perpetuated in most subsequent commentary about the bombs, although they probably are conservative in themselves and obviously fail to take into account bomb-related deaths subsequent to mid-1946. For the usual political reasons, after 1946 neither the U.S. nor Japanese government chose to revise the initial estimates or call attention to the on-going toll of *hibakusha* deaths. It now appears that the total of immediate and longer-term deaths caused by the bombing of the two cities may be as high as triple the familiar early estimates – in the neighborhood, that is, of three hundred thousand or more individuals.[16]

15 Akiro Iwasaki, *Nihon Gendai Taikei: Eiga Shi* [Outline of contemporary Japan: Film history] (Tokyo, 1961), 226–7; Matsuura, *Senryoka no Genron Danatsu*, 192–5. Iwasaki was part of the project filming the aftermath of the bombs in Hiroshima and Nagasaki, which was conducted by the Nichiei studio.
16 The United States Strategic Bombing Survey, *The Effects of Atomic Bombs on Hiroshima and Nagasaki* (Washington, 1946), 3–5. Accurate estimates of atomic bomb related deaths are made problematic by many factors; the demographic turmoil that prevailed in Japan at war's end, especially in urban areas; the extraordinary destructiveness of the bombs, which obliterated whole neighborhoods, along with the records pertaining to their residents; the chaos prevailing after the bombs were dropped, including hasty cremations of victims to prevent disease; and the absence of clear, coordinated, publicly accessible records of subsequent *hibakusha* illnesses and deaths. Useful data on fatalities, and the difficulty of calculating them, appears in the voluminous 1979 Japanese report translated into English as *Hiroshima and Nagasaki* (footnote 2 above); see 113–15, 367, 369, 406. Although conflicting figures are given here, the general conclusion is that total long-term *hibakusha* deaths were approximately double the 1946 figures for each city. In 1994, when the Japanese parliament belatedly debated legislation concerning death-benefits compensation to *hibakusha* families (see footnote 18 below), Ministry of Health and Welfare statistics commonly were cited indicating that between 300,000 and 350,000 *hibakusha* had died prior to 1969, with all but 50 to 70,000 of these deaths occurring prior to 1958; see *Asahi Shimbun*, 27 October and 3 November 1994. Persistent replication of the outdated initial low estimates of fatalities has contributed to perpetuation of one of the enduring misleading statements in standard accounts of the war – namely, that many more people were killed in the Tokyo air raid of 9 and 10 March 1945 than by the atomic bombs in each city. Official Japanese estimates for fatalities in the Tokyo raids are less than one

Disregard for the victims extended beyond sanitized reporting, suppressed film footage of the human aftermath, and disregard of the real death toll. Unsurprisingly, the United States extended no aid to survivors of the atomic bombs. Among other considerations, to do so could have been construed as acknowledging that use of the bombs had been improper. Aid to victims also might have opened the door to claims for compensation or special treatment by victims of conventional U.S. incendiary bombing. The well-known Atomic Bomb Casualty Commission (ABCC) established by the U.S. government in Japan at the beginning of 1947 was set up exclusively to collect scientific data on the long-term biological effects of the bombs. Whether fairly or not, to many Japanese the ABCC thereby earned the onus of simply treating the *hibakusha* residents of Hiroshima and Nagasaki as experimental subjects or guinea pigs a second time.[17]

More surprisingly, perhaps, the Japanese government only began extending special assistance to the bomb victims after the occupation ended in 1952. In the aftermath of the devastation of Hiroshima and Nagasaki, local treatment was largely dependent on local resources – and this from municipalities that had come close to annihilation. One of the several legacies of this callous early history of neglect has been to make identification of victims and precise quantification of the effects of the bombs even more problematic than might otherwise have been the case.[18]

In the localities themselves, suffering was compounded not merely by the unprecedented scale of the catastrophe, as well as by the absence of large-scale governmental assistance, but also by

hundred thousand. Indeed, the Ministry of Health and Welfare estimates that *total* Japanese deaths from the conventional U.S. bombing of some sixty-four Japanese cities apart from the two nuclear targets was in the neighborhood of three hundred thousand persons – that is, equal to or less than the fatalities associated with Hiroshima and Nagasaki.

17 On the ABCC see John Beatty, "Genetics in the Atomic Age: The Atomic Bomb Casualty Commission, 1947–1956," in *The Expansion of American Biology*, ed. Keith R. Benson, Jane Maienschein, and Ronald Rainger (New Brunswick, 1991), 284–324; and M. Susan Lindee, *Suffering Made Real: American Science and the Survivors at Hiroshima* (forthcoming, Chicago).

18 Passage of a comprehensive "*hibakusha* relief law" remained a subject of parliamentary debate in the final months of 1994 and was widely covered in the Japanese press. For concise critical commentary on the national government's relative neglect of the *hibakusha* see Masae Shiina, *Hibakusha Engoho* [*Hibakusha* relief law] (Tokyo, 1992).

the fact that public struggle with this traumatic experience was *not permitted*. It is at the local level that U.S. censorship was most inhumane. With but rare exceptions, survivors of the bombs could not grieve publicly, could not share their experiences through the written word, could not be offered public counsel and support. Psychological traumas we now associate with the bomb experience – psychic numbing and the guilt of survivors, for example, along with simply coping with massive bereavement and mutilation and grotesque protracted deaths – could not be addressed in open media forums. Nor could Japanese medical researchers working with survivors publish their findings so that other doctors and scientists might make use of them in treating the *hibakusha*. U.S. occupation authorities began easing restrictions on the publication of personal accounts by survivors only after more than three years had passed since the bombings. And it was not until February 1952 – two months before the occupation ended, and six and one half years after the residents of Hiroshima and Nagasaki were bombed and irradiated – that Japanese academic associations were able to engage freely, openly, and independently in investigating atomic bomb injuries.[19]

American isolation of the *hibakusha* was compounded by ostracism within Japanese society itself, for the bomb, of course, stigma-

19 The general U.S. policy of media censorship in occupied Japan began to be eased in late 1948 and was formally terminated in mid-1949. It was not until the February 1952 meeting of the Hiroshima Association of Medical Sciences, however, that academic societies were allowed to engage freely in investigation and discussion of the medical effects of the bombs. See *Hiroshima and Nagasaki*, 513. In 1994, some Americans, including several Nisei who had been involved in censorship at the local level, argued that they were sensitive to these matters and would have been lenient if the Japanese had submitted noninflammatory writings on their bomb experiences. Such writings, the ex-censors said, simply were not submitted. See *Asahi Shimbun*, 16 May 1994. Such claims are unpersuasive, however, given the clear top-level opposition to such writings, plus concrete examples of local suppression of such materials, plus the deplorable ban on scientific writings until the very end of the occupation (which apparently involved bureaucratic complications in Washington, and not just Tokyo). In the three years from 1946 through 1948, a total of seven published books and articles, plus twenty-seven written testimonies, were recorded in Hiroshima, most of them appearing in 1946: *Hiroshima and Nagasaki*, 586. U.S. restrictions on scientific findings concerning the effects of the bombs were so severe that, even in the closing years of occupation, American medical investigators working with Japanese *hibakusha* for the ABCC were uninformed of the existence of earlier studies pertinent to their own research. See James N. Yamazaki, M.D., and Louis B. Fleming, *Children of the Atomic Bombs: Nagasaki, Hiroshima, and the Marshall Islands* (forthcoming, Durham).

tized its victims. Some were disfigured. Some were consigned to slow death. Some, in utero on those fateful midsummer days, were mentally retarded. Many could not cope well with the so-called real world to which most other Japanese (including survivors of combat as well as conventional incendiary bombing) returned after the war. And all initially were presumed to carry the curse of the bombs in their blood. *Hibakusha* were not welcome compatriots in the new Japan. Psychologically if not physically, they were de-formed reminders of a miserable past. Given the unknown genetic consequences of irradiation, they were shunned as marriage pros-pects. The great majority of Japanese, overwhelmed by their own struggles for daily survival, were happy to put them out of mind. So was the Japanese government, which did not even establish its own research council to conduct surveys of bomb survivors until November 1953.[20]

In this milieu, where time was so peculiarly warped, the Japa-nese as a whole did not begin to really *visualize* the human conse-quences of the bombs in concrete, vivid ways until three or four years after Hiroshima and Nagasaki had been destroyed. The first graphic depictions of victims seen in Japan were not photographs but drawings and paintings by the wife-and-husband artists Toshi Maruki and Iri Maruki, who had rushed to Hiroshima, where they had relatives, as soon as news of the bomb arrived. The Marukis published a booklet of black-and-white Hiroshima drawings in 1950 under the title *Pika-don* ("Flash-bang," a euphemism pecu-liar to the blinding flash and ensuing blast of the atomic bombs). In 1950 and 1951, they were permitted to exhibit five large murals of *hibakusha* entitled "Ghosts," "Fire," "Water," "Rainbow," and "Boys and Girls." This was the beginning, as it turned out, of a lifelong series of collaborative paintings addressing the human di-mensions of World War II in Asia.[21]

20 *Hiroshima and Nagasaki*, 512–13.
21 Iri Maruki and Toshiko Akamatsu [Toshi Maruki], *Pika-don* (Tokyo, 1950). The Marukis's remarkable series of collaborative paintings, which eventually extended beyond the atomic bombs to deal with such subjects as the rape of Nanking and Auschwitz, are reproduced in Dower and Junkerman, *The Hiroshima Murals*. A docu-mentary film of the artists' work by Junkerman and Dower, entitled *Hellfire: A Jour-ney from Hiroshima*, is available from First Run Features, New York.

As the Marukis later recalled, they began attempting to paint Hiroshima in 1948 not merely because they remained haunted by what they had witnessed but also because they believed that if they did not put brush to paper there might never be a visual eyewitness account of these events for Japanese to see. Actual photographs of the effects of the bombs in Hiroshima and Nagasaki were not published in Japan until after the occupation ended in the spring of 1952 – and in theory never should have been available from Japanese sources to publish at all, since occupation policy forbade even possessing such negatives or prints.

In the print media, the easing of censorship in late 1948 finally paved the way for publication of reminiscences, poems, essays, and fictional re-creations by *hibakusha*. A minor publishing boom developed in this area, led by a remarkable outpouring of writings by Takashi Nagai, a widowed young father dying of radiation sickness in Nagasaki. Nagai, ironically enough, had been a medical researcher specializing in radiology and was a devout Catholic. His wife had been killed outright in the Nagasaki blast. He lived in a tiny hut in the ruins of Nagasaki with his young son and daughter – reflecting on the meaning of his city's fate, writing furiously before death caught him (which it did on 30 April 1951, killing him with heart failure caused by leukemia). Nagai was extraordinarily charismatic in his prolonged death agony and captured popular imagination to a degree unsurpassed by any other Japanese writer about the bombs until the mid-1960s, when the distinguished elderly novelist Masuji Ibuse, a native son of Hiroshima prefecture, published *Kuroi Ame* (Black Rain).

Nagai's interpretation of the nuclear holocaust was apocalyptically Christian. The bombs were part of God's providence, a divine act of suffering and death out of which world redemption would arise. And in his view, it was not mere happenstance that the second and last nuclear weapon fell on Nagasaki, a city with a long Christian tradition – exploded, indeed, above the great cathedral at Urakami. "Was not Nagasaki the chosen victim," Nagai wrote in a typically passionate passage, "the lamb without blemish, slain as a whole-burnt offering on an altar of sacrifice, atoning for the sins of all the nations during World War II?"

There is no evidence that the Japanese who flocked to buy Nagai's writings, or wrote him in great numbers, or made pilgrimages to his bedside, were fundamentally moved by his Christianity. More obviously, they were moved by his courage, his struggle to make sense of his fate, and the pathos of the two youngsters he soon would leave orphaned. And regardless of what one made of messianic Christian theology, Nagai's sermon that Japan had been divinely chosen to endure unique and world-redemptive suffering clearly struck a resonant chord in the Japanese psyche. Even Emperor Hirohito, who had been formally recostumed as "the symbol of the State and the unity of the people" under the new constitution, undertook a pilgrimage to Nagai's bedside in 1949.[22]

In his own telling, Nagai conceived the idea for his most famous book, *Nagasaki no Kane* (The Bells of Nagasaki), on Christmas Eve of 1945 and completed the manuscript around 9 August 1946 – the first anniversary of the Nagasaki bomb that had killed his beloved wife, also a devout Christian, and scores of medical coworkers. The book was not approved for publication until the beginning of 1949, however, and its handling at the time captured the lingering nervousness of U.S. occupation authorities on these matters. Between the same covers, the publisher was required to pair Nagai's abstract and emotional reflections with an extended graphic account of Japanese atrocities in the Philippines. This coupling was fairly ironic, for it unwittingly subverted the official U.S. position that the use of the bombs had been necessary and just. Japanese readers, that is, could just as easily see the juxtaposition of the Hiroshima/Nagasaki bombings and the rape of Manila as suggesting an equivalence between American and Japanese atrocities. Despite this crude and revealing intervention, in any case, *Nagasaki no Kane* not only became a best-

22 The Marist priest Paul Glynn published a book-length homage to Nagai entitled *A Song for Nagasaki* (Hunters Hill, Australia, 1988). In Nagai's eschatology, after singling out Nagasaki, God then inspired the emperor to issue the sacred proclamation ending the war. These views emerge vividly in Glynn, esp. 115–21, but the ideological logic of the connection between the patriotic Christian visionary and erstwhile Shintoist god-emperor, who had portrayed himself as intervening to prevent the apocalypse in the surrender proclamation of 15 August 1945, is generally overlooked. Nagai's radiation sickness, incidentally, apparently was contracted from his research prior to the bombing of Hiroshima, although his suffering from the bomb is beyond dispute.

seller but also soon was turned into a popular movie with an equally well-known theme song.[23]

Nagai's breakthrough essentially opened the door to the publication of books, articles, poems, and personal recollections by *hibakusha* beginning in 1949.[24] By the time the occupation ended, a distinctive genre of atomic bomb literature had begun to impress itself on popular consciousness — often, as in Nagai's case, associated with a vivid sense of martyrdom. In 1951, two years after completing "Summer Flowers," one of the classic stories about Hiroshima, for example, Tamiki Hara committed suicide by laying down on a railway crossing near his Tokyo home. Sankichi Toge, by far the most esteemed poet of the atomic bomb experience, wrote most of his verses in an extraordinary burst of creativity while hospitalized in 1951 for a chronic bronchial condition complicated by exposure to radiation in Hiroshima. Toge died on the operating table in March 1953, with friends from the Japan Communist Party clustered nearby while a compatriot read the "Prelude" to his *Genbaku Shishu* (Poems of the Atomic Bomb). Later engraved on a memorial in the peace park in Hiroshima, "Prelude" became the single best-known Japanese cry of protest against the bombs:

Bring back the fathers! Bring back the mothers!
Bring back the old people!
Bring back the children!

23 For an English translation of this book see Takashi Nagai, *The Bells of Nagasaki*, trans. William Johnston (Tokyo, 1984). Prior to *Nagasaki no Kane*, Nagai had been permitted to publish a moving, sentimental account entitled *Kono Ko o Nokoshite* [Leaving these children behind], reflecting on the future of his soon-to-be-orphaned children. This became an immediate "top ten" best-seller in 1948 and remained on the top-ten list in 1949, where it was joined by *Nagasaki no Kane*; see Minobu Shiozawa, *Showa Besutosera Seso Shi* [Social history of Showa best-sellers] (Tokyo, 1988), 108–10.

24 According to records compiled in Hiroshima, atomic bomb writings pertaining to that city alone totaled 54 books, essays, and stories plus 284 testimonials from 1949 through 1952. By 1971, the total was 500 published books and short pieces and 2,234 written testimonials; *Hiroshima and Nagasaki*, 586. In 1983, major literary writings on the atomic bomb experience were collected in a fifteen-volume series entitled *Nihon no Genbaku Bungaku* [Japanese atomic bomb literature] (Tokyo, 1983). See also the thirty-article series on atomic bomb literature during the occupation published in *Chugoku Shirnbun*, the leading Hiroshima-area newspaper, between 30 June and 12 August 1986. For English translations of some of this extensive literature see Oe Kenzaburo, ed., *The Crazy Iris and Other Stories of the Atomic Aftermath* (New York, 1958); Kyoko and Mark Selden, eds., *The Atomic Bomb: Voices from Hiroshima and Nagasaki* (Armonk, NY, 1989); and Richard H. Minear, ed. and trans., *Hiroshima: Three Witnesses* (Princeton, 1990).

Bring me back!
Bring back the human beings I had contact with!

For as long as there are human beings, a world of human beings,
bring us peace,
unbroken peace.[25]

Among the many things that the paintings of the Marukis and the writings and reminiscences by *hibakusha* provided was a vocabulary and iconography of nuclear annihilation that soon became familiar to most Japanese. Textually and visually, the closest existing approximation to the experience of 6 and 9 August 1945 was to be found in medieval writings and pictorial scrolls depicting the horrors of the Buddhist hell. Phrases such as "it was like hell" or "hell could not be more terrible than this," were the most commonly heard refrain in recollections by survivors. The first detailed Japanese survey of the effects of the atomic bombs – made public on 23 August 1945, a week before the American victors arrived – described Hiroshima and Nagasaki as a "living hell."[26] In the Marukis' paintings, the fire that consumed men, women, and children in Hiroshima was painted in the same manner that medieval artists had used in rendering the flames of the underworld – and indeed, the only real Japanese precedents for the naked, mutilated figures in the Marukis' depictions of atomic bomb victims were the tormented sinners in these old Buddhist hell scrolls. Years later, in selecting a title for a collection of drawings by *hibakusha*, Japan's public television network turned naturally to the phrase "unforgettable fire."[27]

The "procession of ghosts" that was the subject of the Marukis' first, stark, India-ink mural – depicting naked, stunned, maimed *hibakusha* with hands outstretched, skin peeling from them – captured another enduring image of the bomb experience. In this

25 Minear, ed. and trans., *Hiroshima*, 305. Hara's "Summer Flowers" and Toge's "Poems of the Atomic Bomb," are both translated in full by Minear, along with another early classic of atomic bomb literature, Ota Yoko's 1950 narrative "City of Corpses." In his commentary, Minear calls attention to the implicit anti-Americanism in many of Toge's poems; 295–7.
26 *Asahi Shimbun*, 23 August 1945.
27 For the English version of this stunning collection see Japan Broadcasting Corporation (NHK), comp., *Unforgettable Fire: Pictures Drawn by Atomic Bomb Survivors* (New York, 1977).

instance, the nuclear reality resonated with traditional depictions of ghosts and ghouls, who also moved with eerie slowness, hands stretched before them (many bomb survivors had their hands severely burned when they covered their eyes against the blinding flash of the bombs and almost invariably walked holding their hands palms down in front of them because this eased the pain).

Benign images grotesquely transformed also emerged as unforgettable metaphors of the nuclear disaster. Water, for example, became a central fixation in several forms – the parching thirst that victims felt (the most often heard last words spoken by victims were "*mizu kudasai*," or "water please"); the enduring guilt that survivors experienced because usually they did not heed these pleas (the Japanese had been told, as a matter of general principle, not to give water to injured people); the seven great rivers of Hiroshima, running out to the beautiful Inland Sea when the bomb fell, all clogged with corpses (people threw themselves into the rivers to escape the fires, and drowned or died there of their injuries).

Black rain fell after the bombs had transformed the clear-day atmosphere. The ominous rainfall stained skin and clothing and became in time an indelible metaphor of the unprecedented aftereffects of the new weapons. Although subsequent research by the ABCC found no lethal connection between the black rain and radioactive fallout in Hiroshima and Nagasaki, in popular consciousness the rain became associated with the terrible radiation sickness that soon killed thousands of individuals who appeared to have survived the bombings. After a few hours or days, they experienced nausea, vomiting, diarrhea, abnormal thirst, and sometimes convulsions and delirium. Beginning in the second week after the bombs were dropped, apparent survivors found blood in their spit, urine, and stools; bruise-like discolorations (*purpura*) appeared on their bodies; their hair fell out in clumps. At the time no one knew what such grotesqueries portended. The Japanese government report made public on 23 August captured the local horror by describing what we now know to be radiation sickness as an "evil spirit."[28]

28 The nonlethal consequences of the "black rain" are noted in Yamazaki and Fleming, *Children of the Atomic Bomb*, and attributed to the relatively high altitude at which the Hiroshima and Nagasaki bombs were detonated. This is in contrast to the conspicuously lethal fallout from the 1954 U.S. hydrogen-bomb test in the Marshall Islands.

Other traditionally benign symbols also were transmogrified. Mother and infant, universal icon of love and life, were transposed into a symbol of the broken life bond – mothers attempting to nurse dead babies, infants attempting to suck at the breasts of dead mothers. (Classic medieval texts such as the early thirteenth-century *Hojoki* had offered such fractured images as evidence of *mappo*, the Buddhist apocalypse or "latter days of the Buddhist law.") Bizarre iconographies became commonplace in August 1945: monstrously mutilated people, of course, unrecognized by neighbors and loved ones – but also a man holding his eyeball in his hand; hopping birds with their wings burned off; live horses on fire; permanent white shadows on scorched walls (grass, ladders, people), where what had made the shadow no longer existed; people standing like black statues, burned to a crisp but still seemingly engaged in a last energetic act; legs standing upright, without bodies; survivors as well as corpses with their hair literally standing on end; maggots swarming in the wounds of the living.

All this, and much more, became familiar to most Japanese when those who witnessed Hiroshima and Nagasaki began to express what they had experienced.

III

The delayed timing of these first intense Japanese encounters with the human tragedy of Hiroshima and Nagasaki had unanticipated consequences. For example, censorship began to be lifted at approximately the same time that the Tokyo war-crimes trials ended (in December 1948). The culminating moment of the protracted Allied juridical campaign to impress Japanese with the enormity of their wartime transgressions thus coincided with the moment that many Japanese had their first encounters with detailed personal descriptions of the nuclear devastation that the Americans had visited upon them. While former Japanese leaders were being convicted of war crimes, sentenced to death, and hanged, the Japanese public simultaneously was beginning to learn the details of Hiroshima and Nagasaki for the first time. For many Japanese, there seemed an immoral equivalence here.

Of even greater political consequence, the Japanese really confronted the horrors of nuclear war three years or more after Americans and other unoccupied peoples did – at a time when China was being won by the Communists, the Soviet Union was detonating its first bomb, hysteria in the United States had given rise to rhetoric about preventive war and preemptive strikes, runways all over occupied Japan and Okinawa were being lengthened to accommodate America's biggest bombers, and, in a short time, war came to Korea. In effect, the Japanese confronted the bombs and the most intense and threatening moments of the Cold War simultaneously. They did so, moreover, at a level of intimate concern with the human consequences of nuclear weapons that ran deeper than the generally superficial American impressions of a large mushroom cloud, ruined cityscapes, and vague numbers of abstract "casualties."

The impact of John Hersey's classic text *Hiroshima* in the United States and Japan can be taken as a small example of the ramifications of this aberrant collapse of time. Hersey's terse portraits of six victims of the Hiroshima bomb stunned American readers when first published in 1946. His account originally was written for the urbane *New Yorker* magazine, however, and reached a rather narrow upper-level stratum of the American public. By 1949, moreover, when anti-Communist hysteria had taken possession of the American media, the initial impact of the book had eroded. By this time, Hersey's masterwork had no conspicuous hold on the American mind. A Japanese translation of *Hiroshima*, on the other hand, was not permitted until occupation censorship was terminated in 1949. The translation became a best-seller in 1950 – four years after Hersey's account first appeared in the United States – and reinforced popular Japanese sentiment against active commitment to U.S. military policy in the Cold War.

It was in this context that the Japanese "peace movement" (*heiwa undo*) took shape between 1949 and the mid-1950s. Vivid recollections and re-creations of the old war coincided with confrontation with new Cold War realities – including, beginning in July 1950, Japanese rearmament and, beginning in April 1952, the indefinite maintenance of U.S. military bases in sovereign Japan. In attempting to mobilize public support behind a more neutral position for their country, liberal and leftist intellectuals starting with the prestigious

"Peace Problems Symposium" (*Heiwa Mondai Danwakai*) adopted a policy of promoting pacifism by appealing to the personal experience of Japanese in the war just passed – essentially appealing, that is, to the Japanese sense of victimization.

An internationalist peace consciousness, this liberal and left-wing argument went, was like the outermost ring in a series of concentric circles. To promote such a consciousness, one had to begin at the center, with the intimate experience of suffering in the recent war, and strive to extend the aversion to war to the outer rings of a national and ultimately international outlook. The atomic bomb literature contributed to this. So did a complementary vogue of publications evoking the experiences of other Japanese who had suffered in the war. Conspicuous here were collections of the wartime letters of student conscripts killed in battle.[29] Even on the Left, in short, victim consciousness was seen as the essential core of a pacifist and ultimately internationalist consciousness.

By the early 1950s, fear of a nuclear World War III had become almost palpable in Japan. President Truman's threat to use nuclear weapons in the Korean conflict in November 1950 inflamed these fears; and even after a truce had been arranged on the battle-grounds next door, a great number of Japanese remained alarmed by the continued testing of nuclear weapons by the American and Soviet superpowers, extending now to hydrogen bombs. When fallout from a U.S. thermonuclear test on the Bikini atoll irradiated the crew of a Japanese fishing boat misnamed *Lucky Dragon 5* on 1 March 1954, the public was primed to respond with intense emotion to this concrete presentiment of a second cycle of nuclear

---

29 For a broad annotated discussion of Cold War struggles within Japan in general see John W. Dower, "Peace and Democracy in Two Systems: External Policy and Internal Conflict," in *Postwar Japan as History*, ed. Andrew Gordon (Berkeley, 1993), 3–33. By far the most influential collection of student-conscript letters was Nihon Senbotsu Gakusei Shuki Henshu Iinkai, ed., *Kike – Wadatsumi no Koe: Nihon Senbotsu Cakusei no Shuki* [Listen – the voice of the ocean: Testimonies of conscripted Japanese students] (Tokyo, 1949). Like Takashi Nagai's *Bells of Nagasaki*, this also was quickly refashioned as a popular movie. This collection of student letters tapped not only an earlier postwar collection of wartime letters by Tokyo Imperial University conscripts but also a wartime series of such letters published in the Tokyo Imperial University student newspaper – a striking example indeed of war words becoming peace words. After Japan's defeat, such wartime writings often were reinterpreted as evidence of peaceful, idealistic, and even antiwar sentiments – as well, of course, as intimate examples of the tragic loss of talented and attractive young men in a foolhardy and misguided war.

victimization (one fisherman eventually died from exposure to these "ashes of death").

A campaign to ban all nuclear weapons, initiated by Japanese housewives in May 1954, for example, soon collected an astonishing thirty million signatures.[30] This same turbulent period also saw the birth, in November 1954, of Godzilla, Japan's enduring contribution to the cinematic world of mutant science-fiction monsters spawned by a nuclear explosion. In serious cinema, the director Akira Kurosawa followed his triumphant *Seven Samurai*, a 1954 production, with an almost incoherent 1955 film entitled *Record of a Living Being*, in which the fear of atomic extinction drives an elderly man insane.

This was the milieu in which, in 1955, a memorial peace museum and peace park were opened in Hiroshima and the first national coalition against atomic and hydrogen bombs was established. The latter development gave temporary coherence to the antinuclear movement – and simultaneously delivered the movement into the hands of fractious political professionals and ideologues.[31] As a consequence, in the decades that followed, popular remembrance of Hiroshima and Nagasaki can be characterized as having gone through cycles of renewal – or, put differently, through cycles of rehumanization, in which individuals or grass-roots movements reacted against the ritualization and gross politicization of remembrance. While the professional peace advocates warred over whether socialist nuclear weapons were as objectionable as capitalist ones, and while the organizers of formal antinuclear observances negotiated on seating on the speakers' platforms, certain writers, artists, and projects succeeded in casting new perspectives on the human costs of the bombs.

Beginning in 1963, for example, the gifted writer Kenzaburo Oe

30 The appeal is reproduced in Nihon Jyanarisumu Kenkyukai, ed., *Showa "atsugen" no Koroku* [A record of Showa pronouncements] (Tokyo, 1989), 138–9.
31 Gensuikyo, short for Gensuibaku Kinshi Nihon Kyogikai [Japan Council Against Atomic and Hydrogen Bombs] was founded in September 1955. Its domination by the Japan Communist Party led to the splintering off of rival organizations in the 1960s. In 1961, the centrist Democratic Socialist Party and conservative Liberal Democratic Party formed the National Council for Peace and Against Nuclear Weapons (Kapukin Kaigi, short for Kakuheiki Kinshi Ha Kansetsu Kokumin Kaigi), and in 1965 the Japan Socialist Party formed the Japan Congress Against Atomic and Hydrogen Bombs (Gensuikin, short for Gensuibaku Kinshi Nihon Kokumin Kaigi). Factionalism on the Left has continually plagued the antinuclear movement.

began to use reports about the annual peace observations in Hiroshima as a vehicle for criticizing "the strong odor of politics" that
hovered over the peace park, and rediscovering "the true Hiroshima" in the ordinary citizens who still lived with and died from
the legacies of the bomb.[32] Masuji Ibuse's *Black Rain*, a masterful
fictional reconstruction of death from radiation sickness based on
the diary of a Hiroshima survivor plus interviews with some fifty
hibakusha, was serialized in 1965–6 and enjoyed perennial strong
sales in book form thereafter. Ibuse himself had been born in
Hiroshima prefecture in 1898, and his evocation of the rhythms
and rituals of ordinary life restored the human dimension to the
horror of nuclear destruction with immense dignity.[33]

In the early 1970s, Keiji Nakazawa, a cartoonist for children's
publications who had been a seven-year-old in Hiroshima when
the bomb was dropped, achieved improbable success with a
graphic serial built on his family's own experiences as victims and
survivors. Nakazawa's *Hadashi no Gen* (Barefoot Gen) was serialized in a boy's magazine with a circulation of over two million and
ran to some one thousand pages before the series was terminated –
surviving thereafter as both an animated film and a multivolume
collection.[34] In a very different form of popular graphics, Japanese
public television solicited visual representations by *hibakusha* in
the mid-1970s and received several thousand drawings and paintings of scenes that had remained burned in the memories of the
survivors. These intensely personal images became the basis of
television broadcasts, traveling exhibitions, and publications.[35]

As time passed, popular perceptions of Hiroshima and Nagasaki
were transformed in ways both predictable and unpredictable.
Through painstaking demographic reconstructions – an immense

32 For an English translation of Oe's early essays, which originally appeared in the
    monthly *Sekai*, see his *Hiroshima Notes*, trans. Yonezawa Toshi and ed. David L.
    Swain (Tokyo, 1981).
33 For an English translation see Masuji Ibuse, *Black Rain*, trans. John Bester (New York,
    1969). This is without question the classic Japanese literary reconstruction of the
    atomic bomb experience. The Japanese film version of *Black Rain*, directed by Shoehi
    Imamura, did not appear until 1988.
34 Three volumes from the *Barefoot Gen* series (originally published in Japanese by
    Shobunsha, Tokyo) are available in English translation from New Society Publishers,
    Philadelphia.
35 See footnote 27 above for an English rendering of NHK's edited collection of
    hibakusha drawings.

task, since entire families and neighborhoods and all their records had been obliterated – higher estimates of nuclear fatalities became generally accepted. And with the passing of years, the "late effect" medical consequences of the bombs became apparent in higher incidences among survivors of leukemia, thyroid cancer, breast cancer, lung cancer, stomach cancer, malignant lymphoma, salivary gland tumors, hematological disorders, and cataracts.

Belated sensitivity to the enduring social and psychological legacies of the bombs introduced new euphemisms into the lexicon of nuclear victimization. One spoke not merely of "A-bomb orphans," such as the children Takashi Nagai left behind, but also of the "elderly orphaned," in reference to old people bereft of the children who ordinarily would have supported them in old age. The painful disfiguring scars known as keloids were said to have a spiritual counterpart in "keloids of the heart," just as the radiation-caused leukemia had its psychological counterpart in "leukemia of the spirit" among survivors. In the cruel vernacular of everyday discourse, youngsters who were born mentally retarded due to exposure to radiation while in the womb were known as "*pika* babies," in reference to the blinding flash of the bombs.[36]

IV

Such new information and perceptions gave greater concreteness to the victim consciousness that always had accompanied popular recollections of Hiroshima and Nagasaki. At the same time, however, fixation on Japan's nuclear victimization proved unexpectedly subversive – for the closer the Japanese looked at Hiroshima and Nagasaki, the clearer it became that more nationalities than just the Japanese had been killed there. Hiroshima prefecture was one of the major areas from which Japanese immigrated to the United States. After Pearl Harbor, many second-generation Japanese Americans who had temporarily gone to Japan were stranded there – and it is estimated that around thirty-two hundred may have been in Hiroshima when the bomb was dropped. If that is

36 These later developments in demographic, medical, and linguistic understandings are scattered throughout the chaotic but invaluable *Hiroshima and Nagasaki* (footnote 2 above).

true, then extrapolating from overall casualty rates it is probable that at least one thousand American citizens were killed by the Hiroshima bomb.[37]

While these American deaths in Hiroshima are of slight interest in Japan (and, involving ethnic Japanese, of negligible interest to most Americans), by the early 1970s the Japanese found themselves confronting a more troublesome question of victimization. For it had become apparent by then that thousands of Koreans also were killed in Hiroshima and Nagasaki. As a Japanese colony, Korea was a source of extensively conscripted and heavily abused labor in wartime Japan, and it was belatedly estimated that between five and eight thousand Koreans may have been killed in Hiroshima, and fifteen hundred to two thousand in Nagasaki.[38] Such laborers were, in effect, double victims – exploited by the Japanese and incinerated by the Americans. By the same token, the Japanese were revealed as being simultaneously victims and victimizers. Indeed, as the story unraveled, it was learned that even in the immediate aftermath of the nuclear holocaust, Korean survivors were discriminated against when it came to medical treatment and even cremation and burial.

A small number of Japanese read a large lesson in this, concerning the complexities of both victimization and responsibility. In 1972, for example – over two decades after they first started portraying the Japanese victims of the bombs in their collaborative paintings – the Marukis exhibited a stark mural entitled "Ravens," depicting the black scavengers descending on a mound of Korean dead, plucking out eyes. In the Hiroshima peace park itself, however, the guardians of memory thus far have succeeded in keeping a memorial to the Korean victims from violating the central, sacred ground. Even in the peace park, the Japanese unwittingly reveal themselves to be both victims and victimizers.

These tensions – racial and ethnic bias and dual identity as vic-

37 Rinjiro Sodei, *Watakushitachi wa Teki Datta no ka: Zaibei Hibakusha no Mokushiroku* [Were we the enemy? – A record of *hibakusha* in the United States] (Tokyo, 1978).
38 *Hiroshima and Nagasaki*, 471, 474. Korean groups place the figures of Korean casualties much higher. See ibid., 468. See also Kurt W. Tong, "Korea's Forgotten Atomic Bomb Victims," *Bulletin of Concerned Asian Scholars* 23 (January–March 1991): 31–7. Apart from the previously mentioned American POWs killed in Hiroshima, the atomic bombs also killed small numbers of Chinese, Southeast Asian, and European individuals.

tim and victimizer – never will be entirely resolved in Japan. Since the 1970s, however, they have become more transparent and openly debated, Acknowledgment of the Korean victims of the atomic bombs in the early 1970s, for example, coincided with restoration of Japanese relations with the People's Republic of China – and, with this, renewed attention by liberal and left-wing writers to Japanese atrocities in China, beginning with the rape of Nanking. Until then, and despite the zealous didacticism associated with the war-crimes trials conducted by the Allied victors during the occupation period, it seems fair to say that most Japanese regarded Hiroshima and Nagasaki as the preeminent moments of atrocity in World War II in Asia, towering above all other acts of war just as the mushroom cloud had towered over Hiroshima on 6 August 1945.

Belatedly encountering China changed this. Here, again, memory was reconstructed after an abnormal interlude of silence, during which defeat followed by Cold War politics isolated Japan from China and essentially smothered recollections of Japan's aggression and atrocious war behavior there.[39] The struggle to reshape memory of the war has become more intense since then – increasingly so as other Japanese atrocities have been exposed, such as the murderous medical experiments carried out by Unit 731 in Manchuria and the forced recruitment of Asian women to serve as prostitutes (*ianfu*, or "comfort women") for the emperor's loyal troops. To the extent that popular consciousness of victimization and atrocity has changed in contemporary Japan, this has entailed greater general acknowledgment of Japan's own war crimes vis-à-vis fellow Asians.[40]

39 This reencounter with China, and with Japanese war atrocities there, began with nongovernmental contacts in the mid-1960s, before the formal restoration of relations in 1972. The key Japanese writer in bringing the rape of Nanjing to public attention was the well-known progressive journalist Katsuichi Honda, whose influential writings from China were published in newspapers and magazines in 1971 and subsequently collected in a volume entitled *Chugoku no Tabi* [Travels in China] (Tokyo, 1972). The ensuing contentious debates on this topic in Japan are concisely summarized in Yang Daqing, "A Sino-Japanese Controversy: The Nanjing Atrocity as History," *Sino-Japanese Studies* 3 (November 1990): 14–35.

40 In 1994, in anticipation of the fiftieth anniversary of the dropping of the atomic bombs, officials associated with the memorial museum in Hiroshima announced that they would expand their exhibitions beyond depictions of Japanese victimization to include reference to Hiroshima's military role since the Meiji period, Japanese aggres-

Even this remains contested, of course, as the May 1994 resignation of the newly appointed minister of justice, Shigeto Nagano,
attests. Nagano was forced to step down after calling the Nanjing
massacre a "fabrication," characterizing the *ianfu* as "public prostitutes," and referring to the war in Asia by the patriotic old name
"Great East Asia War" (*Dai Toa Senso*).[41] In all this, he was repudiated by his government, which formally acknowledged that the
war against Asia had been a war of aggression. That same month,
however, in the face of considerable domestic pressure, the same
conservative coalition government also canceled plans for the emperor, Hirohito's son, to visit Pearl Harbor while on a state visit to
Hawaii. This, it was argued, was too great a concession – for, after
all, no American head of state ever had visited Hiroshima or
Nagasaki, or even expressed regrets for those terrible deaths.[42]

For most Japanese, the war against other Asians was different and
more regrettable in a moral sense than that against the Americans;
and Hiroshima and Nagasaki account for much of this difference.[43]

sion and atrocities in World War II, and the presence of Korean and Chinese forced
laborers in Hiroshima at the time of the bombs.

41 Convenient compilations of Nagano's statements appear in *Asahi Shimbun*, 7 and 19
May 1994. Although the government officially repudiated Nagano's comments, his
remarks accurately reflect a mainline conservative view in Japan.

42 *Asahi Shimbun*, 20 May 1994. There were other arguments against the state visit as
well, including the liberal and left-wing criticism that it would involve repoliticizing
the role of the emperor in significant ways. The nuances of these acts of symbolic
politics are subtle and convoluted.

43 In the realm of popular symbolic "equations," the most extreme expression of Japanese victimization involves pairing the Holocaust in Europe and "nuclear holocaust"
of Hiroshima/Nagasaki. In the more specifically Asian context, the most familiar
equation pairs the rape of Nanjing and the nuclear destruction of the two Japanese
cities. Americans are most likely to conjoin Pearl Harbor and Hiroshima/Nagasaki,
but this is a view that has little credence in Japan. Here again, the issue is a contentious
one. Whereas the U.S.-dominated Tokyo war-crimes trials portrayed Pearl Harbor as a
deep-seated "conspiracy" against peace, the more persuasive view in Japan is that the
attack was an ill-conceived response to a collapsing world order – and best compre-
hended in the capitalistic, imperialistic, and colonial terms of the time. The Japanese
also tend to place greater emphasis than Americans do on the fact that the imperial
government had intended to break off formal relations with the United States at the
eleventh hour, minutes prior to the Pearl Harbor attack, and only failed to do so
because of a clerical breakdown in the Japanese embassy in Washington. In this construction, Pearl Harbor emerges more as a tactical and technical blunder than as a
treacherous and atrocious act.

Illustrations

Figure 1. Wartime *Enola Gay*. Source: Don Breman, Harry S. Truman Library.

Figure 2. "Little Boy" type nuclear weapon that destroyed Hiroshima. Source: Harry S. Truman Library.

Figure 3. "Fat Man" type nuclear weapon that destroyed Nagasaki. Source: Harry S. Truman Library.

Figure 4. Atomic explosion over Nagasaki, 9 August 1945. Source: Harry S. Truman Library.

Figure 5. Atomic bomb damage to Hiroshima. Source: Harry S. Truman Library.

Figure 6. Atomic bomb damage to Nagasaki. Source: Harry S. Truman Library.

Figure 7. Atomic bomb damage to Nagasaki. Source: Harry S. Truman Library.

Figure 8. The head of one of the Saints lying by the front gate of the Urakami Cathedral, Nagasaki, September 1945. Source: Eiichi Matsumoto.

Figure 9. Japanese Premier Shigemitsu signs the formal document of surrender on board the *U.S.S. Missouri* in Tokyo Bay, Japan. Source: Harry S. Truman Library.

Land of the Rising Sons

Figure 10. Facist wartime propaganda helped shape early responses to the atomic bombing of Japan. Source: *Atlanta Constitution*, 8 August 1945.

Figure 11. *36 Hour War*. In this dreamscape of the nuclear future, technicians measure radioactivity in the rubble of Manhattan as the marble lions of the New York Public Library direct their unblinking gaze over the devastated city. Source: *Life*, November 1945.

Figure 12. A sit-in in front of the Hiroshima peace park, demanding immediate total prohibition of nuclear weapons tests, 27 January 1994. Hiroshima citizens have protested against nuclear tests on every occasion a test was announced or detected and since 1984 have joined the "Nevada Day" (28 January) campaign that was initiated in the United States in 1951. Source: *Chugoku Shimbun*.

Figure 13. Wartime "comfort women" for Imperial Japanese servicemen and their supporters demonstrating in Tokyo, demanding that the Japanese government provide them with indemnities, 6 June 1994. Source: *Kyodo* News.

Figure 14. The restored fuselage of the *Enola Gay*. From the *Enola Gay* exhibition at the Smithsonian's National Air and Space Museum. Source: Carolyn Russo/NASM.

6

Exotic Resonances: Hiroshima in American Memory

PAUL BOYER*

The fiftieth anniversary of the atomic bombing of Hiroshima invites reflection on the role of this event in American memory. And "Exotic Resonances," the topic of a 1978 physics conference at Hiroshima University, seems an apt title for such an essay. Since 1945, "Hiroshima" has indeed resonated in U.S. culture and public discourse, and the resonances have often been exotic, as the word's meaning has been debated, contested, and exploited. For me, a 1958 visit to Hiroshima drove home the ambiguous quality of the memory. As my train entered the station, several Japanese passengers around me, smiling and apparently full of civic pride, repeated "Hiroshima: atomic bomb. Hiroshima: atomic bomb" for the benefit of the visiting American. How to respond? I felt acute embarrassment, yet my seatmates seemed clearly pleased to remind me of the event that had made their city famous. This memory now mingles with earlier recollections of my first confused encounter with Hiroshima, in a newspaper on 6 August 1945, four days after my tenth birthday. With the Hiroshima-Nagasaki bombings now half a century in the past, perhaps the moment is opportune to explore our long effort to come to terms with "Hiroshima," the city, the event, and the symbol.[1]

---

*My thanks to Professor Richard Minear for a careful reading of this essay.

1 Michael Perlman *Imaginal Memory and the Place of Hiroshima* (Albany, 1988), explores the topic from a Jungian perspective. Martin J. Sherwin's "Hiroshima and Modern Memory," *Nation*, 10 October 1981, 1, 349–53, discusses two recently published works – Paul Fussell's essay justifying the use of the atomic bomb (see below) and a scientific report on the bomb's physical and medical effects – and assesses President Truman's decision to drop the bomb. For suggestive theoretical and cross-cultural perspectives see Lawrence Langer, *The Holocaust and the Literary Imagination* (New

143

At least since the Romans leveled Carthage in 146 B.C., thereby imposing the first "Carthaginian peace," the names of certain sites have taken on powerful symbolic meaning. "Waterloo" evokes irrevocable defeat; "Gettysburg," the Civil War's turning point. "Verdun" has become shorthand for the futility of trench warfare, while "Guernica" and "Dresden" stir thoughts of the slaughter of innocent civilians from the air. Allusions to "Pearl Harbor" rallied Americans during World War II, while the Chambers of Commerce of Buchenwald and Dachau face an uphill task in extricating their towns from associations that are only too familiar. In more recent times, "Dienbienphu" and "Bay of Pigs" took on their own symbolic resonances.

Certain place-names, in short, serve a shorthand role in cultural discourse, based on a shared understanding of their symbolic meaning. When the event alluded to is sufficiently remote, the name is drained of emotion and serves a purely rhetorical function. We speak of a "Carthaginian peace" or say that someone "met his Waterloo" with little conscious awareness of the specific events or the specific towns in North Africa or Belgium that gave rise to these expressions. "Hiroshima" is another place-name set apart by history, but unlike "Carthage" or "Waterloo," its symbolic meaning continues to evoke passionate emotional responses.

For many Americans, that meaning is clear and unambiguous. Since 1945, Hiroshima, paired with Nagasaki, has been a synecdoche for the destructive capability of nuclear weapons.[2] In medieval cartography, Jerusalem was the navel of the world. In the nuclear geography of our minds, Hiroshima stands at the center. In *We Can Do It!* (1985), a "Kid's Peace Book" with definitions for each letter of the alphabet, the entry for *h* reads:

H is for Hiroshima. *Hiroshima* is a city in Japan, where an atomic bomb was dropped many years ago in 1945. Thousands of people lost their lives and the city was destroyed. That's why we say "NO MORE HIRO-

Haven, 1975); and Kurihara Sadako, "The Literature of Auschwitz and Hiroshima," trans. Richard H. Minear, *Holocaust and Genocide Studies* 7 (Spring 1993): 77–106.
2 On the role of such sites as Hiroshima, Nagasaki, and Bikini in popular discussion of the nuclear threat see Michael J. Carey, "Psychological Fallout," *Bulletin of the Atomic Scientists* 38 (January 1982): 20–4, esp. 23.

SHIMAS!" H is also for *hope, happiness,* and *harmony.* That's what the world needs instead. Another H is for *hug.*[3]

The page is illustrated with a drawing of a boy hugging his grand-mother as she writes a protest letter, while grandpa sits nearby knitting a scarf with the slogan: "No more Hiroshimas!" In this rhetorical usage, to which we shall return, "Hiroshima" was re-moved from history and treated as a semimythic symbol of atomic menace. In the passive voice of the above passage, for example, the bomb *was dropped,* a city *was destroyed,* with no hint of *who* dropped the bomb or destroyed the city, or *why.* Such dehistoricizing characterizes not just juvenile peace litera-ture but much of the rhetorical invocations of "Hiroshima" by antinuclear activists over the years.

But the peace activists' use of "Hiroshima" is only part of a multivocal discourse. At the other end of the spectrum, millions of Americans have over the years shared the view enunciated by Presi-dent Harry S. Truman when he announced that a new weapon had destroyed the "military base" of Hiroshima: that the atomic bomb was a wholly justified means of defeating a treacherous foe. In Truman's geographic calculus, "Hiroshima" avenged "Pearl Har-bor." More importantly, the argument runs, the bomb saved thou-sands of American lives that would have been lost in an invasion of Japan. In the immediate postwar period, most Americans em-braced this view. As Eugene Rabinowitch, editor of the *Bulletin of the Atomic Scientists,* recalled in 1956: "With few exceptions, public opinion rejoiced over Hiroshima and Nagasaki as demon-strations of American technical ingenuity and military ascen-dency." In a *Fortune* magazine poll late in 1945, only 5 percent of the respondents opposed the atomic bombing of Hiroshima and Nagasaki, and a significant minority wished that the United States had dropped *more* A-bombs on the Japanese.[4]

The lack of detailed visual evidence of the bomb's effects re-inforced this initial positive response. U.S. occupation authorities censored reports from the city and suppressed the more horrifying

3 Dorothy Morrison, Roma Dehr, and Ronald M. Bazar, *We Can Do It! A Kid's Peace Book,* illus. Nola Johnston (Vancouver, 1985).
4 Eugene Rabinowitch, "Ten Years That Changed the World," *Bulletin of the Atomic Scientists* 12 (January 1956): 2; "The Fortune Survey," *Fortune,* December 1945, 305.

films and photographs of corpses and maimed survivors. Americans initially saw only images of the awesome mushroom cloud, which, as historian James Farrell has observed, presented the bomb as "a new but natural event, free of human agency." Indeed, Farrell notes, both elements of the quickly adopted compound term "mushroom cloud" suggested an unmediated natural phenomenon.[5]

Henry L. Stimson's 1947 *Harper's Magazine* article "The Decision to Use the Atomic Bomb" was part of a high-level effort to justify the use of the bomb and thus to define the meaning of "Hiroshima and Nagasaki" for Americans. Harvard president James Conant, a key figure in nuclear policymaking, not only prodded Stimson, the former secretary of war, to publish his apologia but edited the first draft (ghostwritten by McGeorge Bundy) to make sure it struck the appropriate justificatory note.[6] Hollywood reinforced this view in the 1946 movie *The Beginning or the End* and again in *Above and Beyond* (1953), a formulaic drama of marital discord and reconciliation supposedly based on the life of *Enola Gay* pilot Paul Tibbets that justified the bomb as an appropriate retribution for Pearl Harbor.[7] Despite much revisionist scholarship on Truman's decision, the mantra "the atomic bomb prevented an invasion and saved American lives" is still repeated, particularly by veterans convinced that it saved *their* lives.

This argument, more often expressed orally than in print, found its boldest — not to say its most reckless — articulation in Paul Fussell's 1981 *New Republic* essay "Hiroshima: A Soldier's View," revised and issued in book form in 1988. Having spent the spring and summer of 1945 as an infantryman in France expecting imminent reassignment to the Pacific, Fussell implied that only persons in

5 James J. Farrell, "Nuclear Friezes: Art and the Bomb from Hiroshima to Three Mile Island," *Twenty/One: Art and Culture*, Fall 1989, 59–75. Quoted passages, 59.
6 James G. Hershberg, *James B. Conant: Harvard to Hiroshima and the Making of the Nuclear Age* (New York, 1993), 294–300. See also Barton J. Bernstein, "Seizing the Contested Terrain of Early Nuclear History: Stimson, Conant, and Their Allies Explain the Decision to Use the Atomic Bomb," *Diplomatic History* 17 (Winter 1993): 35–72.
7 Jack G. Shaheen and Richard Taylor, "The Beginning or the End," in *Nuclear War Films*, ed. Jack G. Shaheen (Carbondale, IL, 1978), 3–10; Michael J. Yavenditti, "Atomic Scientists and Hollywood: *The Beginning or the End*," *Film and History* 8 (1978): 73–88; Mick Broderick, *Nuclear Movies: A Critical Analysis and Filmography of International Feature Length Films Dealing with Experimentation, Aliens, Terrorism, Holocaust, and Other Disaster Scenarios, 1914–1989* (Jefferson, NC, 1988), 10 (on *Above and Beyond*).

his precarious situation had the moral authority to evaluate the A-bomb decision. He pointed out that one critic of that decision, political scientist Michael Walzer, was only ten years old in 1945. Revisionist historian Michael Sherry, he jeered, "was eight months old, in danger only of falling out of his pram." "The farther from the scene of horror," he said, "the easier the talk." "The invasion was definitely on," Fussell asserted, "as I know because I was to be in it." With equal assurance he dismissed the claim that postwar power calculations influenced Truman's decision: "Of course no one was focusing on anything as portentous as that, which reflects a historian's tidy hindsight. The U.S. government was engaged not in that sort of momentous thing but in ending the war conclusively, as well as irrationally Remembering Pearl Harbor with a vengeance."[8]

Certainly the testimony of historical actors is useful, but Fussell moved beyond merely presenting the combat soldiers' perspective to an anti-intellectualism that ignored a large body of scholarship directly relevant to his topic. Fussell notwithstanding, most historians now view Japan as teetering on the brink of collapse by early August 1945 and agree that postwar considerations did indeed influence Truman's decision.[9] James Hershberg has recently shown that James Conant, a member of the Interim Committee that advised Stimson and Truman on atomic matters, believed that dropping the bomb on a city would most effectively demonstrate its horror and thus strengthen the case for international control.[10] By ignoring or ridiculing the relevant scholarship, Fussell vastly over-

---

8   Paul Fussell, "Hiroshima: A Soldier's View," *New Republic*, 22 and 29 August 1981, 26–30, reprinted in idem, *Thank God for the Atom Bomb, and Other Essays* (New York, 1988). Quoted passage from the 1988 version, 19, 23, 27. See also Stephen Harper, *Miracle of Deliverance: The Case for the Bombing of Hiroshima and Nagasaki* (London, 1985). For a critique of Fussell see Sherwin, "Hiroshima and Modern Memory," 350–1.

9   The large bibliography on these topics, familiar to all diplomatic historians, includes Gar Alperovitz, *Atomic Diplomacy: Hiroshima and Potsdam: The Use of the Atomic Bomb and the American Confrontation with Soviet Power* (New York, 1965; expanded and updated ed., New York, 1985); Martin J. Sherwin, *A World Destroyed: The Atomic Bomb and the Grand Alliance* (New York, 1975); Barton J. Bernstein, "Roosevelt, Truman, and the Atomic Bomb, 1941–1945: A Reinterpretation," *Political Science Quarterly* 90 (Spring 1975): 23–69; Robert L. Messer, "New Evidence on Truman's Decision," *Bulletin of the Atomic Scientists* 41 (August 1985): 50–6; and Rufus E. Miles, Jr., "Hiroshima: The Strange Myth of Half a Million American Lives Saved," *International Security* 10 (Fall 1985): 121–40.

10 Hershberg, *Conant*, 229.

simplifies highly complex issues. Nevertheless, his outburst merits notice as an articulation of a widely held and culturally influential view of the bomb decision – and of the meaning of Hiroshima.[11]

But the more familiar cultural role of Hiroshima has been as a symbol of what must never happen again: the definitive object lesson of nuclear horror. If the bomb's full meaning in terms of human suffering did not at first grip the American consciousness, the fact of the destruction of a *city* certainly did. In this sense, Conant's view of the salutary effects of actually dropping the bomb on a crowded metropolis proved prescient: While the obliteration of two cities did not lead to international control, as Conant had hoped it would, it did help to inspire successive antinuclear campaigns. The cautionary theme emerged quickly. Within hours of Truman's announcement, radio commentators and editorial writers somberly noted that the fate of Hiroshima could await any American city. For many atomic scientists, euphoria over the Alamogordo test and the Hiroshima blast quickly changed to dismay as the human toll became apparent in classified reports. Many Manhattan Project veterans plunged into the campaign for international control with speeches and articles in which future Hiroshimas figured as the fearful alternative to the Acheson-Lilienthal Plan.[12] The image of "Hiroshima" as a preview of the atomic future gripped the American consciousness in August 1945, not to be dislodged thereafter.

John Hersey's "Hiroshima," published in the *New Yorker* in August 1946 and then in book form, deepened popular perceptions of the word's meaning: not just the destruction of "a city," but the death and suffering of scores of thousands of individual men, women, and children, each with his or her own story. A seasoned journalist, Hersey translated the mind-numbing statistics

---

11 Unsurprisingly, Paul Tibbets has long contributed to this literature of justification. See his "How to Drop an Atomic Bomb," *Saturday Evening Post*, 8 June 1946; and his autobiography, Paul W. Tibbets, Clair C. Stebbins, and Harry Franken, *The Tibbets Story* (New York, 1978), reissued as *Flight of the Enola Gay* (Reynoldsburg, OH, 1989). At a 1976 air show in Texas, Tibbets piloted a restored B-29 in a reenactment of the Hiroshima bombing.

12 Alice Kimball Smith, *A Peril and a Hope: The Scientists' Movement in America, 1945–47* (Cambridge, MA, 1970); Paul S. Boyer, *By the Bomb's Early Light: American Thought and Culture at the Dawn of the Atomic Age* (New York, 1985), 3–26, 49–106; Gregg Herken, "Mad About the Bomb," *Harper's*, December 1983, 49 (on the scientists' initial reaction to Hiroshima).

into a gripping interwoven narrative of six individuals. Of the first
339 readers to write Hersey, 301 offered glowing praise. Such
articles were essential, observed one, "to counteract the 4th of July
attitude most people hold in regards to the atom bomb." Another
described "a fitful, dream-laden night" after finishing the article.[13]
The San Francisco poet William Dickey would later recall his initial encounter with Hersey's work:

> I sat in the car one summer
> during lunch breaks at the frozen food plant, reading *Hiroshima*
> when it first came out. The picture that is in my mind
> is of people, vaporized by an unexpected sun
> and only their shadows left burned into the wall behind them.
> In their eyes it was the shock of noon forever.[14]

While Hersey's work deepened emotional sensibilities, it had a
broader cultural impact as well. As William F. Buckley, Jr., would
later observe, its appearance in a leading periodical "was both a
spiritual acknowledgment of the transcendent magnitude of the
event, and an invitation to analytical meditation on its implications." With his cool, understated prose, Hersey helped position
Hiroshima at the core of the debate over nuclear weapons – past,
present, and future. In successive campaigns against the nuclear
arms race, "Hiroshima" would offer a stark one-word encapsula-
tion of the alternative. In the lexicon of symbolic geography, it was
often linked to Alamogordo and Bikini as representations of the
three faces of atomic danger: the menace of modern science, of the
bomb itself, and of more terrible instruments of thermonuclear
destruction around the corner.[15]

But the politicocultural role of Hiroshima memories, brought to

13 Joseph Luft and W. M. Wheeler, "Reaction to John Hersey's 'Hiroshima,' " *Journal of
    Social Psychology* 28 (1948): 135–40, quoted letters, 136. See also Michael J.
    Yavenditti, "John Hersey and the American Conscience: The Reception of *Hiro-
    shima*," *Pacific Historical Review* 43 (February 1974): 24–49; Boyer, *By the Bomb's
    Early Light*, 203–10; Allan M. Winkler, *Life Under a Cloud: American Anxiety about
    the Atom* (New York, 1993), 31–2.
14 William Dickey, "Armageddon," in *Writing in a Nuclear Age*, ed. Jim Schley (Hanover,
    NH, 1984), 42.
15 William F. Buckley, Jr., "To the Readers of the *National Review*," *National Review*, 1
    April 1983, 352–3; David Bradley, *No Place to Hide* (Boston, 1948), on Bikini; James
    J. Farrell, "The Crossroads of Bikini," *Journal of American Culture* 10 (Summer
    1987): 55–66. The 1979 Three Mile Island crisis added another locale to the symbolic
    geography that has shaped the nation's nuclear discourse.

a keen edge by John Hersey in 1946, would fluctuate over the years, paralleling the shifting cycles of activism and quiescence in America's decades-long encounter with the nuclear threat. As Michael Mandelbaum observed in 1984: "Americans have normally ignored the nuclear peril. Each episode of public anxiety about the bomb has given way to longer periods in which nuclear weapons issues were the preoccupation of the nuclear specialists alone." With the onset of the Cold War, the Soviet A-bomb test in 1949, and Truman's green light to the hydrogen-bomb project, Hiroshima and Nagasaki, like nuclear awareness in general, faded from public consciousness. Takashi Nagai's *We of Nagasaki* (1951) offered gripping testimony similar to that of Hersey's *Hiroshima*, but in an altered cultural and political climate, the work attracted much less attention.[16]

Activism revived in the mid-1950s, however, now centered on a campaign to halt nuclear testing. As U.S. and Soviet H-bomb tests pumped strontium-90 and other poisons into the atmosphere, protesters warned not only of nuclear war but also of the immediate hazard of radioactive fallout. The test-ban campaigners again invoked Hiroshima, now as an example of the lethal effects of radiation and as a benchmark to demonstrate the escalating nuclear threat. The H-bomb, they repeatedly emphasized, was "a thousand times more powerful" than the Hiroshima bomb.

The resurgence of Hiroshima memories that accompanied the test-ban campaign had many sources. Michihiko Hachiya's classic *Hiroshima Diary* (1955), published on the tenth anniversary of the bombing, brought the event sharply back into focus. So, too, did the "Hiroshima Maidens," twenty-five disfigured survivors of the blast who in 1955 arrived in the United States for reconstructive surgery. The project had originated with Kiyoshi Tanimoto, a Methodist minister featured in Hersey's *Hiroshima*. Promoted by antinuclear activist Norman Cousins, editor of the *Saturday Review*, the project gained national attention on 11 May 1955, when Ralph Edwards's popular television show *This is Your Life* show-

16 *We of Nagasaki: The Story of Survivors in an Atomic Wasteland*, ed. Takashi Nagai and trans. Ichiro Shirato and Herbert B. L. Silverman (New York, 1951); Michael Mandelbaum, "The Anti-Nuclear Weapons Movement," *PS* (American Political Science Association) 17 (Winter 1984): 27; Boyer, *By the Bomb's Early Light*, 334–51.

cased Tanimoto. The program evoked the terror of the bombing and featured a handshake between Tanimoto and Captain Robert Lewis, copilot of the *Enola Gay*, who gave the minister a check for the Hiroshima Maidens. Edwards invited viewers to contribute, and twenty thousand letters poured in. The 138 operations performed on the young women had mixed results, and the death of one from cardiac arrest under anesthesia clouded the project. But despite criticism in Japan about the "publicity stunt" and the U.S. State Department's reservations, the project helped restore Hiroshima to the forefront of memory while furthering the test-ban cause.[17]

As the test-ban campaign intensified, so, too, did the cultural resonance of Hiroshima. "Nuclear War in St. Louis" (1959), a documentary-style narrative written by St. Louis antinuclear activists and based on data from Hiroshima and Nagasaki, was reprinted in Norman Cousins's *Saturday Review*. Edita Morris's novel *Flowers of Hiroshima* (1959), an exploration of the bomb's physical and psychological effects, was the work of an antinuclear activist who with her husband operated a center in Hiroshima for atomic bomb survivors. Betty Jean Lifton's documentary film *A Thousand Cranes*, on child-victims of the bomb, appeared in 1962.[18]

In a different medium, Alain Resnais's 1959 film *Hiroshima, Mon Amour*, widely shown in the United States, portrayed a brief affair between a Hiroshima architect (played by Eiji Okada) and a French actress (Emmanuelle Riva) who has come to the city to make an antiwar film. With a screenplay by Marguerite Duras, *Hiroshima, Mon Amour* juxtaposed grainy images of the devastated city of 1945 with the actress's recollections of a doomed wartime romance with a German soldier. As the images of destruction give way to scenes of bustling postwar Hiroshima, so the

17 Michihiko Hachiya, M.D., *Hiroshima Diary: The Journal of a Japanese Physician, August 6–September 30, 1945*, trans. and ed. Warner Wells (Chapel Hill, 1955); Rodney Barker, *The Hiroshima Maidens: A Story of Courage, Compassion, and Survival* (New York, 1985), esp. 3–12, 95, 135–41.

18 Greater St. Louis Citizens' Committee for Nuclear Information, "Nuclear War in St. Louis: One Year Later" (St. Louis, September 1959, 4 pp), reprinted as "The Bombing of St. Louis: Report and Epilogue," *Saturday Review* 42 (28 November 1959): 15–18, 40; Edita Morris, *The Flowers of Hiroshima* (New York, 1959); Paul Brians, *Nuclear Holocausts: Atomic War in Fiction, 1895–1984* (Kent, OH, 1987), 266.

actress's wartime memories fade. But though the theme is one of forgetfulness, the atomic bomb scenes early in the movie surely conveyed their own message to audiences of 1959.[19]

This cycle of antinuclear activism and heightened cultural attention to Hiroshima faded as the Limited Nuclear Test Ban Treaty of 1963 barred atmospheric tests and thus allayed fallout fears. But in 1967 came a belated product of the activist campaign: Robert Jay Lifton's *Death in Life: Survivors of Hiroshima*. In 1962, as the test-ban campaign had crested, Lifton, an associate professor of psychiatry at Yale, had interviewed in Hiroshima some seventy *hibakusha* (pronounced hi-*bak*-sha and meaning "explosion-affected persons"). Reporting his findings in *Death in Life*, he advanced the concept of "psychic numbing" to explain how survivors dealt with their bomb memories and their guilt over remaining alive when so many had perished. Broadening his focus, Lifton speculated that "psychic numbing" could also illuminate societal patterns of nuclear denial. "The encounter of people in Hiroshima with the atomic bomb has specific bearing upon all nuclear age existence," he wrote; "a better understanding of what lies behind this word [Hiroshima], this name of a city, might enable us to take a small step forward in coming to terms with that existence."[20] British science writer Jacob Bronowski, reviewing *Death in Life*, made the point explicitly. The psychic numbing exhibited by the *hibakusha*, he suggested, could help explain the decline of nuclear awareness in the later 1960s:

Twenty years is too long for sorrow, which time does not so much heal as blunt. . . . In that ebb tide of conscience, . . . the moral impulse of 1945 has been eroded. We might have supposed that the sense of guilt had been washed away without a trace, had not Professor Lifton discovered it still haunting (of all people) the survivors of Hiroshima. The discovery gives his quiet and penetrating book a kind of cosmic irony that, more than any burst of righteousness, ought to shake us all out of our somnambulism.[21]

19   H. Wayne Schuth, "Hiroshima, Mon Amour," in Shaheen, ed., *Nuclear War Films*, 17–24. Roy Armes, *The Cinema of Alain Resnais* (London, 1968) insightfully discusses *Hiroshima, Mon Amour* and its reception. For interesting reflections on the film see Roger Rosenblatt, "A Vision of Ourselves," *Time*, 19 July 1985, 55.
20   Robert J. Lifton, *Death in Life: Survivors of Hiroshima* (New York, 1967), 14.
21   Jacob Bronowski, "The Psychological Wreckage of Hiroshima and Nagasaki," *Scientific American*, June 1968, 131–2, 134–5, quoted passages 131, 135.

Lifton and Bronowski thus contributed to what by 1967 had become a well-established practice of using Hiroshima heuristically. The fate of this city and its inhabitants in 1945, they suggested, could illuminate the larger psychic dynamics of the nuclear age.

The next surge of U.S. nuclear activism arose in the late 1970s, fed by rising concerns about nuclear power and by protests in Europe against the deployment of Pershing and cruise missiles. Spurred by the Reagan administration's belligerent rhetoric and military buildup, this cycle of activism peaked in 1982–3 in a campaign to freeze the testing and deployment of nuclear weapons. Late in 1981, New England town meetings adopted freeze resolutions. Media attention to the nuclear threat increased dramatically, and in June 1982, seven hundred thousand antinuclear demonstrators jammed New York's Central Park. Jonathan Schell's 1982 best-seller *The Fate of the Earth*, which both reflected and intensified the antinuclear mood, graphically described a nuclear attack on New York City, pondered the implications of human extinction, and proposed world government as the only alternative to global destruction. One critic compared Schell's work to Charles Reich's *The Greening of America* (1970) as *"Zeitgeist* books that tell more about their times than about anything else."[22] But the zeitgeist soon changed as President Reagan's "Star Wars" speech of 23 March 1983 subtly undermined the freeze campaign. Professing to share the freeze advocates' desire to end the nuclear threat, Reagan proposed a futuristic laser-based shield against missile attack. As debate shifted to the merits of Reagan's proposal (and as the stalled arms-control talks resumed), the freeze movement faded. By the end of the decade, with the Cold War breaking up and the nuclear arms race ending, one long cycle of Americans' engagement with nuclear weapons was drawing to a close.

While it lasted, however, the freeze campaign once more brought Hiroshima to the cultural forefront. As in the late 1950s and early

22 Theodore Draper, "How Not to Think about Nuclear War," *New York Review of Books*, 15 July 1982, 36. On the upsurge of nuclear awareness and activism in the early 1980s see Boyer, *By the Bomb's Early Light*, 359–67; Winkler, *Life Under a Cloud*, 187–208; Nigel Young, "The Contemporary European Anti-Nuclear Movement: Experiments in the Mobilisation of Public Power" (Oslo, 1983); Fox Butterfield, "Anatomy of the Nuclear Protest," *New York Times Magazine*, 11 July 1982, 14ff; and Howard Kohn, "Nuclear War and TV: Are the Networks Playing Fair?" *TV Guide*, 15 January 1983, 8.

1960s, activists again contrasted the puny Hiroshima bomb with modern nuclear firepower. The poet Sharon Doubiago, for example, noting that the missiles carried by one Trident submarine packed the explosive might of 2,040 Hiroshimasize bombs, wrote in 1982:

Say the word Hiroshima
Reflect on its meaning for one second
Say and understand Hiroshima again.
Say and understand Hiroshima two thousand and forty times.[23]

Testament, a 1983 television movie set in a northern California town as radiation from an attack on San Francisco creeps nearer, included an impaired Japanese-American boy called Hiroshi – a common Japanese name, but one obviously chosen for its historical resonances. The courses on nuclear war introduced on many college and university campuses in the early 1980s typically began with Hiroshima and assigned John Hersey's now-classic work. For several years, Wisconsin antinuclear activists launched paper lanterns on the Mississippi River on 6 August, emulating an annual commemorative ceremony held in Hiroshima on that date. Robert Penn Warren's 1983 poem "New Dawn" imagined the moment just after the Hiroshima blast, as the *Enola Gay* streaks away:

Now, far behind, from the center of
The immense, purple-streaked, dark mushroom that,
	there, towers
To obscure whatever lies below,
A plume, positive but delicate as a dream
Of pure whiteness, unmoved by breath
	of any wind,
Mounts

Above the dark mushroom,
It grows high – high, higher –
In its own triumphant beauty[24]

Hiroshima also provided freeze advocates with a wealth of medical evidence. In 1947 the National Academy of Sciences, with funding from the Atomic Energy Commission, had launched a

23 Sharon Doubiago, "Ground Zero," in Schley, ed., *Writing in a Nuclear Age*, 20.
24 Robert Penn Warren, "New Dawn," *The New Yorker*, 14 November 1983, 46–8.

research project in Hiroshima on the bomb's radiological effects. By the 1980s, links had emerged between A-bomb exposure and heightened incidence of cataracts, leukemia, multiple myeloma, and other cancers. Persons exposed in utero or in infancy exhibited abnormally high levels of small head and body size and mental retardation. Antinuclear organizations such as Physicians for Social Responsibility (PSR) used this evidence to build opposition to nuclear weapons. References to Hiroshima dotted *The Final Epidemic*, a 1981 collection of essays by scientists and physicians on the effects of nuclear war. At a 1982 Washington conference of educators concerned with the nuclear threat, Dr. Stuart Finch of Rutgers Medical School presented medical data from Hiroshima and expressed the hope that it would help deter "any future use of nuclear energy as an instrument of war."[25]

Meanwhile, Robert Jay Lifton continued to explore the larger applicability of "psychic numbing." The *hibakusha*, he wrote in 1979, "resemble us more than we realize."[26] At the 1982 conference mentioned above, Lifton again stressed Hiroshima's heuristic value: "Hiroshima is important to us, it is a text for us, and we must embrace it and learn from it." In addressing the probable psychic effects of a global nuclear war, as contrasted to the *fear* of such a conflict, however, Lifton stressed that Hiroshima could be a misleading text. Just as the "small" 1945 bomb served to dramatize the vastly larger destructive power of the H-bomb, so Lifton contrasted the *hibakusha* experience with the incompa-

25 Robert Jay Lifton, "In a Dark Time," J. Carson Mark, "Nuclear Weapons: Characteristics and Capabilities," Stuart C. Finch, M.D., "Occurrence of Cancer in Atomic Bomb Survivors," all in *The Final Epidemic: Physicians and Scientists on Nuclear War*, ed. Ruth Adams and Susan Cullen (Chicago, 1981), 7–20, 93–109, 151–65; Stuart C. Finch, M.D., "Hiroshima: Immediate and Long-Term Medical Effects," in *Proceedings of the Symposium: The Role of the Academy in Addressing the Issues of Nuclear War. Washington, D.C., March 25–26, 1982* (Geneva, NY, 1982), 23–32, quoted passage, 31. See also James V. Neel, Gilbert W. Beebe, and Robert W. Miller, "Delayed Biomedical Effects of the Bombs," *Bulletin of the Atomic Scientists* 41 (August 1985): 72–5; and Paul Boyer, "Physicians Confront the Apocalypse," *Journal of the American Medical Association*, 2 August 1985, 633–43. Initially called the Atomic Bomb Casualty Commission (ABCC), the U.S.-sponsored Hiroshima research project became the Radiation Effects Research Foundation in 1975. A comprehensive report by Japanese scientists, *Hiroshima and Nagasaki: The Physical, Medical, and Social Effects of the Atomic Bombings* (New York, 1981), contributed to this body of technical data as well.
26 Robert Jay Lifton, *The Broken Connection: On Death and the Continuity of Life* (New York, 1979), 367.

rably greater psychological impact of global thermonuclear war. At Hiroshima, outsiders had quickly arrived to aid the survivors; in a full-scale thermonuclear war, little outside aid would be available – the whole world would become "Hiroshima." Beyond the statistics of death and destruction and long-term medical consequences, Lifton contended, Hiroshima had introduced a "new image" into human self-awareness: a "radical sense of futurelessness" that undercut the hope of "living on" through one's work or one's offspring that can soften death's sting. After August 1945, such forms of "immortality" could no longer be assumed. All this, he suggested, lay embedded in the historical meaning of Hiroshima and set it forever apart from other cities that had become symbols of war's horror.[27]

A variety of literary works helped reawaken Hiroshima memories in the late 1970s and early 1980s. Eleanor Coerr's children's book *Sadako and the Thousand Paper Cranes* (1979) told of the young bomb survivor dying of leukemia who tried to fold a thousand paper cranes, believing this would cure her. She died short of her goal, but her classmates completed the project. In 1982 Harper's issued a paperback edition of *Children of Hiroshima*, a long-out-of-print collection of writings by youthful survivors. *Atomic Aftermath*, an anthology of short stories about Hiroshima by Japanese authors, published in Japan in 1983, appeared in U.S. bookstores in an English edition the following year. In Kim Stanley Robinson's 1984 science-fiction story "The Lucky Strike," the *Enola Gay* crashes on a practice run, killing all aboard. The bombardier of the back-up crew has qualms of conscience and releases the bomb far outside the city, with few casualties. This "demonstration shot" ends the war, but the bombardier is executed for disobeying orders. The activist climate of the early 1980s also assured a larger audience for Masuji Ibuse's brilliant *Black Rain*, a novel exploring the long-term effects of the Hiroshima bombing on a young woman and her relatives. Originally serialized in a Japanese magazine, Ibuse's work had appeared in English in 1967–8 in the small-circulation *Japan Quarterly*, but it

27 Lifton, "Beyond Nuclear Numbing: A Call to Teach and Learn," in *Proceedings of the Symposium*, 65–9 passim. See also Robert Jay Lifton and Kai Erikson, "Nuclear War's Effect on the Mind," *New York Times*, 15 March 1982; and Lifton, *The Broken Connection*, 363–8.

was a 1985 Bantam paperback edition that introduced it to a wider public.[28]

PSR lecturers, instructors in college nuclear history courses, and organizers of nuclear freeze rallies made effective use of films of Hiroshima's devastation and photographs of survivors, including the horrifying (and once suppressed) documentary film *Hiroshima-Nagasaki 1945*. But the visual evocations of Hiroshima came in many forms. The artist Robert Morris's ambitious 1981 installation "Journado del Muerto," a highly theatrical and politically engaged work exhibited by Washington's Hirshhorn Museum in 1981–2, included large photographs of Hiroshima in ruins and close-ups of burn victims, together with replicas of missiles and photographs of Manhattan Project scientists. *Unforgettable Fire* (1977) offered gripping water colors by Hiroshima survivors originally shown on Japanese television. In the preface, Japanese TV executive Soji Matsumoto stressed its contemporary relevance:

Thirty years have passed since the A-bomb was dropped. The memory of how things were in Hiroshima at that time is being forgotten. It is therefore necessary to appeal to the people of Japan and of the world that there be "No More Hiroshimas." . . . To publish a collection of these pictures as a book is very significant, since we are living in a world in which the diffusion of nuclear weapons is threatening the existence of all humanity.[29]

In 1982, a San Francisco publisher issued "I Saw It," cartoonist Keiji Nakazawa's comic-book-format account of the bombing, which he had lived through as a boy. In 1985 came a U.S.

28 Eleanor Coerr, *Sadako and the Thousand Paper Cranes* (New York, 1979); Dr. Arata Osada. comp., *Children of Hiroshima* (New York, 1982); Kenzaburo Oe, ed., *Atomic Aftermath: Short Stories about Hiroshima and Nagasaki* (Tokyo, 1984); Kim Stanley Robinson, "The Lucky Strike" in *Universe 14*, ed. Terry Carr (Garden City, 1984), 1–35; Masuji Ibuse, *Black Rain* (New York, 1985); Brians, *Nuclear Holocausts*, 161, 291; Lifton, *Death in Life*, 543–55 (on *Black Rain*). For a listing of all works by Japanese atomic bomb survivors in English translation see *Hiroshima: Three Witnesses*, ed. and trans. Richard H. Minear (Princeton, 1990), 389–91.

29 *Unforgettable Fire: Pictures Drawn by Atomic Bomb Survivors*, ed. Japanese Broadcasting Corporation (NEK) (New York, 1977), 5; Howard N. Fox, *Metaphor: New Projects by Contemporary Sculptors* [Catalog of an exhibition at the Hirshhorn Museum and Sculpture Garden] (Washington, 1981), 62; Winkler, *Life Under a Cloud*, 194. The title of Morris's work, "Journado del Muerto" (day's journey of death, or day's work of death), was the traditional name of the desert valley near Los Alamos where the first atomic bomb was tested.

edition of the powerful "Hiroshima Murals" by the Japanese
artists Iri and Toshi Maruki. A 1986 documentary film about the
Marukis and their work, by historian John Dower and film-
maker John Junkerman, received an Academy Award nomina-
tion. Toshi Maruki also wrote and illustrated *Hiroshima No
Pika* (1982), a children's book about a Hiroshima family caught
in the bombing.[30] Like Hersey's *Hiroshima*, these fresh visual
images – from naïve water colors, "comic books," and children's
stories to works by well-known artists – restored human and
historical immediacy to an image constantly at risk of being
dulled by familiarity or drained of specificity by repeated use for
symbolic or rhetorical purposes.

Like the Hiroshima Maidens in 1955, now-aging Hiroshima
survivors added emotional intensity to the nuclear freeze campaign. Several *hibakusha* spoke at the June 1982 Central Park rally
and participated in a television special on the Public Broadcasting
System. At a Washington forum arranged by Senate sponsors of
the freeze resolution, four survivors recounted their memories.
One, Dr. Mitsuo Tomosawa, fifteen years old in 1945, recalled
lying awake all night on 6 August listening to the moans from a
nearby hospital.[31]

The fortieth anniversary of the Hiroshima-Nagasaki bombings
in 1985, coming at a moment when nuclear anxiety, though diminishing, remained high, attracted much notice. *Time* featured a
cover photograph of the mushroom cloud over Hiroshima and a
special section, "The Atomic Age," that included a lengthy essay
about Yoshitaka Kawamoto, director of Hiroshima's Peace Memorial Museum and himself a bomb survivor. The *Bulletin of the
Atomic Scientists* published a special anniversary issue. Yale sociologist Kai Erikson, in an anniversary essay in the *Nation*, saw an
inexorable momentum for dropping the bomb built into the Man-

30 Keiji Nakazawa, *I Saw It: The Atomic Bombing of Hiroshima* (San Francisco, 1982);
    John W. Dower and John Junkerman, eds., *The Hiroshima Murals: The Art of Iri
    Maruki and Toshi Maruki* (Tokyo and New York, 1985) and *Hellfire: A Journey
    from Hiroshima* (film) (New York, 1986); Toshi[ko] Maruki, *Hiroshima No Pika*
    (Tokyo, 1980; English trans., New York, 1982); Brians, *Nuclear Holocausts*, 256.
    For biographical background on the Marukis see Minear, *Hiroshima: Three Wit-
    nesses*, 371–8.
31 "Hiroshimans Recall a 'Desert of Death' in Asking Arms Halt," *Harrisburg Patriot*, 23
    March 1982; "Hiroshima Survivors" sound recording (Washington, 1982).

hattan Project itself. The successful Alamogordo test propelled the project forward, so that alternatives such as a demonstration shot followed by a pause barely merited notice. Typically, Erikson cited Hiroshima's significance for the present: "We need to attend to such histories as this, . . . because they provide the clearest illustrations we have of what human beings can do . . . when they find themselves in moments of crisis and literally have more destructive power at their disposal than they know what to do with. That is as good an argument for disarming as any that can be imagined."[32]

Hiroshima memories were often explicitly used by freeze activists to awaken people to the nuclear danger. As the editor of *Atomic Aftermath* put it: "The short stories included herein are not merely literary expressions, composed by looking back at the past. . . . They are also highly significant vehicles for thinking about the contemporary world over which hangs the awesome threat of vastly expanded nuclear arsenals." More luridly, Peter Wyden's 1984 popular history *Day One: Before Hiroshima and After* contained a stark frontispiece that began: "One millisecond after you read this, you and one billion other people could begin to perish."[33]

From the autumn of 1945 through the 1980s, in short, the role of Hiroshima in American memory has been linked to the shifting rhythms of confrontation with the threat of nuclear war and with campaigns to reduce that threat. In an official environment marked by concealment and evasion, Hiroshima remained jaggedly real. The missiles were out of sight, underground or underwater, their horror only potential; what happened at Hiroshima (and Nagasaki) could be instantly grasped and invoked: the print of a woman's blouse fabric burned into her skin, a battered pocket watch forever frozen at 8:15 A.M., shadow images of human beings vaporized by the blast. Such evidence offered a permanent reminder that the nuclear threat was not simply potential or theoretical: An actual city had been destroyed, actual human beings had died. As Robert Jay Lifton wrote in 1980:

32 Kai Erikson, "Of Accidental Judgments and Casual Slaughters," *Nation*, 3/10 August 1985, 1, 80–5, quoted passages 1, 85.
33 *Atomic Aftermath*, 15; Peter Wyden, *Day One: Before Hiroshima and After* (New York, 1984), 14.

We require Hiroshima and its images to give substance to our own terrors, however inadequately that city represents what would happen now if thermonuclear weapons were dropped on a human population. As much as we must decry the atomic bombings of Hiroshima and Nagasaki, it is possible that these cities already have contributed significantly to our tenuous hold on the imagery of extinction. They have kept alive our imagination of holocaust and, perhaps, helped to keep us alive as well.[34]

Hiroshima memories subversively undercut the techno-rational vocabulary of the nuclear theorists. Artifacts from the shattered city, whether survivors' narratives, photographs or water colors, or the prose of a Hersey or an Ibuse, cut through the strategists' bloodless prose. As Jean Bethke Elshtain has observed:

Human beings think most often in images; a terrible or delightful picture comes into our minds and then we seek to find words to express it, to capture it, to make it somehow manageable. Thus it is with the possibility of nuclear war. Our images are fixed. The scenes of utter destruction at Hiroshima and Nagasaki; two cities laid waste; people disappeared, remaining as shadows on cement or persisting in a terrible and painful twilight zone of lingering death from radiation.[35]

But precisely how, if at all, did Hiroshima memories actually affect nuclear policy? Evidence of *direct* influence on policymakers is scant. Former Secretary of Defense Robert S. McNamara, asked in 1985 if he could recall any film, novel, painting, or other imaginative work that had shaped his view of nuclear war, candidly replied: "No I don't think so. . . . I was so associated with the Defense Department and writings related to the Defense Department that were . . . scientific, or technical, or political in character

34 Robert Jay Lifton, "Nuclear Awareness – 'In a dark time the eye begins to see,' " *Humanities* (National Endowment for the Humanities newsletter), January/February 1980, 1.
35 Jean Bethke Elshtain, "Nuclear Discourse and Its Discontents" (Lecture at Northwestern University, 25 February 1989). See also Carol Cohn, "Sex and Death in the Rational World of Defense Intellectuals," *Signs* 12 (Summer 1987): 687–718; Brian Easlea, *Fathering the Unthinkable: Masculinity, Scientists and the Nuclear Arms Race* (London, 1983); and Paul Chilton, "Nukespeak: Nuclear Language, Culture, and Propaganda," in *Nukespeak: The Media and the Bomb*, ed. Crispin Aubrey (London, 1982), 94–112.

that I think it was those rather than artistic expression that influenced my thinking."[36]

But the effect of Hiroshima images on grass-roots opinion, and thus in defining the parameters within which the policymakers operated, while difficult to quantify, has surely been important. From 1945 through the 1980s, antinuclear activists used films, photographs, paintings, journalistic accounts, firsthand testimony, fiction, and poetry based on the Hiroshima and Nagasaki bombings to convey the human meaning of nuclear attack, rouse awareness of the continuing threat, and build support for disarmament.

A few scholars, usually antinuclear activists themselves, have attempted to measure this effect. In the late 1960s, disturbed by widespread apathy about the nuclear threat, sociologists Donald Granberg and Norman Faye showed the harrowing documentary film *Hiroshima-Nagasaki 1945* to students at the University of Missouri and then measured the results by questionnaire. After several screenings they reported: "It was our impression that the film was doing what we wanted: making concrete something that is ordinarily seen as an abstraction, and sensitizing people to the victims and potential victims of nuclear war." The questionnaires confirmed this impression: The film increased most students' "anxiety regarding nuclear war, decrease[d] the desire to survive a nuclear war, raise[d] the sufficient provocation threshold, and lower[ed] the maximum tolerable casualty threshold."[37]

A decade later, a doctoral student in history at Illinois State University devised a teaching unit on Hiroshima and then tested its results on undergraduates at Illinois State and on students in an Indiana high school. The unit included films documenting the devastation and suffering caused by the Hiroshima bombing, as well as material on Truman's atomic bomb decision. The results proved mixed. For example, the high school students who completed the study unit showed greater agreement with the statement "War is not a satisfactory way to settle disputes" and heightened awareness of the "danger of nuclear extinction," but they also showed

36 Paul Boyer interview with Robert S. McNamara, 3 October 1985, transcript in author's possession.
37 Donald Granberg and Norman Faye, "Sensitizing People by Making the Abstract Concrete: Study of the Effect of 'Hiroshima-Nagasaki,' " *American Journal of Orthopsychiatry* 42 (October 1972): 811–15, quoted passages 811, 812.

greater agreement with the statements "The dropping of the atomic bomb was a moral act" and "The bomb was used to save lives and shorten the war."[38] Apparently the visual material from Hiroshima heightened apprehensions about a future nuclear war, while the print material convinced some students that Truman's 1945 decision was justifiable and wise.

Other research suggested that many factors shaped attitudes toward nuclear-related issues, and thus toward the meaning of Hiroshima. In an attitudinal study of 477 Californians conducted in 1969–70, for example, sociologist Vincent Jeffries found the greatest readiness to accept nuclear war in defense of "our national interests" among the generation born before 1927, and the least readiness among those born between 1943 and 1949. In other words, Americans who had learned of Hiroshima as adults, and who had lived with the knowledge the longest, showed a higher tolerance for nuclear war than did those with no direct memories of the event. Such evidence casts doubt on the assumption, often implicit in the antinuclear camp, that the sharper the Hiroshima memories, the greater the aversion to nuclear war. For the older age group, news of the atomic bomb had come in a specific historical context: at the close of a popular war against a hated enemy. The younger and more vehemently "anti-nuclear" group in Jeffries's study, by contrast, knew "Hiroshima and Nagasaki" in a more culturally mediated, less historically rooted framework.[39]

Political ideology as well as age affected how one "read" the Hiroshima story. For example, from the 1950s through the 1980s, antinuclear activists cited medical data from Hiroshima to show the long-term radiological hazards of nuclear war. But others used the same evidence for different purposes. In 1955, just as the Hiroshima Maidens arrived, the conservative *U.S. News and World Report* published an upbeat interview with Dr. Robert H. Holmes,

---

38 Jack Bertrand Nicholson, *The Atomic Bomb and Hiroshima: Historical Impact and Teaching Unit* (Ann Arbor, 1980), 270, 312, 360–3.

39 Vincent Jeffries, "Political Generations and the Acceptance or Rejection of Nuclear War," *Journal of Social Issues* 30 (1974): 119–36, esp. 128, 129. Jeffries also found class and occupational differences in nuclear attitudes, particularly in the older age cohorts. Among those born before 1927, 69 percent of the blue-collar workers were willing to accept nuclear war in defense of America's "national interest," while only 38 percent of the professionals in this age group thought nuclear war acceptable even under these conditions.

director of the Hiroshima research project.[40] The boldface captions accompanying the interview conveyed the magazine's rose-tinted slant on the story: "In 190,000 Survivors: 100 Cases of Leukemia, Some Mild Eye Cataracts, The Next Generation is Normal . . . No genetic changes thus far in the first generation . . . Many within 2,000 meters did not show radiation effects . . . Only 15 percent of deaths due solely to radiation . . . Children of survivors appear happy, well adjusted . . . usually fertility returns with general health . . . The Atomic Age is here, Let's not be afraid of it." Three photographs illustrated the story: a devastated Hiroshima in 1945; a healthy-looking young survivor being measured by a kindly researcher; and three generations of a Hiroshima family, including a boy born before August 1945, one in utero when the bomb fell, and one born after the bombing, all apparently in the bloom of health. At the time this cheerful feature appeared, *U.S. News* was faithfully echoing the government's theme that through civil defense, atomic war would not be so bad. The message was clear: Hiroshima had been destroyed, but recovery had been quick, and all was now well.

Religious beliefs influenced perceptions of Hiroshima's meaning as well. For biblical literalists, the annihilation of two cities, and the prospect of a vastly more destructive nuclear war, represented essential steps in a foreordained sequence of end-time events. Humankind, according to this scenario, must pass through untold horrors before the Second Coming and the Millennium. In this providential narrative, Hiroshima functioned not as a cautionary example but as a prophesied end-time sign pointing to a glorious future as God's divine plan unfolds.[41]

Not only was the meaning of "Hiroshima" contested but the repeated use of this image by activists always carried the risk of exploiting the actual event and of subordinating it to one's own agenda. Paul Goodman addressed this risk in a sardonic and doubtlessly unfair comment on *Death in Life*: "The survivors of Hiroshima, Dr. Lifton has shown us, are certainly fucked up, but they are not so fucked up as Dr. Lifton. After all, it is rather much to

40 "Latest about After-Effects of A-Bomb," *U.S. News and World Report*, 13 May 1955.
41 Paul Boyer, *When Time Shall Be No More: Prophecy Belief in Modern American Culture* (Cambridge, MA, 1992), 115–51.

drop an atom bomb on people and then to come ask them how
they feel about it."[42] Hiroyuki Agawa made a similar point in his
1957 novel *Devil's Heritage*, which bitterly attacked the U.S. medical research project in Hiroshima for treating the *hibakusha* like
guinea pigs.[43] As Hiroshima memories were transmuted into literature and visual images, and as cautionary lessons were drawn from
the ordeal of the city and its inhabitants, the reality of what actually happened on 6 August 1945 – and why – sometimes seemed
to blur. As the Japanese architect repeatedly tells the French actress
in *Hiroshima, Mon Amour*, as she describes the photographs and
artifacts displayed in the city's atomic bomb museum: "You have
seen nothing."

The issues involved in manipulating and imaginatively rework-
ing historical events can become exceedingly complex. In *Death in
Life*, Lifton reflected perceptively on the symbolic status of Hiroshima, distinguishing it from other cities devastated by war:

When we hear reports about the Hiroshima bomb, our emotions are not
exactly the same as when confronted with equivalent evidence of bomb
destruction in London, Amsterdam, Hamburg, Dresden or Tokyo. These
cities, to be sure, convey their own messages of man's capacity and inclination to assault himself. But with Hiroshima (and her neglected historical sister, Nagasaki) something more is involved: a dimension of totality,
a sense of ultimate annihilation – of cities, nations, the world.[44]

Yet this unique emotional power rested in part on extracting "Hiroshima" from history and elevating it to the realm of metaphor.
Lifton himself, with admirable motives, contributed to this process, as he made the psychically numbed *hibakusha* symbols of a
numbed world. But he was hardly alone. Many who spoke out
against nuclear war over the decades used memories of Hiroshima
in this instrumentalist and potentially exploitive fashion. For some
activists, invoking "Hiroshima" became a way to avoid hard thinking, an emotional button that could always be pressed, a high-
voltage jolt to any discourse.

42 Paul Goodman, "Stoicism and the Holocaust," *New York Review of Books*, 28 March
    1968, 17.
43 Hiroyuki Agawa, *Devil's Heritage*, trans. John M. Maki (Tokyo, 1957); Brians, *Nu-
    clear Holocausts*, 107.
44 Lifton, *Death in Life*, 14.

But the effect of this jolt could not always be anticipated. For some, it simply roused terror. The Australian pediatrician and antinuclear activist Helen Caldicott faced criticism in the early 1980s for what some saw as her irresponsible manipulation of fearful images.[45] For others, repeated exposure to the "Hiroshima" image seems to have produced the very numbing that Lifton deplored. Symbols – even the most potent ones – decay over time. As Andy Warhol once observed: "When you see a gruesome picture over and over again, it doesn't really have any effect." Hiroshima was not immune to this process. As early as 1981 a journalist wrote: "Hiroshima has become one more historical cliché, like Lexington or the Battle of New Orleans."[46] Contributing to this deadening process was the ubiquitous practice of using "Hiroshima" as a convenient date marker in book titles, as in *The American Past: A History of the United States from Concord to Hiroshima*; *Cold War America: From Hiroshima to Watergate*; or *From Harding to Hiroshima: An Anecdotal History of the United States from 1923 to 1945*. New imaginative works in different genres helped revive the image, but as 1945 receded further into the past, the loss of immediacy and resonance that eventually envelops even the most horrendous or momentous historical events inevitably took its toll.

In summary, "Hiroshima" has played both a crucial and a complex role in postwar American thought and culture. The slowly dimming memory of 6 August 1945 has functioned as a palimpsest on which many different fears, expectations, and political agendas have been imprinted for half a century.[47] In the realm of cultural images, "Hiroshima" has functioned as a kind of empty vessel that replicated the literal void created in August 1945. As one survivor described his experience immediately after the bombing: "I climbed Hijiyama hill and looked down. I saw that Hiroshima had disap-

---

45 See Paul Boyer, "A Historical View of Scare Tactics," *Bulletin of the Atomic Scientists* 42 (January 1986): 17–19; and P. M. Sandman and J. Valenti, "Scared Stiff – or Scared into Action?" ibid., 12–16.

46 Don Behm, "Nuclear Proponents Deny Hiroshima Lessons," *City Lights*, 12 August 1981, 12. Warhol quoted in Farrell, "Nuclear Friezes," 71.

47 As Americans confronted racism at home, for example, they debated the role of racism in the decision to use the bomb. See John W. Dower, *War without Mercy: Race and Power in the Pacific War* (New York, 1986).

peared. . . . Hiroshima just didn't exist."[48] As the actual city was
rebuilt and became the bustling metropolis of today, the "Hiroshima" of the imagination floated free, playing its ambiguous role in
the first half century of our encounter with nuclear weapons.

And what of the future? Will "Hiroshima" gradually fade from
our cultural and political discourse? The Cold War is over, and
while nuclear menaces remain – the danger of proliferation in
rogue states such as North Korea; the uncertain future of Russia;
the problem of disposing of a half-century's accumulation of radioactive waste – the threat of the superpower nuclear arms race and
the ultimate nightmare of global thermonuclear holocaust have
clearly receded. The National Register of Historic Places is even
considering designating selected nuclear missile silos and command centers as historic landmarks! Under these circumstances,
cultural attention to Hiroshima – always closely linked to broader
cycles of nuclear awareness and activism – diminished sharply.
"For most people," historian Richard Minear observed in 1993,
"Hiroshima has become a non-issue."[49]

Such judgments, of course, are relative. As this volume makes
clear, Hiroshima is obviously in no danger of vanishing entirely
from the arena of either scholarly or cultural discourse. A newly
published anthology of nuclear-age poetry contains several poems
about Hiroshima. Evidence for its continued power to stir the
imagination is provided, too, by a recent three-act play about Hiroshima by Walter A. Davis, a professor of English at The Ohio State
University. The drama begins realistically, with a 1989 book sign-
ing at an Ohio shopping mall by Paul Tibbets, the *Enola Gay* pilot
(an actual event in which Davis participated as a protester bearing

---

48 Hachiya, *Hiroshima Diary*, 54–5.
49 Marcella Sherfy and W. Ray Luce, "Guidelines for Evaluation and Nominating Proper-
    ties that Have Achieved Significance within the Last Fifty Years," *National Register:
    Bulletin*, No. 22 (Washington, 1990); "Interim Guidance: Treatment of Cold War
    Historic Properties for U.S. Air Force Installations" (Paper presented to the Air Force
    Cultural Resource Working Group at the Society for American Archeology Annual
    Meeting, St. Louis, 14 April 1993); Richard Minear to author, 18 October 1993.
    Minear was commenting on the lack of attention given his important 1990 work,
    Hiroshima: Three Witnesses, which in three years had received only three reviews: a
    brief notice in the daily *New York Times*; a short review in *Choice*; and a longer piece
    in the small-circulation *Nuclear Texts and Contexts*. Had this work appeared six or
    seven years earlier, in a very different cultural milieu, it would unquestionably have
    received major attention both in the scholarly press and the general media.

a sign proclaiming: "Mourn: Hiroshima was Mass Murder"). But it soon takes a surreal and expressionistic turn. Tibbets, kidnapped by a historian, recalls his career, and Truman, Stimson, Oppenheimer, and a group of *hibakusha* make appearances. In a hallucinatory final scene suggesting the enduring vitality of the Hiroshima memory, the historian shoots "Tibbets" between the eyes, but the latter "rises from the dead and reclaims his spot and begins again to sign copies of his book for the queue in a never-ending procession."[50]

Meanwhile, however, the ranks of those who actually remember the events of fifty years ago grow thinner. In another twenty-five years, when "Hiroshima" is nearly as remote as "Verdun" is today, what will be its symbolic status? If the danger of nuclear war continues to recede, it will probably join Carthage and Waterloo in the graveyard of dead symbols, drained of urgency, a shorthand convenience for textbook writers.

But given the human capacity for mischief, and the nuclear knowledge that is now an ineradicable part of our mental storehouse, "Hiroshima" seems at least an even bet to again play its symbolic role, as the world confronts the nuclear threat in some new form. In Helen Caldicott's epidemiological language, the virus has entered a latent phase, but it survives. We still live with the new reality encoded in that innocuous-looking metal sphere as it floated six miles down from the *Enola Gay* to a point 570 meters above the Aioi Bridge: epicenter of the nuclear age.

50 *Atomic Ghosts: Poets Respond to the Nuclear Age*, ed. John Bradley (Minneapolis, 1995), 9–23; Walter A. Davis, "The Holocaust Memorial: A Play about Hiroshima" (typescript, Columbus, Ohio, c. 1993). My thanks to Professor Davis for sharing a copy of his play with me.

7

The Quest for a Peace Culture: The A-bomb Survivors' Long Struggle and the New Movement for Redressing Foreign Victims of Japan's War*

SEIITSU TACHIBANA

In the years following their defeat in World War II, the Japanese people identified themselves as the victims, not only of Allied wartime measures but also of the militarism of their government, which mobilized the emperor's subjects into a holy war for the cause of the Greater East Asia Co-Prosperity Sphere. The Japanese, however, have been slow to realize their role as victimizer. Thousands of Asians suffered as a result of Japanese aggression during the war, and during the early 1990s these foreign victims began to voice their long-overdue demands for compensation.[1] In addition, the more than three hundred thousand A-bomb survivors, called *hibakusha*,[2] have also become increasingly vocal in demanding

---

*Unless otherwise noted, English translations of Japanese sources are the author's.

1 From 1990–3, some three thousand citizens of China, Hong Kong, Indonesia, Korea, the Philippines, and Taiwan, in addition to those of the Netherlands and the United Kingdom, either filed or were preparing to file almost thirty separate lawsuits in Japan against the "state" and some private companies of Japan. The plaintiffs included former "comfort women" or sex slaves for Japanese servicemen; laborers who had coercively been brought into Japan and Sakhalin (where most of them have been forced to stay since the end of World War II under Soviet and then Russian jurisdiction); Koreans and Taiwanese convicted of class-B and class-C war crimes for duties they had been forcibly made to assume in POW camps; conscripted civilian employees of the military and forced laborers who became disabled as a result of their duties; servicemen of the Imperial Japanese Army who were denied eligibility to pensions for having lost their "Japanese nationality" after the San Francisco peace treaty; holders of Japanese military currency, into which they had been forced to convert their local Hong Kong currency; holders of Japanese military post-office savings accounts in which they had been forced to deposit; and POWs of the Allied powers. *Asahi Shimbun*, 13 November 1993.

2 "*Hibakusha*," initially coined to mean those who experienced the atomic bombing, has also come to mean those who were exposed to radiation, with two different Chinese

---

that the Japanese government enact a relief law. This essay deals first with some factors that seem to have contributed to the neglected settlement of postwar compensation for the foreign victims. It then addresses the problems of the *hibakusha*, focusing on the evolution of their consciousness and activities and on their gradual impact on the Hiroshima and Nagasaki municipalities, which in recent years have worked for a totally nuclear-free world.

Predominant among the major factors in Japan's failure to follow up on its responsibility to foreign victims of its wartime aggression was the country's overall political setting during the immediate postwar period. Although American occupation authorities initially aimed to completely remake Japan, by 1948, as the Cold War developed, Washington reversed its policy. The U.S.-orchestrated purge of wartime leaders exempted large numbers of politicians, business people, bureaucrats, social leaders, and others who had been involved in overseas expansion and military administration,[3] which made it unlikely that official policy would consider making restitution to the country's foreign victims. Additionally, the International Military Tribunal for the Far East (Tokyo Tribunal) dealt with war crimes committed against the Allied powers but ignored those against the peoples of Asia and the Pacific,[4] thereby giving the impression that the war's Asian victims were unimportant. Moreover, the subsequent execution of seven class-A war criminals produced a general impression that Japan had adequately absolved itself of all war crimes and need not worry about additional compensation in the future.

Another factor preventing Japan from following up on its wartime responsibilities was the Japanese government's turn away

---

characters used for "-baku-" meaning the "bomb" and the "exposure," respectively. The term has been used internationally especially since 1977, when the participants in a symposium declared: "We also are Hibakusha" in the sense that all human beings carry in their bodies man-made radioactivity that would never have been there "but for the nuclear explosions which have followed since 1945." The Japan National Preparatory Committee, ed., *A Call from Hibakusha of Hiroshima and Nagasaki: Proceedings of International Symposium on the Damage and After-Effects of the Atomic Bombing of Hiroshima and Nagasaki, July 21–August 9, 1977, Tokyo, Hiroshima and Nagasaki* (Tokyo, 1978), iv (hereafter *ISDA* 1978).

3 Of about two hundred thousand who were purged from public office, 80 percent were professional servicemen. Yui Daizaburo, *Mikan no Senryo Kaikaku* [The occupation reforms abandoned incompletely] (Tokyo, 1989), 286–7.

4 Awaya Kentaro, *Tokyo Saiban ron* [On the Tokyo Tribunal] (Tokyo, 1989), 156–8.

from democratization. This move was first encouraged by the
Supreme Commander of the Allied Powers and then indepen-
dently pursued in the context of the San Francisco conference, the
September 1951 U.S.-dominated assembly that produced a final
Allied peace treaty with Japan. Among the most important mea-
sures to limit democracy were the "red purge" of the media and
public and private sectors in 1950 in the wake of the outbreak of
war in Korea, the rescission of the occupation purge directive in
April 1952, the enactment of the Subversive Activities Prevention
Law in July 1952, the revival of pensions for service people in
January 1953, the passage of legislation regulating labor strikes in
August 1953, and the centralization of the police force in June
1954. All of these measures weakened democratic elements in
Japan and strengthened the hand of militaristic and conservative
groups. Japan's postwar government also acted to limit the power
of foreign elements in Japanese society. By the time the final peace
treaty went into effect in April 1952, the Japanese government
had moved to strip foreigners who had forcibly been brought to
Japan and its overseas territories during the war, mostly Koreans
and Taiwanese, of their "Japanese nationality," thus making them
"stateless" and ineligible for legal, political, or social security.[5]
This kind of administrative measure made Japan's lack of concern for its foreign victims patently obvious.

Contributing further to Japan's neglected responsibility were the
various settlements between it and the other Asian nations regarding wartime damages. The most notable of these settlements was

---

5   The legal status of the Koreans and Taiwanese in Japan changed precariously. In Decem-
    ber 1945, when suffrage was extended to women, the Koreans and Taiwanese were
    denied the right on the ground that a voter's register would be established on the basis of
    the Family Registration Law, which had not been applied to them. In May 1947, they
    were treated as "aliens" according to the Alien Registration Decree, the last edict to be
    issued by the emperor. In April 1952, the new Alien Registration Law obligated them
    and all other foreigners to register themselves with "finger printing." (Exemption from
    finger printing is allowed only to permanent residents under the revised registration law
    that became effective after 1993.) The Koreans and Taiwanese were also denied the right
    to choose nationality, and the only way for them to acquire Japanese nationality, should
    they so wish, was to apply for naturalization; but the acceptance or rejection of applica-
    tion was at the discretion of the Japanese government. Tanaka Hiroshi, *Zainichi
    Gaikokujin* [Foreign residents in Japan] (Tokyo, 1991), 60–1, 63–9. The various post-
    war aid laws for the former servicemen and the civilian employees of the military have
    not been applicable to the Koreans and the Taiwanese since they had lost Japanese
    nationality. Ibid., 99, 105–7.

the Treaty on Basic Relations with the Republic of Korea (ROK), which was concluded in 1965 after thirteen years of intermittent negotiations.[6] According to this agreement, all problems between Japan and South Korea were deemed "completely and finally" solved and the ROK waived all claims against Japan in exchange for a total of $800 million.[7] Thus, the door was closed to efforts by individual victims of Japanese colonialism and wartime aggression to claim redress for their suffering and losses. Although the Japanese government paid war reparations to other Asian countries — Burma, Indonesia, the Philippines, and South Vietnam — these funds were used for economic reconstruction, not for the compensation of wartime victims.[8] With Cambodia, Laos, Malaysia, Singapore, and Thailand, the Japanese secured confirmation (in varying forms) that wartime problems had been solved;[9] and in 1972, the Chinese government waived claims of war reparations against Japan. The Japanese government entered into negotiations with the Democratic People's Republic of Korea for the establishment of state relations only in 1991.

Yet another factor in Japan's neglect of wartime responsibility was the effect that the Cold War had on Japanese politics. On various issues throughout the postwar period, peace-oriented groups found their efforts to get the government to atone for Japan's wartime conduct stymied by the emerging East-West conflict. With regard to the question of a peace treaty with the Allied powers, for example, the opposition parties, trade unions, students' groups,

6 In Article 3 of the Japan-ROK Basic Treaty, the ROK government is confirmed as "the only lawful Government in Korea."

7 $800 million from the United States included $300 million in grants, $200 million in government loans, and $300 million in private loans. *Asahi Shimbun*, 13 November 1993.

8 Reparations paid in goods, such as heavy industrial and chemical products, machine tools, and manufacturing plants, meant that Japanese manufacturers were securing a stable market among the reparation recipients. Kobayashi Hideo, *Nihon Gunsei-ka no Ajia: "Dai-Toa Kyoeiken" to Gunpyo* [Asia under Japan's military administration: "The Greater East-Asia Co-Prosperity Sphere" and the military currency] (Tokyo, 1993), 194–6.

9 In their 1959 agreements with Japan on economic and technical cooperation, Cambodia and Laos each relinquished the right to reparations. By their 1968 agreements with Japan, Malaysia and Singapore each received money as the solution to the problems of "unfortunate incidents" during WWII. *Asahi Shimbun*, 13 November 1993. Disputes over Japan's debts to Thailand incurred from the "special Yen" account that Japan had opened during the war for procuring local currency and goods were settled in 1955 and 1961. Kobayashi, *Nihon Gunsei-ka no Ajia*, 194.

religious organizations, and intellectuals favored a comprehensive treaty that included the People's Republic of China, the USSR, and other socialist countries and that allowed Japan to play a role as facilitator of an East-West rapprochement.[10] Needless to say, this was not a position favored by the conservative holders of power in 1940s–1950s Japan, nor of their American sponsors, and the comprehensive peace treaty movement died on the vine.[11] Although the movement laid the intellectual and political foundations on which the subsequent peace movement was to build, in the 1950s it fell victim to the realities of the Cold War, thereby illustrating how the East-West struggle worked to keep Japan from accepting responsibility for its wartime conduct.

A final factor preventing Japanese action was the contemptuous view that many Japanese held of their Asian neighbors. This view originated during the period of Japan's modernization late in the nineteenth century.[12] And although it has been denied in name, it seems to have survived in Japan's almost frantic postwar efforts to

10 One of the most representative propositions along this line was expressed on 15 January 1950 by fifty-six noted intellectuals: *Heiwa Mondai Danwa-kai, "(Kowa Mondai ni tsuite no) Seimei"* [Informal forum on problems of peace, statement (on problems of the proposed peace treaty)] *Sekai* No. 51, March 1950, reprinted in ibid., No. 477, extra issue, July 1985, 109–11. In January 1951, the Japan Teachers' Union adopted four principles for peace: a comprehensive peace treaty, neutrality, no foreign military bases, and opposition to rearmament. Its slogan, "Never Send Students to the Battlefields Again," was used for decades. Nihon Kyoshokuin Kumiai, ed., *Nikkyoso 40-nen Shi* [Forty years of the Japan Teachers' Union] (Tokyo, 1989).

11 Two developments need to be mentioned here. (1) In July 1950, a fortnight after the outbreak of hostilities in Korea, the Supreme Commander of the Allied Powers ordered Prime Minister Shigeru Yoshida to set up a "National Police Reserve," leading to Japan's rearmament in contravention of Article 9 of its new constitution on the non-possession of any "war potential," the clause inserted by instructions of General MacArthur himself. Regarding his instructions see Kobayashi Naoki, *Kenpo Dai-Kyujo* [Article 9 of the Constitution] (Tokyo, 1982), 32. (2) On the same day as the San Francisco peace treaty was signed between the Allied powers and Japan in September 1951, a Japan-U.S. security treaty was also signed in the same city, and the latter was superseded by the Treaty of Mutual Cooperation and Security between the United States of America and Japan in 1960. The security treaty setup has since orientated Japan's foreign policy.

12 In a 1885 essay, Yukichi Fukuzawa, a leading ideologist of Japan's modernization, argued that since Japan could not afford to wait for China and Korea to become civilized enough to join it in working for a prosperous Asia, it should take the same course of action that the civilized nations of the Occident were taking, without being too restrained in dealing with the two countries only because they were neighbors but treating them just as the Westerners were doing. *"Datsu-A ron"* [Overcoming Asia], in *Fukuzawa Yukichi Senshu* [Selected works of Fukuzawa Yukichi], ed. Tomita Masafumi and Dobashi Toshikazu (Tokyo, 1981), 7:221–4, and paraphrased from 224.

catch up with the West. As Japan's economy expanded, in fact, certain leading politicians grew increasingly oblivious of their country's wartime treatment of fellow Asians. In 1982, history textbook screeners of the Ministry of Education asked authors to play down Japan's conduct by rewriting accounts of the Second World War – changing "aggression" to "advance," for instance.[13] In 1985, Prime Minister Yasuhiro Nakasone officially worshipped at the Yasukuni Jinja, a Shinto shrine in Tokyo honoring the war dead, including the class-A war criminals. And more than one cabinet minister has made slips of the tongue that either justified or played down the country's past.[14]

If all of these factors prevented immediate Japanese acceptance of wartime responsibility, there are recent signs that this trend is being reversed. The Japanese people were moved when the Federal Republic of Germany's President Richard von Weizsäcker proposed at the Bundestag on 8 May 1985 to assume full responsibility for the past. They were also impressed that in 1988 the United States admitted its wartime "mistake" in relocating and detaining 120,000 Japanese-Americans and provided for restitution to the survivors and that the Canadian government later did the same. Since 1990, historians, teachers, journalists, students, and citizens have held joint meetings in Tokyo and Seoul for the study of history textbooks.[15] The International Hearing Concerning Postwar

13   For the textbook screening system and its negative role see Saburo Ienaga, "The Glorification of War in Japanese Education," *International Security* 18 (Winter 1993/94): 113–33.
14   In 1986, Education Minister Masayuki Fujio claimed that the 1910 Japan-Korea "merger" was achieved in accordance with "negotiations and agreement" both in "de jure and de facto terms." Fujio Masayuki, "'Hogen Daijin' oini hoeru" ["Indiscreet-remarks minister" barks aloud], *Bungeishunju* 64 (October 1986): 125; and the point was substantiated in idem, "'Hogen Daijin' futatabi hoeru" ["Indiscreet-remarks minister" barks again], ibid. (November 1986): 115–17 (the latter was published after his dismissal from the Nakasone cabinet). In 1988, Cabinet Minister Seisuke Okuno, director of the National Land Agency, stated in the Diet that the Japan-China war broke out as a result of an incident that took place "by accident" around Lugou Qiao (Marco Polo Bridge) in 1937. *Asahi Shimbun*, 10 May 1988. In 1989, Prime Minister Noboru Takeshita, who had made a fence-mending trip to Beijing because of Okuno's statement, stated in the Diet that whether the past war should be regarded as a war of aggression or not was a matter "to be evaluated by historians in coming ages." Ibid., 27 February 1989.
15   Ni-kkan Rekishi Kyokasho Kenkyu-kai (hen), *Kyokasho o Ni-kkan Kyoryoku de kangaeru* [Fujisawa Hoei et al., eds., writing school textbooks under Japanese and Korean cooperation] (Tokyo: 1993). This work is reviewed (in Japanese) by Suzuki Ryo in *Rekishigaku Kenkyu* No. 657, April 1994, 45–7.

Compensation of Japan was held in Tokyo on 9 December 1992, with foreign witnesses giving firsthand testimony.[16] While demanding that the Japanese government investigate various damages inflicted on peoples of Asia and the Pacific, concerned intellectuals and citizens in 1993 independently established the Center for Research and Documentation on Japan's War Responsibility with offices in Tokyo and Osaka.[17]

More to the point of this volume, changes have also begun concerning the status of A-bomb survivors. It took years for people to gain unrestricted access to information about conditions of the *hibakusha*. Ten days after Japan's surrender, it was reported that Hiroshima and Nagasaki would remain barren for a period of seventy-five years.[18] Then a news blackout of everything about the atomic bombings was implemented on 18 September 1945.[19] It was only in August 1952, after the San Francisco treaty went into effect, that the first photographs of Hiroshima and Nagasaki and their survivors were published in the news weekly *Asahi Gurafu* (Asahi Picture News).[20]

Two years later, people rediscovered Hiroshima and Nagasaki after the twenty-three crew members of a Japanese tuna boat, the *Fifth Lucky Dragon* (Dai-go Fukuryu-maru), were contaminated with radiation from a U.S. nuclear test off the Bikini atoll in the Pacific.[21] People refrained from eating their favorite fish, and radio-

16 The Executive Committee of the International Public Hearing Concerning Postwar Compensation of Japan, ed., *War Victimization and Japan: International Public Hearing Report* (Osaka, 1993).

17 In the autumn of 1993, the Center for Research and Documentation on Japan's War Responsibility began publication of its quarterly *Senso Sekinin Kenkyu* [Report on Japan's war responsibility] in Japanese.

18 *Asahi Shimbun*, 25 August 1945, quoting U.S. broadcast sources.

19 For the censorship operations see Monica Braw, *The Atomic Bomb Suppressed: American Censorship in Japan, 1945–1949* (Malmo, Sweden, 1986). One of the rare exceptions was Takashi Nagai, *Nagasaki no Kane* [Bells of Nagasaki] (Tokyo, 1948). Its publication was approved on condition that "Japanese Atrocities in Manila," material furnished by the Military Intelligence Division of the Supreme Commander of the Allied Powers, be incorporated in Nagai's work; it was printed in pp. 189–319 in the same book. Ryuzaburo Shikiba, who had labored for three years for the publication of the book, remarked in the preface that while the Japanese bowed to the tragedy of Nagasaki, they must also have "deep remorse" for the Manila incident (p. 2).

20 This extra issue was sold out on the day of publication, and the total number of copies printed reached 520,000.

21 When it was smothered with radioactive ash on 1 March 1954, the 140-ton *Fifth Lucky Dragon* was at a place about 150 kilometers to the east-northeast of the testing

active rain contaminated the earth, affecting the food cycle from vegetables to milk. A panic ensued.

In response to the *Lucky Dragon* incident, Suginoko-kai, a women's reading circle in Tokyo's Suginami ward, initiated a signature collection for the prohibition of atomic and hydrogen bombs. The campaign soon spread; a national council was formed in August; and, after the collection of over thirty million signatures, the World Conference against Atomic and Hydrogen Bombs was held in Hiroshima in August 1955. In September, the National Council for the Signature Collection Campaign against Atomic and Hydrogen Bombs and the Japan Preparatory Committee for the World Conference jointly formed the Japan Council against Atomic and Hydrogen Bombs (Gensuikyo) as a national center of the movement and as an international liaison.[22]

The 1955 World Conference provided *hibakusha* with an opportunity to speak of their experiences for the first time. Most of the conference participants from places other than the two bombed cities also had the new experience of seeing *hibakusha*, hearing them speak, and talking with them in person. Because the Japanese government had provided only immediate medical care for the *hibakusha*, they had been forced to help each other mostly on an individual basis.[23] But after the 1955 conference, they stepped up their organization efforts. In 1956, existing and new groups

site, outside the danger zone designated by the U.S. Atomic Energy Commission. In a scoop on 16 March 1954, *Yomiuri Shimbun* strongly suggested that the test was of a hydrogen bomb. Aikichi Kuboyama, the radio operator, died on 23 September. In 1968, the ship was found anchored in out-of-use condition at a corner of Tokyo Bay. A citizens' campaign saved the ship, which since 1976 has been placed in a permanent display as a reminder of the nuclear threat at the "Dai-go Fukuryu-maru Tenji-kan" (museum) in Tokyo's Yumenoshima under the management and custody of the Dai-go Fukuryu-maru Peace Society and administered by the Tokyo metropolitan government. Early Japanese works on the affected Pacific islanders include Maeda Tetsuo, *Kimin no Gunto: Mikuroneshia Hibaku-min no Kiroku* [The abandoned people of the islands: A record of the Micronesian *hibakusha*] (Tokyo, 1979).

22   For subsequent developments of this movement see footnote 46.
23   The 1942 Wartime Casualties Care Law providing for a sixty-day period of relief activity had expired by 5 October 1945. In April 1952 the Law for Relief of the War Wounded and for Survivors of the War Dead was enacted but was not applicable to the *hibakusha*. See the Committee for the Compilation of Materials on Damage caused by the Atomic Bombs in Hiroshima and Nagasaki, ed., *Hiroshima and Nagasaki: The Physical, Medical, and Social Effects of the Atomic Bombings* (Tokyo, 1981), 554 (hereafter *Hiroshima and Nagasaki*).

formed the Japan Confederation of A-bomb and H-bomb Sufferers Organizations (Hidankyo).

With growing public support, Hidankyo's activities succeeded in getting the Law Concerning Medical Care for A-bomb Victims enacted in 1957 after twelve years of total neglect. Under the law, which has subsequently been revised several times, *hibakusha* received health books and annual health examinations, and the government pledged to pick up the costs of their treatment if recommended by medical institutions. In 1968, Hidankyo also succeeded in getting the Law Concerning Special Measures for A-bomb Survivors enacted. Under this law and its subsequent revisions, *hibakusha* with one of eleven certified illnesses may receive a health maintenance allowance, and those who were within two kilometers of the bomb's hypocenter may receive a health protection allowance if their incomes are below a certain level.

Despite these kinds of measures, however, since 1961 the *hibakusha* have demanded the enactment of a genuine relief law that would admit government responsibility for their plight and provide financial compensation. A 1963 Tokyo District Court decision strengthened the *hibakusha*'s case by declaring that the U.S. atomic bombing "violated fundamental codes of war." But it also decreed that individuals could not appeal for redress from domestic courts in Japan or the United States because neither international nor domestic law upheld any claims against the two states. In light of the magnitude of the *hibakusha*'s suffering, however, the court ruled that the accused (the Japanese state) should take steps to provide "adequate relief measures" beyond the existing Medical Care Law.[24]

Because the damages of the atomic bombing were brought about "by the [Japanese] state's act of war," and because in the San Francisco treaty the Japanese government "waived all claims" against the United States for any damage arising out of the war, the *hibakusha* urged the Japanese government to accept its moral and legal responsibilities to compensate them.[25] Official opposition to

24 The Tokyo District Court lawsuit had been filed by three *hibakusha*. The court ruling of 7 December 1963 is reprinted in Matsui Yasuhiro, *Senso to Kokusaiho: Genbaku Saiban kara Rasseru Hotei made* [War and international law: From the A-bomb trial to the Russell tribunal] (Tokyo, 1968), 183–206.

25 The first quotation is from the Supreme Court ruling of 30 March 1978 on the case of

such a relief law has been based on the conviction that state compensation should be limited to military personnel and their dependents.[26] But this principle has been violated twice before, as the government compensated landowners in 1965 for losses caused by postwar land reforms and those who returned from former overseas territories in 1967 for the loss of the assets they left behind.[27]

Urged by Hidankyo and others, the minister for health and welfare in June 1979 appointed a Council on Basic Problems Regarding Measures for A-bomb Victims (Kihonkon). But its report, submitted in 1980, was far from what the *hibakusha* would have liked. First, it dismissed the *hibakusha*'s claim to special status by asserting that people had to "tolerate" wartime sacrifices equally. More important, it closed the door to any official acceptance of responsibility for the *hibakusha* by claiming that because the state could not legally be charged with its political acts (acts of governance) such as declaring war and concluding peace, the *hibakusha* had no way to seek legal redress.

Kihonkon went on to conclude that what the government had already done for the *hibakusha* was proper and should continue but ruled out direct financial compensation by the state. It was unfair for the *hibakusha* to claim such payments by saying that they were being made to former servicemen and their dependents, it asserted, because those payments were due to the servicemen's "special legal relations with the state." The *hibakusha*, who were private citizens, had no such legal relationship, and measures to support them to the exclusion of others would constitute a "striking imbalance," since all these measures were to be financed by taxes and almost all people had suffered from the war in one form or another.[28]

Son Jin-doo, a Korean *hibakusha*, which stated that the Korean *hibakusha* should be treated on equal terms with the Japanese *hibakusha*. Later, the government acted accordingly. Both Japanese and foreign *hibakusha* residing abroad, however, have to bear the cost of travel to and from Japan to receive health examinations and medical treatment. The waiver of claims is provided for in Article 19(a) of the San Francisco peace treaty.

26 Health and Welfare Minister Kunisuke Saito is quoted as reconfirming the government position in "Suwarikonda Hibakusha-tachi" [The *hibakusha* who staged a sit-in] *Sekai*, No. 338, January 1974, 123.

27 *Hiroshima and Nagasaki*, 556.

28 The Kihonkon's report of 11 December 1980, "Genbaku Hibakusha Taisaku no Kihon Rinen oyobi Kihonteki Arikata ni tsuite" [On the basic concept and basic direction of measures for the A-bomb victims], submitted to the minister of health and welfare, is

The *hibakusha*'s response to the Kihonkon's report was not positive. In a 1984 rebuttal, "Never Again Produce Hibakusha Any More," Hidankyo indicated their plan of action and appealed for public understanding and support.[29] Given their firsthand experience with the effects of radiation, the *hibakusha* condemned the existence of all nuclear weapons, whether for security or under the pretext of deterrence. They demanded that the Japanese government disseminate information throughout the world on the actual effects of the atomic bombings; enact a law on three nonnuclear principles;[30] pledge not to come under the nuclear umbrella of any country; lobby all nuclear states to totally abolish nuclear weapons; and work for a nuclear-free Asia and the Pacific. The *hibakusha* also demanded that the U.S. government acknowledge that the atomic bombings constituted a violation of the principles of humanity and international law and apologize to the *hibakusha*; scrap its own nuclear weapons, thereby taking the lead toward their complete abolition; discontinue deployment of nuclear weapons in Japan; and immediately withdraw nuclear war-related facilities. They further demanded that the nuclear powers conclude a treaty for the total abolition of nuclear weapons, scrap nuclear war-related facilities in their own and other countries, and dissolve all military alliances.

With regard to the specific issue of a relief law, Hidankyo made four demands: (1) that the Japanese state compensate the *hibakusha* for their damages and pledge that no more *hibakusha* would be produced; (2) that the bereaved receive condolence money and pensions; (3) that the *hibakusha*'s health care, medical treatment, and recuperation be the responsibility of the state; and (4) that all *hibakusha* receive pensions, with a bonus for the handicapped. At-

reprinted in *Ishida Tadashi, Genbaku Higaisha Engo-ho: Han-Genbaku Ron-shu II* [A relief law for A-bomb victims: A collection of essays against the atomic bomb, Vol. 2] (Tokyo, 1986), 177–85 (hereafter *Ishida II 1986*).
29 Hidankyo, *Genbaku Higaisha no Kihon Yokyu – futatabi Hibakusha o tsukuranai tameni* [Basic demands of the A-bomb victims – Never again produce *hibakusha* any more], a pamphlet, 18 November 1984.
30 Three nonnuclear principles: nonmanufacture, nonintroduction, and nonpossession of nuclear weapons, first referred to by Prime Minister Eisaku Sato in 1967 as part of his "four nuclear principles," which included "U.S. nuclear deterrent" as a premise. The government has subsequently said that it would abide by the three principles but has refused to codify them in law.

taining these demands, said Hidankyo, was "the mission assigned to the hibakusha by history."

But how had the *hibakusha* come to realize this historic mission? For the *hibakusha*, their suffering was "neither momentary nor passing," but rather has "endured for decades." Even after acute aftereffects, such as alopecia, diarrhea, bleeding, and other symptoms ceased, survivors suffered from the fear that they might any day fall ill unexpectedly.[31] Tadashi Ishida has analyzed the "life history" of individual *hibakusha* and concluded that their thought processes are characterized by two patterns: "floating" and/or "protest." Every individual *hibakusha* wavers and struggles between these patterns, depending on what position he or she takes vis-à-vis the atomic bomb: One can become conscious of one's own "floating" only by transcending "floating" and moving on to the position of "protest."[32]

After the A-bomb demolished the human and material basis of a community that had sustained "life," survivors might have been

31 Shinji Takahashi, "Relief for the Hibakusha," *Bulletin of the Atomic Scientists* 40 (October 1984): 25–6. The Ministry of Health and Welfare (MHW) made nationwide surveys on the conditions of the *hibakusha* in 1965, 1975, and 1985. The third survey findings are compiled in Koseisho Iryo-kyoku, *Showa 60-nendo Genshi-bakudan Hibakusha Jittai Chosa (Seizon-sha Chosa)* [MHW Medical Treatment Bureau, 1985 surveys on the actual conditions of A-bomb victims (survivors surveys)], June 1987. The average age of the *hibakusha* in 1985 was 59.9 years. In addition, two independent surveys were made. The first, in 1977 by the Japan National Preparatory Committee for ISDA, included items that had not been covered by the MHW surveys, such as information on the dead, *hibakusha*'s medical data (symptoms and treatments), life history, and demands. For its three interim reports see *ISDA* 1978, 26–9, 192–242. From November 1985–March 1986, Hidankyo made its own surveys, because it decided that the MHW's surveys had been limited to "statistical grasping" of the "present conditions of life and health" and "aging status" of the *hibakusha* but had not covered items regarding their sufferings and anxieties that were brought about by the atomic bombings and that no analysis had been shown either of the causes of the data collected or of the problems involved in the data. (Hidankyo, "Hibakusha wa Genbaku o 'Junin' shinai" [*Hibakusha* do not "tolerate" the atomic bomb], 1987.) Hidankyo survey findings in Japanese include First report (commentary edition), 6 December 1986; and Second report (interim report on the A-bomb dead), 10 March 1988. English publications include English Translation Group, *The Witness of Those Two Days: Hiroshima and Nagasaki August 6 & 9, 1945*, Vols. I & II (accounts of one thousand *hibakusha* selected from among some thirteen thousand), October 1989; and *The Deaths of Hibakusha: The Days of the Bombings to the End of 1945*, Vol. I (memories of the dead family members as told by some three hundred survivors), September 1991.

32 Ishida Tadashi, *Genbaku Taiken no Shiso-ka: Han-Genbaku Ron-shu I* [Conceptualization of the A-bomb experiences: A collection of essays against the atomic bomb, Vol. I] (Tokyo, 1986), 134–6.

overwhelmed by the instinct of self-preservation and become inhuman. While some of them strove to maintain human dignity, others showed egotistic and inhuman actions that they could justify by the extraordinary circumstances in which they were placed. Even the latter, however, eventually became conscious of their "guilt" or "shame" as they placed themselves in relation to those killed: They feared that their lives might have been purchased by the deaths of those who died not as human beings but as objects. This thought of "atrocious death" would not disappear.[33]

Many *hibakusha* sought moral rehabilitation, wondering who was responsible for robbing them of their humanity, and they gradually came to realize that the dehumanization took place as a result of the atomic destruction of the community that had sustained their lives. Thus, they began to resist war and the A-bomb, thereby linking "the dead" (the past) with "themselves" (the present) and their "successors" (the future).[34] The *hibakusha* are in the process of conceptualizing their individual experiences into a universal ideology of nuclear pacifism.

The *hibakusha*'s awakening, coupled with developments of national and international public opinion, gradually came to exert an influence on the stance of the Hiroshima and Nagasaki municipalities. Over time, the mayors of Hiroshima and Nagasaki came to use the occasion of the anniversary of the atomic bombings to express the municipal authorities' position regarding nuclear war.[35] Following the Bikini incident in 1954, for instance, Hiroshima mayor Shinzo Hamai warned that with the advent of the hydrogen bomb, human beings were facing "the possibility of self-extinction" and

33 Tadashi Ishida, "Idealization [Conceptualization] of the A-Bomb Experience," in *ISDA 1978*, 126–7. Ishida's bibliographic commentator points out that his grasping of *hibakusha*'s "guilt" consciousness is quite different from Robert J. Lifton's concept of "guilt over survival priority," which is described as a "survivor's impaired formulation" in his *Death in Life: The Survivors of Hiroshima* (Harmondsworth, 1971), 559–60. See Masaharu Hamatani, "Kaidai," in *Ishida II 1986*, 236.

34 Ishida, "Idealization," 127.

35 English translation of these statements by Hiroshima mayors are in Hiroshima Peace Culture Foundation, *Peace Declarations Delivered by the Mayors of Hiroshima [1947–1986]*. The texts of 1947–1956 and 1962 were translated in 1985. And the texts of 1987–1993 in English translation, courtesy of the same foundation. English translation of Nagasaki mayors' declarations, 1987–1991 and 1993, courtesy of the Nagasaki Foundation for the Promotion of Peace. Quotations from declarations of the other years were translated by this author.

appealed for "the total abolition of war and for the proper control of nuclear energy throughout the world." In 1955, Nagasaki mayor Tsutomu Tagawa said that the renunciation of atomic weapons and the condemnation of war by the great scientists made him believe that "the dawn of a lasting world peace" would be seen in the near future.[36]

According to Hamai, the partial nuclear test ban treaty of 1963 was a step toward a total abolition of nuclear weapons and a complete renunciation of war. But in 1964 Tagawa pointed to "the explosive world situation being aggravated" by the parallel existence of the utterly exhausted countries and of those countries demonstrating their superiority by "going all out for the production and possession of nuclear weapons." To counteract this danger, in 1967 Hiroshima mayor Setsuo Yamada proposed a "new world order" in the spirit of the "solidarity of mankind." One year later, he warned that regarding nuclear weapons as an "effective war deterrent" would only "serve to spur the nuclear race." Reacting to the prevailing fear that nuclear weapons would be used in Vietnam, in 1970, Mayor Yamada stated that the continued call from Hiroshima – "supported by the world-wide opinion" – for the abolition of nuclear weapons contributed to prevent their use. In 1971, he proposed that in order to build a new world structure "all nations [must] relinquish their military sovereignty completely" by transferring it to a world organization binding mankind in solidarity. And in 1973, Mayor Yamada condemned individual states for invoking national security in justifying continued nuclear war preparations tests, calling such action a "criminal act against all mankind."

Over time, the municipalities of Hiroshima and Nagasaki moved beyond the Peace Declaration formula in spreading their anti-nuclear message. On 14 July 1975, on the eve of the thirtieth anniversary of the bombings, the municipal assemblies of the two cities unanimously approved the Agreement on Hiroshima and Nagasaki Partnership for Peace Culture Cities, vowing to contribute to world

36 The scientists' statement referred to by Tagawa is "The Russell-Einstein Manifesto," signed by the eleven scientists and published in London, 9 July 1955. The text is in J. Rotblat, *Scientists in the Quest for Peace: A History of the Pugwash Conferences* (Cambridge, MA, 1972), 137–40.

peace and human welfare by fulfilling their mission as A-bomb cities.[37] The two cities set about launching a series of activities both at home and internationally and were encouraged by revitalized action on nuclear disarmament and other global issues by various international nongovernmental organizations.[38] Eighteen months later, Mayors Takeshi Araki of Hiroshima and Yoshitake Morotani of Nagasaki asked the United Nations to take "appropriate measures" toward a total abolition of nuclear weapons and general and complete disarmament.[39]

Over time, pronouncements in peace declarations grew more concrete. In 1979, Nagasaki mayor Hitoshi Motoshima strongly urged the Japanese government to work for nuclear disarmament as "the central task of [its] diplomacy."[40] In 1981 he asked Prime Minister Zenko Suzuki to "tell the people the truth" regarding the government's decision to allow U.S. nuclear-arm-delivery vessels to call at Japanese ports and U.S. nuclear-bomb-carrying planes to land on Japanese soil.

Recent efforts at nuclear-weapons limitation have met with mixed reactions from municipal authorities. In 1988, Hiroshima mayor Araki welcomed the INF treaty between the United States and the Soviet Union as a "worthwhile historic first step" toward comprehensive nuclear disarmament, as did Nagasaki mayor Motoshima. But both still called for total nuclear disarmament. In 1990, as the Cold War drew to an end, Mayor Araki urged all countries to make "greater efforts for total disarmament across

37 Kamata Sadao, ed., *Hiroshima-Nagasaki no Heiwa Sengen* [Peace declarations of Hiroshima and Nagasaki] (Tokyo, 1993), 91.
38 In 1976, the Hiroshima Peace Culture Foundation, first set up in 1967 as a branch of the municipal office, became a nonprofit foundation with citizens' participation. The Nagasaki Foundation for the Promotion of Peace, established in 1983 under the auspices of the municipality and with the membership from among citizens, also became a nonprofit foundation in 1984. Citizens are encouraged to take their own initiatives both in cooperation with and in addition to municipality-sponsored events such as the "UN Disarmament Week" annually observed in Nagasaki around the UN Day on 24 October.
39 Hiroshima-Nagasaki, *To The United Nations*, 1976, 2. The sixty-eight-page document includes "Appeal to the Secretary General of the United Nations" and "Actual Conditions of Atomic Bomb Damages in Hiroshima and Nagasaki," a paper edited by the Expert Committee for Compilation of Data to Appeal to the United Nations.
40 Assuming office in 1979, Nagasaki mayor Motoshima instituted a new system of securing assistance of a committee of learned and experienced citizens in drafting annual declarations.

the board." Thus, in 1993, Hiroshima mayor Takashi Hiraoka and Nagasaki mayor Motoshima both expressed opposition to the 1968 Nuclear Non-Proliferation Treaty not being extended indefinitely at its final review conference in 1995 and urged that an international agreement for the complete abolition of nuclear weapons be concluded.

At the same time, the two mayors worked on behalf of the *hibakusha*. In 1980, when the minister of health and welfare's advisory committee was working on the previously discussed report, they asked the government to enact a relief law based on the principle of state compensation. The request has since been repeated.[41] They also began to suggest what they regarded as unique contributions to be made by A-bombed cities. In 1982, Hiroshima mayor Araki renewed his proposal that a world summit conference on disarmament be held in Hiroshima.[42] He also proposed that an international institute for research on peace and disarmament be set up there. In 1985, Nagasaki mayor Motoshima asked Prime Minister Yasuhiro Nakasone to exert efforts to see that disarmament conferences currently held in New York and Geneva also meet in Nagasaki and Hiroshima. Regarding an international center for *hibakusha*, which he had proposed in 1983 for Nagasaki, Motoshima reported in 1993 that the city was carrying on a joint project with the Nagasaki prefecture and Nagasaki University in establishing the Nagasaki Association for *hibakusha*'s Medical Care to accept foreign physicians for training, to send Japanese physicians abroad, and to provide medical treatment for foreign *hibakusha*.

Hiroshima and Nagasaki officials have also been working to convince the government to pay more attention to the plight of foreign victims of Japan's war. In a recognition of his nation's victimizer past, Motoshima in 1989 challenged Japanese to "think deeply about the events from the attack on Pearl Harbor through

41 A *hibakusha* relief bill was passed in 1989 in the House of Councilors when the opposition parties held sway there but was dropped in the House of Representatives, with which the legislative authority rests; another bill was passed in the former house in 1992 but was dropped again in the latter house in 1993.

42 Speaking in Vladivostok in July 1986, Mikhail Gorbachev, then general secretary of the Communist Party of the Soviet Union, suggested that Hiroshima could be a suitable place for an Asia-Pacific version of the Conference on Security and Cooperation in Europe (CSCE).

to the destruction of Nagasaki" and "reflect with sincerity on the war," praying for the repose of the souls of the more than twenty million Japanese and foreign victims of the "dark chapter in history." In 1990, he invited special attention to the "moral responsibility" for having ignored the plight of foreign *hibakusha* for forty-five years, especially those Koreans and Chinese who were forcibly brought into Japan, treated inhumanely, and exposed to the atomic bombing in a foreign land. Immediate steps should be taken, the Nagasaki mayor proposed, "to offer apologies, to conduct investigations, and to provide assistance" for these *hibakusha*.[43] Takashi Hiraoka was first among Hiroshima mayors to state in 1991 that there was no excuse for Japan's inflicting "great suffering and despair on the peoples of Asia and the Pacific" during its reign of "colonial domination and war."

In the meantime, the World Conference of Mayors for Peace through Intercity Solidarity emerged out of the twin-city initiatives. "The Role of Cities in Building Peace – Toward the Total Abolition of Nuclear Weapons" has remained the conference's keynote theme, but the changing world situation and broadening representation in the conferences has led to the expansion of future themes.[44] The "Hiroshima-Nagasaki Appeal" from the 1993 conference included a pledge to strengthen efforts for mobilizing international public opinion in favor of the abolition of

43 In 1990, the Japanese government for the first time promised to make a donation of 4 billion yen to a fund for the Korean *hibakusha* in South Korea. *Asahi Shimbun*, 15 August 1990. Early works on the conditions of Korean *hibakusha* include Hiraoka Takashi, *Henken to Sabetsu: Hiroshima soshite Hibaku Chosenjin* [Prejudice and discrimination: Hiroshima and the A-bombed Koreans] (Mirai-sha, 1972); Kamata Sadao, ed., *Hibaku Chosen-Kankokujin no Shogen* [Testimonies of the A-bombed Koreans (in South Korea and those citizens of the ROK and the Democratic People's Republic of Korea who are residing in Japan)] (Tokyo, 1982).

44 Although originally unintended when it first met in 1985, the conference resolved to reconvene every four years. The first conference was represented by 98 cities in 23 countries, and the second in 1989 by some 130 mayors from more than 30 countries. Hiroshima Peace Culture Foundation, Secretariat Office, ed., *1st World Conference of Mayors for Peace through Inter-City Solidarity, Hiroshima & Nagasaki 1985*, and *2nd World Conference of Mayors for Peace through Inter-City Solidarity, Hiroshima & Nagasaki 1989*. While citizens of the two cities were provided with opportunities to sit at conferences and listen to discussions, it has been suggested that the municipal authorities should devise a forum that would ensure more "positive" participation by citizens other than *hibakusha*'s statements. Yabui Kazuo, "Overview of Hiroshima City's Effort toward the Coalition of Anti-Nuclear Cities in the World – 'World Conference of Mayors for Peace through Inter-City Solidarity,' 1982–1992" (in Japanese), *Peace Studies* (Heiwa Kenkyu), 17 (November 1992): 34–48, and quoted from 45.

nuclear, chemical, and biological weapons. Special emphasis was placed on deepening respect for human rights and "peaceful multiethnic coexistence," particularly among the coming generation. The abolition of "hunger, poverty, and discrimination on all levels," including that against refugees and foreign workers, was reaffirmed as one of the conference's goals. All national governments and international organizations were called upon to take relevant measures along these lines. The United Nations in particular was urged to take the initiative in holding a disarmament conference in 1995 on the occasion of the fiftieth anniversary of the atomic bombings and of its own founding.[45]

The *hibakusha*'s long struggle and the new movement to redress foreign victims of Japan's colonial rule and war of aggression share an emphasis on the reestablishment of basic human rights. Their underlying message is to change the political culture of Japan, moving it toward peace. This is a formidable task given the Japanese government's position on the problem of postwar compensation alone, and all the more so in light of its recent attempts at rising to the status of a global power, which include assigning an overseas role to the "Self-defense Forces" closer to that of the armies of the Great Powers and pursuing permanent status in a restructured UN Security Council. Criticisms, especially from other countries, of the Japanese government's attitude have been extremely instrumental in highlighting the issues involved in war responsibility.

On the other hand, different elements in the peace movement have much to do to cultivate their own peace culture by learning how to cooperate with one another more effectively.[46] What suc-

---

45   3rd World Conference of Mayors for Peace through Inter-city Solidarity, "Hiroshima-Nagasaki Appeal," Nagasaki, 9 August 1993. The conference was represented by 122 cities in 42 countries.

46   Reference may here be made to the Japanese movement for the abolition of nuclear weapons, the launching of which, as previously mentioned, encouraged *hibakusha* to organize themselves. Over time, the movement began to face difficulties in overcoming effects of the Cold War that have since plagued it. In 1959, Gensuikyo took the position that the proposed revision of the Japan-U.S. security treaty would pave the way for Japan's nuclear arming and dispatch overseas of its Self-Defense Forces, and the ruling Liberal Democratic party labeled it a "disguised peace movement." In 1961, some outside organizations formed the National Council for Peace and against Nuclear Weapons (Kakkin Kaigi), with the support of the Democratic Socialist party, criticizing Gensuikyo for taking a "pro-Communist and anti-American" stance. The

cess could be achieved both by the *hibakusha*'s movement and by the movement for compensation for foreign victims would doubtless contribute to the conversion of Japan's negative asset – its victimizer past – into a positive one – the new political culture for peace.

Soviet resumption of nuclear tests in 1961 evoked a controversy in Gensuikyo over whether or not nuclear tests by any nation should equally be condemned, and another controversy arose in 1963 over the evaluation of the partial nuclear test ban treaty. These led several groups to break with Gensuikyo and form the Japan Congress against A- and H-Bombs (Gensuikin) in 1965, with the support of the Socialist party and the General Council of Trade Unions of Japan (Sohyo, the largest trade union center at the time). The Communist party continued to support Gensuikyo. Hidankyo and some other organizations, including many grassroots groups, remained uncommitted to the organizational antagonism. In 1978–1985, these organizations joined with Gensuikyo and Gensuikin in an ad hoc committee to host annual world conferences. In 1992–1994, Gensuikyo and Gensuikin each worked for the World Court Project to outlaw nuclear weapons by securing an advisory opinion from the International Court of Justice. The movement is still to learn how to make common cause with its diverse elements.

8

*History, Collective Memory, and the Decision to Use the Bomb**

J. SAMUEL WALKER

The roots of collective memory in the United States have attracted considerable scholarly attention in the past few years. The ways in which historical events – such as the Watergate scandal, the assassination of John F. Kennedy, and the reception of immigrants at Ellis Island – are perceived and interpreted in American culture have inspired study and debate among students in several disciplines. One important issue they have examined is the discrepancy, often great, between popular memory and scholarly views of historical events. Michael Schudson, a professor of sociology and communication, complains that popular memories of Watergate lose sight of the constitutional issues involved and instead focus on personalities. In a similar manner, Barbie Zelizer, a former reporter and now a professor of rhetoric and communication, is sharply critical of journalists who, in her opinion, created and continue to shape popular views of the Kennedy assassination for their own purposes. She asserts that journalists "refused to turn the assassination story over to historians because they wanted to remain its authoritative spokespersons," thus perpetuating a division between prevailing collective memory and competing interpretations advanced by scholars.

Perhaps the most vivid example of the gulf between popular perceptions and scholarly knowledge is the report of historian Michael Frisch on the results of a poll he conducted in his Ameri-

*This article expresses the personal views of the author. It does not represent an official position of the U.S. Nuclear Regulatory Commission or any other government agency. The author gratefully acknowledges the comments of Charles J. Errico, Donald A. Ritchie, and Allan M. Winkler.

can history survey course over a period of years. He asked his students at the start of a term to write down the first ten names that came to mind from the beginning of American history to the end of the Civil War, exclusive of presidents, generals, and other prominent public officials. To his astonishment, the consistent and overwhelming winner was the "unsinkable" Betsy Ross for her mythical role in making the American flag.[1]

The same kind of dichotomy between popular views and scholarly findings seems apparent in how President Harry S. Truman's decision to use atomic bombs against Japan is remembered. There is no sure method for ascertaining exactly what constitutes collective memory on any given topic. The studies of the subject are more successful in explaining the influences on collective memory than in defining the content of collective memory, which can be done only with a liberal portion of assumption and extrapolation. In the case of the use of the bomb, collective memory, from all available evidence, regards Truman's action as a sound decision that ended the war without requiring an invasion of Japan and thus saved large numbers of American lives. Most Americans, it seems safe to say, would accept without serious reservation the assertion of President George H. W. Bush in 1991 that dropping the bombs "spared millions of American lives."[2]

One student of collective memory in the United States, John Bodnar, argues that the primary agent for shaping popular views of historical events in recent times has been the federal government. In alliance with state governments, middle-class professionals, and others, it sought to replace "vernacular interests" with "official culture" in order to build unity, foster patriotism, and ensure loyalty. Although Bodnar overstates the role of the federal government in

1   Michael Schudson, *Watergate in American Memory: How We Remember, Forget, and Reconstruct the Past* (New York, 1992); Barbie Zelizer, *Covering the Body: The Kennedy Assassination, the Media, and the Shaping of Collective Memory* (Chicago, 1992), 186; Michael Frisch, "American History and the Structure of Collective Memory: A Modest Exercise in Empirical Iconography," *Journal of American History* 75 (March 1989): 1130–55. For other recent discussions of collective memory see the articles that appear with Frisch's in a special issue on "Memory and American History," *Journal of American History* 75 (March 1989): 1115–1280; Michael Kammen, *Mystic Chords of Memory: The Transformation of Tradition in American Culture* (New York, 1991); and John Bodnar, *Remaking America: Public Memory, Commemoration, and Patriotism in the Twentieth Century* (Princeton, 1992).
2   *Washington Post*, 2 December 1991.

creating collective memory, in the case of the decision to use atomic bombs against Japan, his findings are applicable.[3]

Recent scholarly work by James G. Hershberg and Barton J. Bernstein has shown how former government officials consciously and artfully constructed the history of the decision. James B. Conant, anxious to head off criticism, convinced former Secretary of War Henry L. Stimson to publish an article explaining and justifying the use of the bomb. In his widely publicized article, which appeared in *Harper's* in early 1947, Stimson suggested that the atomic attacks had avoided more than one million American casualties. Truman later drew on Stimson's estimate to support his claim that the bomb had saved as many as half a million American lives. Those figures formed the basis for popular views of Truman's action and decisively influenced collective memory of the reasons for his decision.[4]

Scholars now know better. One key finding of the past few years is that U.S. casualty estimates did not begin to approach one million and the projected American deaths from an invasion, in the unlikely event that an invasion was necessary, were much lower than one half million. Estimated deaths from an invasion were, in a worst case, about forty-six thousand. As military historian John Ray Skates has recently concluded: "The record does not support the postwar claims of huge Allied casualties to be suffered in the invasion of Japan." The evidence of the casualty figures that military planners presented to top policymakers in the summer of 1945 has added a new dimension to the historiographical controversy over the use of the bomb. The debate, ignited by the publication of Gar Alperovitz's *Atomic Diplomacy* in 1965 and carried on at varying levels of intensity ever since, has centered on the ques-

3 Bodnar, *Remaking America*, esp. chaps. 1, 8. Kammen, *Mystic Chords of Memory*, demonstrates how public memories of historical events are shaped by a variety of cultural influences as well as by the government. For a critique of Bodnar's emphasis on the role of the federal government see Dwight T. Pitcaithley's contribution to a roundtable on "Government-Sponsored Research: A Sanitized Past?" *Public Historian* 10 (Summer 1988): 40–6.

4 Barton J. Bernstein, "Writing, Righting, or Wronging the Historical Record: President Truman's Letter on His Atomic-Bomb Decision," *Diplomatic History* 16 (Winter 1992): 163–73; idem, "Seizing the Contested Terrain of Early Nuclear History: Stimson, Conant, and Their Allies Explain the Decision to Use the Atomic Bomb," ibid. 17 (Winter 1993): 35–72; James G. Hershberg, *James B. Conant: Harvard to Hiroshima and the Making of the Nuclear Age* (New York, 1993), 279–304.

tion of whether Truman was motivated primarily by military or political/diplomatic considerations in deciding to drop the bomb. It has produced a deluge of new information and a rich variety of intriguing arguments. While scholars continue to disagree on many points, a broad consensus emerged.[5]

According to the scholarly consensus, the United States did not drop the bomb to save hundreds of thousands of American lives. Although scholars generally agree that Truman used the bomb primarily to shorten the war, the number of American lives saved, even in the worst case, would have been in the range of tens of thousands rather than hundreds of thousands. Specialists also view political/diplomatic objectives as a secondary objective in the decision. They have not fully accepted the revisionist claim, articulated most trenchantly by Alperovitz, that Truman acted primarily to impress the Soviets and advance American political objectives, but it seems clear that the political implications of the use of the bomb figured in the administration's deliberations. The scholarly consensus holds that the war would have ended within a relatively short time without the atomic attacks and that an invasion of the Japanese islands was an unlikely possibility. It further maintains that several alternatives to ending the war without an invasion were available and that Truman and his close advisers were well aware of the options.[6]

The broad agreement among scholars differs markedly from the justifications presented by Stimson, Truman, and others, and from popular views of American actions. The discrepancy has much to do with the foundations of collective memory. David Lowenthal,

5 Barton J. Bernstein, "A Postwar Myth: 500,000 U. S. Lives Saved," *Bulletin of the Atomic Scientists* 42 (June/July 1986): 38–40; Rufus B. Miles, Jr., "Hiroshima: The Strange Myth of Half a Million American Lives Saved," *International Security* 10 (Fall 1985): 121–40; Martin J. Sherwin, *A World Destroyed: Hiroshima and the Origins of the Arms Race*, rev. ed. (New York, 1987); Robert A. Pape, "Why Japan Surrendered," *International Security* 18 (Fall 1993): 154–201; John Ray Skates, *The Invasion of Japan: Alternative to the Bomb* (Columbia, SC, 1994), 74–83.
6 J. Samuel Walker, "The Decision to Use the Bomb: A Historiographical Update," in this volume. For an essay that analyzes earlier writings on the bomb see Barton J. Bernstein, "The Atomic Bomb and American Foreign Policy, 1941–1945: An Historiographical Controversy," *Peace and Change* 2 (Spring 1974): 1–16. For a good example of the ongoing debate over the use of the bomb see the views that Gar Alperovitz and Robert L. Messer exchanged with Bernstein, "Correspondence: Marshall, Truman, and the Decision to Drop the Bomb," *International Security* 16 (Winter 1991/92): 204–21.

in his book *The Past Is a Foreign Country*, identifies three basic sources of public perceptions of the past – history, memory, and relics. Lowenthal suggests that history is generally the most important of these, and clearly it is in the case of the decision to use the bomb. As Paul Boyer points out elsewhere in this volume, the ranks of those who remember Hiroshima are diminishing. And those who remember often do not have a full or accurate picture of the reasons for Truman's decision. The best example of the distortion that memory can cause is Paul Fussell's celebration, aptly titled *Thank God for the Atom Bomb*. One can sympathize with the vast relief of Fussell and other infantrymen who learned that they would not have to invade Japan, and he writes that he received many letters from former compatriots who "cheered themselves hoarse" in response to his tribute to the bomb. But their perceptions as soldiers in the field are of little value in understanding why U.S. policymakers made the choices they did.[7]

In a similar manner, relics are of limited application in studying the reasons behind the Truman administration's action. Artifacts can be helpful in visualizing and grasping the terrible destruction that the bomb produced and in serving as grim reminders of the costs of nuclear warfare. But whatever their value in understanding the effects of the bomb, they have little to contribute to understanding the reasons that Truman elected to authorize the atomic attacks.

That leaves historical documentation and presentation as the principal means of informing collective memory. In a rich array of books, articles, pamphlets, documentary collections, films, docudramas, and television programs, the sources that reach more students than any other are American history textbooks. This is particularly true of secondary school texts, which, in theory at least, impress the historical consciousness of nearly every high school student in America. As Frances FitzGerald has pointed out, the history that those students learn is often the version of events that will stay with them for the rest of their

---

7   David Lowenthal, *The Past Is a Foreign Country* (Cambridge, England, 1985), 255–9; Paul Boyer, "Exotic Resonances: Hiroshima in American Memory," in this volume; Paul Fussell, *Thank God for the Atom Bomb and Other Essays* (New York, 1988), 45. For a critique of an earlier version of Fussell's essay see Martin J. Sherwin, "Hiroshima and Modern Memory," *Nation*, 10 October 1981, 329, 349–53.

lives. She adds that long after facts have been forgotten, general impressions remain: "What sticks to the memory from those textbooks is not any particular series of facts, but an atmosphere, an impression, a tone."[8]

The information that leading secondary school textbooks provide on the decision to use the bomb generally gives an impression that Truman and his advisers would hardly find objectionable. Their discussion of the bomb would probably have pleased Conant, who urged Stimson to write his article as a way to preempt "sentimentalism" that might show up among school teachers. He worried that they might influence future generations by advancing "a distortion of history" about why the bomb was dropped.[9]

A sampling of secondary school texts shows that some accept the explanations of the Truman administration by reporting that the president had to choose between the bomb and an invasion that could cause the loss of one million American lives (a higher number than Truman himself cited).[10] Others, which Conant would probably find less satisfactory, cite the figure of a possible one million deaths, but also make clear that alternatives to the bomb were available and that Truman's decision stirred controversy.[11] One text, James West Davidson and Mark H. Lytle's *The United States: A History of the Republic*, departs from the pattern. It does not mention projected casualties or suggest that an invasion was likely without the bomb. A college textbook by the same authors and three collaborators, however, states that military leaders thought that an invasion would be necessary to end the war and that it would result in "half a million to a million casualties."[12] The explanation for the use of the bomb that prevails in high

8   Frances FitzGerald, *America Revised: History Schoolbooks in the Twentieth Century* (New York, 1979), 16–18.
9   Bernstein, "Seizing the Contested Terrain," 40; Hershberg, *James B. Conant*, 294.
10   Daniel J. Boorstin and Brooks Mather Kelley, with Ruth Frankel Boorstin, *A History of the United States* (Lexington, MA, 1986); Henry F. Graff, *America: The Glorious Republic* (Boston, 1990).
11   Henry W. Bragdon, Samuel P. McCutchen, and Donald A. Ritchie, *History of a Free Nation* (New York, 1993); Andrew R. L. Cayton, Elizabeth Israel Perry, and Allan M. Winkler, *American Pathways to the Present* (Englewood Cliffs, NJ, 1994).
12   James West Davidson and Mark H. Lytle, *The United States: A History of the Republic* (Englewood Cliffs, NJ, 1990); James West Davidson, William B. Gienapp, Christine Leigh Heyrman, Mark H. Lytle, and Michael B. Stoff, *Nation of Nations: A Narrative History of the American Republic* (New York, 1990).

school texts is summarized in a recent issue of *Cobblestone: The History Magazine for Young People*, a magazine aimed at secondary school students. It notes that alternatives to the bomb existed but concludes that Truman made his "difficult choice" because he wanted to avoid "losing an estimated one million Americans." Given the alternatives that are outlined in textbooks, it is highly probable that most high school students would agree with those in an Indiana survey that Truman made the right decision.[13]

The treatment of the use of the bomb in secondary school texts is not surprising in light of the demands of powerful state textbook selection committees and the inherent pressures to avoid controversy. The general impression that they deliver is that Truman faced a stark choice between the bomb and an extremely costly invasion, although some suggest that Truman's options were less clear-cut. Without the need to cater to selection committees and with a better educated and more mature audience to target, one might expect a more sophisticated treatment of the issue in college survey textbooks. In some ways, collegiate texts offer a richer and more subtle discussion of the issue. In other ways, however, many college textbooks perpetuate the same myths and simplifications as leading secondary school texts.

In general, college textbooks reflect the consensus among scholars that the Truman administration used the bomb primarily to shorten the war and secondarily to impress the Soviets.[14] They do

13   "World War II: Americans in the Pacific," *Cobblestone: The History Magazine for Young People* 15 (January 1994): 34–40; Boyer, "Exotic Resonances."

14   The discussion of college texts is drawn from a survey of eighteen books. For the sake of brevity, multi-author volumes will be cited hereafter by the name of the first-listed author. The texts, in addition to Davidson, *Nation of Nations*, are: Thomas A. Bailey and David M. Kennedy, *The American Pageant*, 9th ed. (Lexington, MA, 1991); Bernard Bailyn, Robert Dallek, David Brion Davis, David Herbert Donald, John C. Thomas, and Gordon S. Wood, *The Great Republic: A History of the American People*, 4th ed. (Lexington, MA, 1992); John M. Blum, William S. McFeely, Edmund S. Morgan, Arthur M. Schlesinger, Jr., Kenneth M. Stampp, and C. Vann Woodward, *The National Experience: A History of the United States*, 8th ed. (Fort Worth, 1993); Paul S. Boyer, Clifford E. Clark, Jr., Joseph E. Kett, Neal Salisbury, Harvard Sitkoff, and Nancy Woloch, *The Enduring Vision: A History of the American People*, 2d ed. (Lexington, MA, 1993); Alan Brinkley, Richard N. Current, Frank Freidel, and T. Harry Williams, *American History: A Survey*, 8th ed. (New York, 1991); Joseph R. Conlin, *The American Past: A Brief History* (San Diego, 1991); Robert A. Divine, T. H. Breen, George M. Fredrickson, and R. Hal Williams, *America: Past and Present*, 3d ed. (New York, 1991); John A. Garraty, *A Short History of the American Nation*, 6th ed. (New York, 1993); Winthrop D. Jordan and Leon F. Litwack, *The United States*,

not fully accept a revisionist interpretation, but they are influenced by it. Without exception, college survey texts do not celebrate the destruction of Hiroshima and Nagasaki as something for which to "thank God." John M. Blum and his coauthors, for example, call the decision "the most tragic in the long course of American history."[15] A few texts make it clear that Truman's decision was more complex than simply a choice between the bomb and an invasion. John A. Garraty calls it "the most controversial decision of the entire war."[16]

Nevertheless, the treatment of the atomic bomb decision in many college textbooks is surprisingly dated, and in some cases, misleading and superficial. The most common shortcoming is that the vast majority of the books under review state or imply that the bomb avoided the need for an extremely costly invasion. In some cases, the authors present this view as an incontrovertible fact; in others they hedge slightly by saying that Truman was convinced that the bomb would bring victory without an invasion of Japan. Even when they discuss other options that might have ended the war, most texts fail to make clear that an invasion was a remote possibility, even without the bomb.

As a corollary, most textbooks assert that by replacing the need for an invasion, the bomb spared large numbers of American lives. Some writers use the numbers cited by Stimson and Truman or some slight variation. Others use descriptive rather than quantitative terms — such as "untold thousands" or "colossal bloodbath."[17] No

7th ed. (Englewood Cliffs, NJ, 1991); Robert Kelley, *The Shaping of the American Past*, 5th ed. (Englewood Cliffs, NJ, 1990); Arthur S. Link, Stanley Coben, Robert V. Remini, Douglas Greenberg, and Robert C. McMath, Jr., *The American People: A History*, 2d ed. (Arlington Heights, IL, 1987); James Kirby Martin, Randy Roberts, Steven Mintz, Linda O. McMurry, and James H. Jones, *America and Its People*, 2d ed. (New York, 1993); Gary B. Nash, Julie Roy Jeffrey, John R. Howe, Peter J. Frederick, Allen F. Davis, and Allan M. Winkler, *The American People: Creating a Nation and a Society*, 2d ed. (New York, 1990); Mary Beth Norton, David M. Katzman, Paul D. Escott, Howard P. Chudacoff, Thomas G. Paterson, and William M. Tuttle, Jr., *A People and a Nation: A History of the United States*, 3d ed. (Boston, 1990); George Brown Tindall with David E. Shi, *America: A Narrative History*, 3d ed. (New York, 1992); Irwin Unger, *These United States: The Questions of Our Past*, 5th ed. (Englewood Cliffs, NJ, 1992); and R. Jackson Wilson, James Gilbert, Stephen Nissenbaum, Karen Ordahl Kupperman, and Donald Scott, *The Pursuit of Liberty: A History of the American People*, 2d ed. (Belmont, CA, 1990).

15 Blum, *The National Experience*, 779.
16 Garraty, *Short History of the American Nation*, 472.
17 Kelley, *Shaping of the American Past*, 660; Unger, *These United States*, 792.

textbook mentions the much smaller numbers of deaths and casualties that have been cited by specialists on the subject, although a few sidestep the issue by avoiding the use of numbers or descriptive terms altogether. The articles that first refuted the myths of one half million deaths or one million casualties appeared in the mid-1980s, which would seem to allow ample time to be included in more recent editions of textbooks. One popular reading book for students, James West Davidson and Mark H. Lytle's *After the Fact*, notes that the casualty figures have been "quite controversial."[18] But the recent findings that the anticipated casualties in the summer of 1945 did not approach one million even in the worst scenarios have not been disputed by specialists on the subject.

The questions of the need for an invasion and the estimates of casualties go to the heart of understanding the reasons for the use of the bomb. Textbook authors do their readers an injustice if they simplify the alternatives faced by Truman and overstate both the chances and the costs of an invasion. Incorporating the information that scholars have reported over the past few years would not necessarily change the prevailing textbook interpretation of why Truman opted for the bomb. A case can be made that the prospect of saving forty-six thousand American lives in the unlikely but conceivable event that an invasion proved necessary (or a smaller number if the war dragged on for several weeks even without an invasion) provided sufficient military justification to use it.[19] But the new information about casualty estimates introduces more ambiguity into the question of why the United States dropped the bomb. This kind of ambiguity is apparently what Stimson and Truman sought to avoid with their inflated casualty figures. Textbook writers should not fall into the trap of accepting those numbers uncritically. Even if inclusion of the recent findings makes textbook discussions of the bomb less tidy, it is preferable to treat-

18 James West Davidson and Mark H. Lytle, *After the Fact: The Art of Historical Detection*, 3d ed. (New York, 1992), 286.
19 Barton J. Bernstein argues that no single alternative to the bomb would have ended the war as quickly. He concludes that it seems "very likely, though certainly not definite," that a combination of Soviet entry into the war, modifying the unconditional surrender demand, and continuing the blockade and heavy conventional bombing would have ended the war before the planned invasion of Kyushu on 1 November 1945. See Bernstein, "Understanding the Atomic Bomb and the Japanese Surrender: Missed Opportunities, Little-Known Near Disasters, and Modern Memory," in this volume.

ments that are clear but inaccurate. Indeed, the best college text-book accounts of the decision to use the bomb – those of Blum, Boyer, Winthrop D. Jordan, and Mary Beth Norton – are among the least categorical in explaining Truman's motives.

In addition to their failure to grapple with important new find-ings on the decision to use the bomb, many textbooks suffer from factual errors or dubious assertions. Most of the lapses are trivial, such as citing the wrong date for the Alamogordo test or claiming that "many" atomic scientists opposed the use of the bomb.[20] Other errors are more serious. Some books state explicitly and others imply that Truman made his decision only after thorough deliberation and careful weighing of the alternatives. Stimson made this point in his 1947 article. But in a book published in 1988, McGeorge Bundy, his "scribe" for the article, expressed doubt that the use of the bomb received the consideration it de-served. "Whether broader and more extended deliberation would have yielded a less destructive result we shall never know," Bundy wrote. "Yet one must regret that no such effort was made."[21]

Some of the factual mistakes in textbooks are inexplicably fla-grant. Davidson's textbook, *Nation of Nations*, asserts that the radiation effects of the atomic blasts were "unexpected by many of the scientists who built the bomb," when, in fact, those scientists were well aware of the hazards of exposure to high levels of radia-tion. Arthur S. Link contends that Truman and his advisers appar-ently did not realize that Japan was on the verge of collapse in the summer of 1945. George Brown Tindall submits that Truman "had no idea" that an atomic bomb could "destroy virtually an entire city." Such errors would perhaps be less worthy of mention if they did not show the Truman administration in a more favor-able light than a more accurate presentation of the facts would suggest.[22]

Many American history survey textbooks, in sum, sustain myths

20 Kelley, *Shaping of the American Past*, 659 (Alamogordo); Blum, *The National Experi-ence*, 777 ("many" scientists).
21 Garraty, *Short History of the American Nation*, 472; Martin, *America and Its People*, 895, 897; Unger, *These United States*, 792; Wilson, *The Pursuit of Liberty*, 929–30; McGeorge Bundy, *Danger and Survival: Choices about the Bomb in the First Fifty Years* (New York, 1988), 97.
22 Davidson, *Nation of Nations*, 1076; Link, *The American People*, 746; Tindall, *Amer-ica*, 1215.

about and questionable explanations for the use of the bomb. Even while accepting revisionist views to a point, they reinforce many of the key arguments that have prevailed since the 1940s, especially the conclusion that Truman used the bomb to avoid an invasion and save huge numbers of American lives. Even allowing for the need for brevity, the desire for clarity, and the lead times for incorporating new scholarship, the treatment of the atomic bomb decision by many textbook authors is regrettably flawed. In general, it reflects the historiography of the mid-1970s and fails to consider or include new findings. The contribution that a large majority of college textbooks make to collective memory seems likely to underscore the interpretations or impressions that students receive from high school history books.

The misleading or simplified version of the use of the bomb that many textbooks advance is echoed in popular history accounts. Perhaps this is understandable in older books that were written before the discovery and publication of new evidence on Truman's decision. It is much less defensible in more recent books. The most popular and presumably most influential of these is David McCullough's best-selling, highly acclaimed, and Pulitzer Prize-winning blockbuster, *Truman*. McCullough's discussion of the atomic bomb is defiantly traditional. He informs his readers that Truman opted for the bomb to avoid the dreadful prospect of an invasion and to save many American lives, though he is uncertain about how many lives. He acknowledges that in the summer of 1945, military leaders estimated casualties in the first thirty days of an invasion in a range of 30,000 to 50,000 (which, using a death to casualty ratio of 1:4 or 1:5, would have placed the number of deaths in the range of 6,000 to 12,500). But he adds that one estimate placed the number of American deaths in the range of five hundred thousand to one million. This, McCullough asserts, "shows that figures of such magnitude were then in use at the highest levels." If McCullough had consulted Bernstein's article on projected casualties, he would have learned that the document that cited estimates of five hundred thousand to one million deaths was not taken seriously by military planners and was not circulated at the "highest levels." Later, McCullough suggests that the use of the bomb prevented 250,000 American casualties.

In this case and throughout his discussion of the bomb, Mc-Cullough dismisses the findings of scholars and the documentary evidence that raise questions about his own interpretation. His bibliography indicates that he did not bother to read the works of many leading scholars, including Alperovitz, Robert L. Messer, Leon V. Sigal, Michael S. Sherry, and Melvyn P. Leffler, and he lists only one edited book and one article of Bernstein's many important publications on the bomb. McCullough surely has an obligation to acquaint himself with the analyses of those scholars and, perhaps as a result, with the complexities involved in the decision to use the bomb. Scholars might well be justified in simply disregarding Mc-Cullough's arguments as too shallow to be taken seriously. But the book's impact on popular views and collective memory will entrench even more deeply the misconceptions about the decision to use the bomb that Stimson, Truman, and others created.[23]

Despite the prevalence of the conclusions that McCullough advances, students and the general public are exposed, at least potentially, to other interpretations. Even students who are assigned textbooks in survey courses and actually read them can get differing views from supplementary readings, lectures, or classroom discussions. Other materials are available for use either inside or outside the classroom. They include mass market books (though the mass is smaller than for McCullough), such as Richard Rhodes's *The Making of the Atomic Bomb* and Peter Wyden's *Day One*.[24] Newspaper and magazine articles that are critical of Truman appear on occasion, usually around the anniversary of Hiroshima, and reach a larger audience than most scholarly histories. Several documentary films, an admirable television docudrama, *Day One*, and a woeful movie, *Fat Man and Little Boy*, dissent from the popular image of Truman's decision.

The influence of those books, articles, and films on prevailing views, although impossible to measure, seems limited. Perhaps this is because those accounts focus on the building or the effects of the

---

23 David McCullough, *Truman* (New York, 1992), 436–44. For criticisms of McCullough's discussion of the atomic bomb decision see, for example, Walter Isaacson, "Where the Buck Stopped," *Time*, 29 June 1992, 80; and Gar Alperovitz and Kai Bird, "Giving Harry Hell," *Nation*, 10 May 1993, 640–1.

24 Richard Rhodes, *The Making of the Atomic Bomb* (New York, 1986); Peter Wyden, *Day One: Before Hiroshima and After* (New York, 1984).

bomb rather than on the decision to use it. Perhaps the authoritative tone of textbooks and the prestige of their authors give their interpretations the aura of gospel. In any event, textbooks play a key role in shaping collective memory. As Sara Evans and Roy Rosenzweig have suggested, "Textbooks are the single most important written source through which college students learn about the past." Or perhaps Truman has become such a folk hero, an image enhanced by McCullough's portrait of him, that the burden of proof on those who question the standard version of events is insurmountable.[25]

The chasm between scholarly views and collective memory could be narrowed if textbooks at both the secondary school and college levels and popular histories would incorporate new findings and their implications into their discussions of the use of the bomb. This does not mean that, by doing so, they necessarily have to fully accept a revisionist interpretation or condemn Truman for ordering the atomic attacks. But it does mean that they should make clear the alternatives that were available to Truman, the potential costs as projected before the attacks were authorized, and the complexities of the considerations that led to the destruction of Hiroshima and Nagasaki. Scholars have been working hard for years to make sense of new information so that we can gain a better understanding of one of the monumental decisions of the twentieth century. Authors who describe the bases for Truman's reasoning to students or the general public have an obligation to do the same. Otherwise, collective memory will remain poorly informed by an incomplete and oversimplified version of events, and textbook presentations and popular accounts will continue to reinforce the justifications and misconceptions that have skewed explanations of the decision to use the bomb for nearly half a century.

25 Sara Evans and Roy Rosenzweig, "Textbooks and Teaching: Introduction," *Journal of American History* 78 (March 1992): 1377–9.

9

The Enola Gay Controversy: History, Memory, and the Politics of Presentation

MICHAEL J. HOGAN

It was an "eerie sight," reported the *Washington Post* on Thanksgiving Day 1994. Two nights before, observers in the nation's capital had been dumbstruck to see the fuselage of a B-29 bomber being hauled down Independence Avenue to the Smithsonian's Air and Space Museum. It was the *Enola Gay*, the giant four-engine Superfortress that had dropped the atomic bomb on Hiroshima, Japan, in the early morning of 6 August 1945. Named after the mother of its pilot, Colonel Paul W. Tibbets, the *Enola Gay* had disappeared from sight after its deadly mission. Stored outdoors in three states, it had been home to field mice and other critters before taking up residence in Building 20 at the Smithsonian's storage yard in Suitland, Maryland. There, technicians had worked for years to restore the bomber before shrink-wrapping its fuselage for protection and moving it to the Air and Space Museum for an exhibit that was to open in May 1995.[1]

Shrouded in white plastic as it traveled down Independence Avenue, the fuselage looked vaguely like a blowup of the "Little Boy" atomic bomb it had dropped on Hiroshima. A group of demonstrators assembled near the museum to protest the public display of a warplane whose payload had taken the lives of so many Japanese soldiers and civilians. For them, the *Enola Gay* was a symbol of

1 *Washington Post*, 24 November 1994, B2. See also Arthur Hirsch, "Deadly Courier Retains Its Place in History," *Baltimore Sun*, 24 March 1994, A1; and Thomas B. Allen, "Flying into Controversy: Enola Gay a Target Decades after Hiroshima," *Phoenix Gazette*, 6 August 1994, B13. Although it has not always been possible to identify the section as well as the page number of particular newspaper stories, this information is included in the citations whenever available. The byline is also included whenever available.

the atomic carnage that had ended World War II and launched the Cold War. For others, however, the giant B-29 bomber was a lifesaver, a peacemaker, "a totem of American technological triumph," as Arthur Hirsch reported in the *Baltimore Sun*, that deserved center stage in an exhibit marking the fiftieth anniversary of the atomic bombing of Japan.[2]

These competing symbols were at the heart of a bitter controversy over the proposed exhibit, finally entitled "The Last Act: The Atomic Bomb and the End of World War II."[3] At stake in this controversy was whether the exhibit would commemorate the atomic bombing of Japan or investigate the circumstances surrounding that event. Would Hiroshima loom as the last act in a bloody struggle or the first in a long and dangerous arms race? The answers to these and similar questions would determine whose story the exhibit recounted. Although American veterans wanted an exhibit that spoke for them, it was not at all clear if their memories could be reconciled with a careful analysis of the motives that drove President Harry S. Truman's resort to atomic warfare. Nor would it be easy to balance their narrative of the war against the silent voices of those who had perished at Hiroshima and Nagasaki, the Japanese city that was destroyed by a second atomic bomb three days after Hiroshima.

To a large extent, everything depended on who controlled the process by which the exhibit was framed. Curators at the Air and Space Museum based their right to interpret the past on their scholarly credentials, on their mastery of the historical record, and on the advice they received from professional historians. American veterans appealed to the authenticity of personal experience. They equated their collective memory with historical reality and asserted their authority over that of the curators. These differences might have been reconciled, and some balance between history and memory achieved, had it not been for the intervention of organized interests, including the American Legion, the Air Force Association, and conservative politicians in Congress. These groups appro-

2 Hirsch, "Deadly Courier Retains Its Place in History," *Baltimore Sun*, 24 March 1994, A1.
3 The exhibit was originally entitled "The Crossroads: The End of World War II, the Atomic Bomb, and the Origins of the Cold War."

priated the memory of American veterans to defend a conventional, patriotic picture of the past. Determined to deny history if it subverted their sense of American identity, they censored alternative voices and forced the Smithsonian to cancel its original plans. To be sure, the fuselage of the *Enola Gay* would still be displayed at the Smithsonian's Air and Space Museum, but the exhibit would no longer tell the bomber's story or recount the memories, and commemorate the sacrifices, of American veterans.

II

The curators at the National Air and Space Museum understood better than most that historical commemorations are socially constructed and often contested events. At stake in such commemorations is nothing less than the control of history itself, or at least the process by which historical representation gives voice to the past. The question is: Whose voice will be heard? In addressing this question the curators knew they were walking a "tightrope," to borrow a word from Tom D. Crouch, chair of the museum's aeronautics department and a leading figure in the *Enola Gay* controversy. "On both sides of the Pacific, the sensitivities on this subject run very deep," he said. "There's very little middle ground." Crouch's colleagues agreed. "When we began discussions of the exhibit," Martin O. Harwit, the museum's director, told a reporter for the *Baltimore Sun*, "there were two points everyone agreed on. One, this is a historically significant aircraft. Two, no matter what the museum did, we'd screw it up."[4]

Harwit worried from the beginning about Japan's reaction to the proposed exhibit and was anxious to include a Japanese voice in the Smithsonian's plans. Early in 1994, Crouch and other curators met with a delegation of Japanese officials from Hiroshima and Nagasaki. The Smithsonian hoped for their cooperation in the commemoration, particularly the contribution of a number of artifacts that could illustrate the awesome power of the atomic bomb

4 Robert L. Koenigk, "Enola Gay Display Evokes Passion," *St. Louis Post-Dispatch*, 9 June 1994, A1; Maurice Weaver, "Japanese Upset by A-Bomb Exhibition," *Daily Telegraph*, 7 January 1994, 14. See also Hirsch, "Deadly Courier Retains Its Place in History," *Baltimore Sun*, 24 March 1994, A1.

and the death and destruction it had brought to Japan. For their part, the Japanese did not want the exhibit to glorify the atomic assault on their homeland or arouse anti-Japanese sentiments in the United States. One Japanese resident in Washington wrote the mayor of Hiroshima that the *Enola Gay* belonged in "the Holocaust Museum," not in the Air and Space Museum. Japanese-Americans had similar concerns, which officials at the Smithsonian tried to assuage. The proposed exhibit, they explained on every occasion, would "reflect all the many arguments" about the atomic bombing of Hiroshima and Nagasaki. To be sure, it would be "an American exhibition," said Michael J. Neufeld, the exhibit's principal curator, but it would nonetheless "present all the differing views."[5]

It was this aspect of the Smithsonian's plan that got it into so much trouble with American veterans of the Second World War. Neufeld had said at the start that he and his collaborators "must be careful not to offend our own veterans." But this was going to be difficult if the curators also acknowledged Japanese concerns and perceptions or addressed some of the controversial issues that have bothered historians for years, which is exactly what they decided to do. For example, early drafts of the exhibit's script dealt with the diplomatic as well as the strategic aspects of Truman's decision to use the atomic bomb, especially with whether that decision had been driven in part by a desire to intimidate the Soviet Union with American military power. They also presented evidence on the degree to which Truman's decision might have been motivated by racist perceptions of the Japanese and by a desire to avenge the Japanese attack on Pearl Harbor. They summarized recent historical studies that question whether an invasion of Japan would have cost hundreds of thousands of American and Japanese lives, and they asked if the atomic bombing of Hiroshima and Nagasaki was the only alternative to such an invasion. Might the Japanese have been induced to surrender by a test demonstration of the bomb, by Soviet entry into the war, or by revising the American demand for unconditional surrender in order to safe-

5 Weaver, "Japanese Upset by A-Bomb Exhibition," *Daily Telegraph*, 7 January 1994, 14; Hirsch, "Deadly Courier Retains Its Place in History," *Baltimore Sun*, 24 March 1994, A1.

guard the position of the Japanese emperor? Historians have been dealing with these difficult issues since 1945, and the curators wanted those who viewed the exhibit to tackle them as well. Visitors would be encouraged to take sides in the historiographical debates, as the curators themselves appeared to do in certain cases. They seemed convinced, for example, that diplomatic considerations had played a part in Truman's decision, and they had their doubts about whether the atomic bomb was the best way to end the war. "In the end," said Neufeld, "there's still a case to be made that the bomb was a better alternative than invading, but it's not as clear-cut as some would say. . . . There are a lot more questions and unknowns."[6]

For the curators, in other words, the exhibit would be much more than a display of historical artifacts; it would be an exercise in historical thinking. Besides the motives behind Truman's decision, they wanted visitors to view that decision less in the context of the Pacific war, more as prelude to the postwar era, and to grapple with its consequences. As a result, the exhibit would begin with the last year of the war, by which time the Japanese were clearly on the defensive. From this beginning, visitors would move through a second section of the exhibit on the American decision to drop the bomb and a third section on the wartime bombing of Japan and the training of the 509th Composite Group, an elite corps of Army Air Force crewmen that included the crew of the *Enola Gay*. This section would feature the fuselage of the *Enola Gay* and a replica of the "Little Boy" atomic bomb it dropped on Hiroshima. The fourth section would constitute the "emotional center" of the exhibit. It would illustrate the destruction at Ground Zero with life-size pictures of Japanese dead and wounded, personal narratives of those who survived, and a variety of artifacts, including a watch with its hands frozen on the moment when the bomb exploded over Hiroshima. A final section would focus on the nuclear arms race that followed the war. This section would speak to the children and

6 See the sources cited in the previous footnote. See also two scripts for "The Last Act," one finished in late May 1994 and the other in late August, in the files of the Organization of American Historians, Bloomington, Indiana (hereafter OAH Files). I am grateful to Arnita Jones, executive secretary of the OAH, for sharing these and other documents with me. My account of the controversy also draws on the first and last scripts of the exhibit, which are in my own possession.

grandchildren of those who had lived through World War II, for whom Hiroshima and Nagasaki marked the start of a fabulously expensive arms race with "megaton warheads, the DEW line, 45-minute warnings, first strike, Mutually Assured Destruction," radio-active fallout, and the danger of nuclear winter. "Part of the purpose of the exhibition," Crouch told National Public Radio, was "to get people to think about the origins" of the "nuclear age and every-thing that's come with it over the past half-century."[7]

Veterans envisioned a different history altogether. While the cu-rators wanted visitors to analyze the Hiroshima bombing and wres-tle with the horrors of war and the dangers of a nuclear arms race, veterans wanted an exhibit that commemorated the sacrifices they had made in a just cause. From their perspective, these sacrifices would be obscured by the exhibit's emphasis on the last year of the struggle, on the death and destruction at Ground Zero, and on the role that diplomatic considerations, racism, and the spirit of ven-geance had played in Truman's decision. Instead of commemorat-ing their sacrifices, the exhibit, in their opinion, would portray the Japanese as victims of American aggression and the atomic bomb-ings as unnecessary, wrongful acts. The Smithsonian's plans were an "insult to every soldier, sailor, marine and airman who fought the war against Japan," complained W. Burr Bennett, Jr., a veteran from Illinois. "They're trying to evaluate everything in the context of today's beliefs," explained Brigadier General Paul Tibbets, who flew the *Enola Gay* on that fateful day, and it's "a damn big insult." Instead of taking up the questions that historians have debated, Bennett, Tibbets, and other veterans urged the Smithso-nian to display the bomber "proudly and patriotically," much as it displayed the Wright Brothers' first airplane or Lindberg's *Spirit of St. Louis*.[8]

As the veterans saw it, the curators were recounting the end of

7 National Public Radio, *Morning Edition*, script for 9 August 1994, OAH Files. See also the layout of the proposed exhibition in *New York Times*, 5 February 1995, E5.

8 Hirsch, "Deadly Courier Retains Its Place in History," *Baltimore Sun*, 24 March 1994, A1; "Plan to Display First Nuclear Bomber Stirs Ire," *Rocky Mountain News*, 23 June 1994, A30; Mike Christensen, "New Attitudes on Display: Changing Focus at Smithso-nian Upsets Some Traditionalists," *Atlanta Journal and Constitution*, 3 May 1994, A4. See also Mario Battista (past commander of the American Legion Post 79, New Port Richey, Florida), "What was Crueler than the Enola Gay? Japan at War," *St. Petersburg Times*, 5 September 1994, 2.

the war from a perspective that privileged a Japanese narrative over their own experience. They were particularly offended by the curators' decision to emphasize the destruction at Hiroshima and Nagasaki. Neufeld and Crouch could not imagine an exhibit that stopped "the story when the bomb leaves the bomb bay." Veterans, Crouch complained, were reluctant to "tell the whole story." Not so, said Bennett. What troubled the veterans was the exhibit's "accent on the effects of the bombing rather than the fact that the bombing ended the war in nine days." By stressing the death and destruction at Ground Zero, the exhibit, according to the veterans, made the Japanese look like victims. "It will leave you with the impression that you have to feel sorry for those poor Japanese," said Tibbets, "because they were only defending their way of life." Still worse, the curators' perspective made American soldiers look like ruthless aggressors rather than selfless heroes. "History has been denigrated," Tibbets complained. "The *Enola Gay* has been miscast and a group of valiant Americans . . . have been denied a historically correct representation to the public." Other veterans made the same point. Manny Horowitz, a B-29 navigator, did not want "school children and their parents born after World War II" to leave the exhibit "with a distorted and incorrect understanding of this important part of our country's history." Ben Nicks, another B-29 pilot who flew his last mission on the day of the Hiroshima bombing, was more specific. The *Enola Gay* was a symbol to generations for whom World War II was only a memory, said Nicks, and he and other veterans wanted a symbol "that reflects credit on us."[9]

To veterans and other critics it was especially galling to see the Air and Space Museum discounting the experiences of those who had lived through the war and whose collective memories supposedly added up to the nation's history. "Let the Smithsonian listen to the voices of those who fought," said the son of a war veteran,

9 "Smithsonian's Plans for Enola Gay Assailed," *Arizona Republic*, 8 May 1994, A21; "Plan to Display First Nuclear Bomber Stirs Ire," *Rocky Mountain News*, 23 June 1994, A30; Thomas B. Allen, "Flying into Controversy," *Phoenix Gazette*, 6 August 1994, B13; Horowitz letter to the editor, *Washington Post*, 14 August 1994, C9. See also Christensen, "New Attitudes on Display," *Atlanta Journal and Constitution*, 3 May 1994, A4; and Guy Gugliotta, "Air and Space Exhibit Gets Flak Even before Takeoff," *Washington Post*, 31 May 1994, A15.

not to historians who would "place the legacy" of the veterans in "a specific ideological camp." Historians had no business challenging "the views of history of those who actually lived it." They could "read the words of their research," but they could not interpret that research "in the atmosphere of the past." By ignoring the authentic voices of the past, according to the critics, the curators had failed to properly contextualize the bombing of Hiroshima and Nagasaki. They had ignored the record of Japan's aggression, the brutality of its war policy, and the fanaticism of its soldiers. Most importantly, they had failed to appreciate how Truman's decision to drop the bomb had saved countless lives that would have been spent in an American invasion of the Japanese home islands.[10]

Anthony Sokolowski, a veteran from Orlando, was offended when he heard a "Smithsonian intellectual historian" report on television that only forty-six thousand Americans would have been killed or injured in an invasion of Japan, not the hundreds of thousands commonly assumed. His LST was scheduled for the invasion and his life "might have been one of the ONLY 46,000 lives cut short on that day." Other veterans felt the same way. Glenn McConnell, a retired air force pilot, "was a POW in Tokyo that August" and could say from experience what the facts were: The bomb saved thousands of lives, "including Japanese lives." Another veteran of the Pacific war wrote his newspaper that "in 1945, instead of invading Japan, I went home." Hal King, whose artillery battalion was scheduled for the invasion, was told by his commanding officer to expect fanatical Japanese resistance and the loss of more than half of his comrades. "We were convinced that this would be our last landing and that we would die on the beaches," King wrote the *Wall Street Journal*. James Potter, a navy veteran whose cruiser had been torpedoed in 1944, made a similar point in a letter to the same newspaper. "The A-bomb saved hundreds of thousands of my compatriots from death or injury in the projected home-island invasion," he wrote. "I'm so glad my friend

10 David J. Smollar, "A War of Words . . . over World War II," *San Diego Union-Tribune*, 1 December 1994, B11; Frank E. Maestrone letter to the editor, ibid., 16 October 1994, G3. See also unsigned letter to the editor, *Pittsburgh Post-Gazette*, 22 December 1994, C3; and Battista, "What was Crueler than Enola Gay? Japan at War," *St. Petersburg Times*, 5 September 1994, 2.

Pat DiGiacomo, who survived the Bataan Death March and spent four years of the war as a slave working in the coal mines in northern Japan, is no longer alive to hear the drivel" coming from the Smithsonian.[11] The same message came from veterans of the Bataan march when they met for their annual reunion, from representatives of the Jewish War Veterans of the U.S.A., from the surviving members of the 509th Composite Group when they held a four-day reunion at the Fairmount Hotel in Chicago, and from a group of B-29 bomber pilots who gathered in front of a war memorial in Battery Park City, New York, to protest the Smithsonian's proposed exhibit.[12]

As these narratives attest, the Smithsonian's exhibit struck not only at the historical memories of American veterans but also at their sense of personal and national identity. They wanted the exhibit to reflect credit on them, to convey an image of themselves as heroes who had risked their lives in a great struggle, not as racist, vindictive warriors. Such an unambiguous narrative was not easily squared with doubts about the necessity of Truman's decision or with an analysis of the motives behind that decision, the alternative strategies for ending the war, and the human cost at Ground Zero. Nor was it easy for veterans to reconcile such an analysis with their image of themselves as Americans. Many of their letters, which poured into newspapers by the dozens, stressed how the bombing of Hiroshima and Nagasaki had saved Japanese lives, not just American lives. In this sense it was an act of mercy that defined Americans as different from the Japanese, and the United States as unique among nations. "For all of our faults," Robert Wilcox wrote the editor of the *Los Angeles Times*, "we have been a kind and just people. We don't boil captives alive as the Japanese did. We don't hold Inquisitions like the Spanish, nor

11 Sokolowski letter to the editor, *Orlando Sentinel*, 11 October 1994, A8; McConnell letter to the editor, *Washington Post*, 14 August 1994, C9; Matthew H. Portz letter to the editor, *Los Angeles Times*, 1 January 1995, E5; King letter to the editor, *Wall Street Journal*, 7 October 1994, A11; Potter letter to the editor, ibid., 12 September 1994, A17.

12 Janine DeFao, "Death March Survivors Remember the Horror," *Sacramento Bee*, 17 October 1994, B1; Eugene L. Meyer and Eric Brace, "Seeking the Survivors," *Washington Post*, 5 December 1994, B7; William Mullen, "WWII Airmen Gather in Storm," *Chicago Tribune*, 2 September 1994, A1; Susan Price, "NY Protest of Bomb Exhibit," *Newsday*, 26 September 1994, A8.

Holocausts like the Germans. We were the first victors not to rape and pillage. Instead, we built up Japan in the Occupation and did the same for Germany through the Marshall Plan." Herbert Jaffe struck the same theme of American exceptionalism in a letter to *Newsday*. The curators, he said, were missing a great opportunity "to show that American compassion is unique among nations." The United States did not seek vengeance or reparations or territory after World War II, but "showed the finest example of reconciliation and magnanimity." It rebuilt the defeated aggressors and "bestowed upon them a monumental gift, the American democratic political system."[13]

III

More was at stake in the controversy than whose history would be told in the Smithsonian's exhibition; involved as well was a struggle to dominate the process of historical representation. The veterans and their supporters aligned themselves on one side of this struggle. Burr Bennett helped to organize the Committee for the Restoration and Display of the *Enola Gay*. Composed of veterans who had flown B-29s during the war, the committee responded to what it heard about the exhibit by circulating protest petitions across the country. By April 1994, Bennett had gathered more than nine thousand signatures. The committee wanted the Smithsonian to abandon its plans for a historical analysis of Truman's decision and its consequences, display the *Enola Gay* without commentary, or give it to a museum that would.[14] Joining Bennett and his associates was the Air Force Association and its publication, *Air Force Magazine*. The association's executive director, retired Air Force General Monroe W. Hatch, Jr., had learned of the Smithsonian's exhibit in late 1993 and had complained to Harwit that it treated Japanese and American war strategies as if they "were morally

---

13 Wilcox letter to the editor, *Los Angeles Times*, 1 January 1995, E5; Jaffe letter to the editor, *Newsday*, 25 October 1994, A35.

14 Hirsch, "Deadly Courier Retains Its Place in History," *Baltimore Sun*, 24 March 1994, A1; Christensen, "New Attitudes on Display," *Atlanta Journal and Constitution*, 3 May 1994, A4; "Smithsonian's Plans for Enola Gay Assailed," *Arizona Republic*, 8 May 1994, A21; Battista, "What was Crueler than Enola Gay? Japan at War," *St. Petersburg Times*, 5 September 1994, 2.

equivalent." During a meeting with Harwit in January 1994, Hatch and John T. Correll, editor-in-chief of *Air Force Magazine*, expressed their concerns and asked to see an early, incomplete version of the exhibit's script. In March, after reviewing the script, the Air Force Association issued a press release criticizing the proposed exhibit. Correll accused the Smithsonian of "politically correct curating." The exhibit, he said in the April issue of *Air Force Magazine*, lacked context and balance, particularly the emotionally loaded section on the destruction at Hiroshima and Nagasaki. By concentrating on the last six months of the war, the exhibit ignored the record of Japan's aggression in the 1930s, not to mention its surprise attack on Pearl Harbor. It made the Japanese look like embattled patriots who were merely defending their country against a vindictive American assault that was racially motivated and unnecessarily brutal.[15]

On the other side of the controversy stood the curators at the National Air and Space Museum and their allies among professional historians. From their point of view, the exhibit should represent historical reality, more than personal memory, and should be framed by professional historians, rather than veterans. The curators, in other words, responded to their critics by citing professional authority and defending their right to guide the process of historical representation. The Smithsonian had "no thought of apologizing for Hiroshima and Nagasaki," Harwit asserted, but at the same time it aimed at an accurate historical account that went beyond the personal perceptions of American veterans. The curators wanted to be "true to the documented facts." Their goal was to "tell the full story surrounding the atomic bomb and the end of World War II," which meant balancing personal narratives against "the reality of atomic war and its consequences."[16]

With this goal in mind, Crouch told the *St. Louis Post-Dispatch*,

15 Gugliotta, "Air and Space Exhibit Gets Flak Even before Takeoff," *Washington Post*, 31 May 1994, A15. See also Correll, "War Stories at Air and Space," *Air Force Magazine* (April 1994): 24–9; and John R. Dichtl, "A Chronology of the Smithsonian's 'Last Act,' " *OAH Newsletter* (November 1994): 9-10.
16 Hirsch, "Deadly Courier Retains Its Place in History," *Baltimore Sun*, 24 March 1994, 1A; Harwit, "Enola Gay and a Nation's Memories," *Air & Space* (August/September 1994): 18, 20–1; idem, "The Enola Gay: A Nation's and a Museum's Dilemma," *Washington Post*, 7 August 1994, OAH Files. See also Harwit letter to the editor, *Air Force Magazine* (May 1994): 4.

the curators had gone to extraordinary lengths to solicit expert advice in drafting the exhibit's script. Harwit drove the same point home on several occasions. The Smithsonian had been guided by an advisory group of distinguished scholars, he said. The group included Edwin Bearss, chief historian of the National Park Service and a veteran of the Second World War; Barton Bernstein, a professor of history at Stanford University who had written widely on U.S. atomic policy; Victor Bond, a doctor with the Brookhaven National Laboratory who specialized in radiation effects; Stanley Goldberg, an expert on the history of the Manhattan Project that produced the first atomic weapons; Richard Hallion, chief historian of the U.S. Air Force; Akira Iriye, a professor at Harvard University who specialized in Japanese-American relations; Edward Linenthal, a professor at the University of Wisconsin at Oshkosh and an expert on American war memorials; Richard Rhodes, author of the Pulitzer Prize-winning book *The Making of the Atomic Bomb*; and Martin Sherwin of Dartmouth College, another specialist on the history of the atomic bomb.[17]

The Smithsonian tried to bolster its own authority, and the credibility of its exhibit, by citing the authority of these distinguished historians. A press release, for example, included favorable comments by members of the advisory board. "A most impressive piece of work," said Hallion, "comprehensive and dramatic, obviously based upon a great deal of sound research, primary and secondary." Bernstein thought the script "reflected the current scholarship on the war" and was "fair, balanced, and historically informed." Iriye praised its "judicious" interpretation of "controversial events."[18] "Everybody signed off on it," said Tom Crouch, himself a published scholar with a doctorate in history from The Ohio State University. The other curators were similarly credentialed. Michael Neufeld, for example, was a specialist in European history and German rocketry, while Martin Harwit had been a professor of astronomy at Cornell University and a member of

17 Ken Ringle, "At Ground Zero: Two Views of History Collide over Smithsonian A-Bomb Exhibit," *Washington Post*, 26 September 1994, A1; Harwit letter to the editor, *Air Force Magazine* (May 1994): 4; idem, "Enola Gay and a Nation's Memories," *Air & Space* (August/September 1994): 18, 20–1.
18 See the news release enclosed in Neufeld to Arnita Jones (OAH executive secretary), 17 August 1994, OAH Files. See also Bernstein to Harwit, 23 May 1994, OAH Files.

NASA's Astrophysics Management Working Group before taking over the directorship of the Smithsonian's Air and Space Museum. The script had the advantage of this combined authority, the Smithsonian seemed to imply, and was therefore a reasonable and balanced document. As proof, Crouch defended the script not only against conservative critics in the Air Force Association but also against Professor Sherwin of Dartmouth, a historian on the "left" who thought that any exhibit of the *Enola Gay* was obscene and would tend to glorify the bombing of Hiroshima and Nagasaki.[19]

Critics quickly challenged the Smithsonian's claim to authority. For one reason or another, they did not view the curators or their historical consultants as disinterested experts. Perhaps it was because their version of history contrasted so sharply with the lived experience of American veterans, whose personal narratives, according to the critics, constituted a collective memory of unimpeachable authority. Perhaps it was because Bernstein and Sherwin were "revisionist" historians who had long been critical of Truman's decision to use the atomic bomb, or because the curators had taken sides in some of the historiographical controversies covered in the exhibit. Perhaps it was because Iriye was a native of Japan, or because Neufeld was a Canadian citizen, or because Harwit had been born in Prague and raised in Istanbul, or because neither Neufeld nor Crouch had served in the armed forces. At least some of the criticism seemed to imply that the exhibit was tainted with un-Americanism. Then, too, the advisory committee had not written the scripts; it had been consulted and the extent of its involvement was the subject of dispute. The committee had gathered only once, and not all of its members could attend the meeting. They kept no record of their discussion, and it was never clear if they had seen or approved the script in all of its variations. Even more important, the consultants themselves apparently disagreed. As noted above, Martin Sherwin of Dartmouth had criticized the original script for glorifying the atomic bombing of Hiroshima and Nagasaki. Even more important was the position taken

19   Ringle, "At Ground Zero," *Washington Post*, 26 September 1994, A1. See also Koenigk, "Enola Gay Display Evokes Passion," *St. Louis Post-Dispatch*, 9 June 1994, 1A; and Correll, "Three Doctors and the Enola Gay," *Air Force Magazine* (November 1994): 8–10, 12.

by Dr. Richard Hallion of the Air Force. The Smithsonian said that Hallion had endorsed the script, and quoted him accordingly, but Hallion argued later that he was consulted only after the first script was finished, at which point the curators dismissed his proposals for fundamental revisions.[20]

Divisions on the advisory board undermined the Smithsonian's efforts to place the expertise of historians over the memory of veterans, the historical document over the personal narrative. Nor was that the worst of it. Disagreement among the curators also raised doubts about their claim to authority and their right to assert their views over those of their critics. Even as the first script was being prepared, the *Washington Post* reported, Smithsonian Secretary Robert McCormick Adams and museum director Harwit had apparently expressed concerns about whether the decision to bomb Hiroshima and Nagasaki was sufficiently contextualized. Harwit raised the same concern in April 1994, as the script was being revised. "We do have a lack of balance," he told the curators; "much of the criticism leveled against us is understandable." Harwit established a so-called Tiger Team of staff advisers to scrutinize the second draft, which the curators finished in mid-May. This process led to additional changes in light of the team's report, but not enough to satisfy the critics.[21]

"There is [more] work to be done," said an official of the Retired Officers Association, which claimed four hundred thousand members. He and other veterans, including Paul Tibbets, still considered the exhibit to be "a pack of insults." To their way of thinking, the curators at Air and Space had hijacked the history of World War II. They had reinterpreted that war in a way that defied the experience of American veterans and gave far too much credence to the Japanese point of view. Hallion, by now a leading critic, had the "overall impression, even from this revised script," that the Japanese, "despite 15 years of aggression, atrocities and brutality, were the victims." Correll agreed. Although Harwit de-

20 Ringle, "At Ground Zero," *Washington Post*, 26 September 1994, A1. See also Eugene Meyer, "Dropping the Bomb," ibid., 21 July 1994, C2; Dichtl, "A Chronology of the Smithsonian's 'Last Act,'" *OAH Newsletter* (November 1994): 9–10; and Correll, "Three Doctors and the Enola Gay," *Air Force Magazine* (November 1994): 8–10, 12.
21 Meyer, "Dropping the Bomb," *Washington Post*, 21 July 1994, C2. See also Ringle, "At Ground Zero," ibid., 26 September 1994, A1.

214 The Enola Gay Controversy

fended the revised script as a balanced account that would allow visitors to "draw their own conclusions," Correll saw it as "a partisan interpretation." It still lacked sufficient context, he explained in the *Washington Post* and in a report to the Air Force Association, and still gave too much attention to the "crackpot theories" promoted by historians, including the notion that Truman's decision might have been motivated by vindictiveness, by racism, or by a desire to influence Soviet diplomacy. In addition, Correll was still convinced that the exhibit put too much emphasis on death and destruction at Ground Zero and too little on Japanese aggression and the suffering of Japan's victims, including American soldiers and prisoners of war. The last section of the exhibit on the postwar legacy of Hiroshima and Nagasaki also showed little regard, in Correll's words, for "military perspectives" on a "military subject." It dismissed the notion that nuclear deterrence had made war between the superpowers impossible, while giving too much attention to the waste, contamination, and cost involved in the nuclear arms race. Most of all, Correll, Hallion, and other critics resented the reluctance of the Smithsonian to acknowledge what they considered to be the principal military justification for Truman's decision to use the atomic bomb: It ended the war and saved hundreds of thousands of Japanese and American lives. The curators, Hallion said, were "still pushing the thesis that the atomic bomb shouldn't have been dropped."[22]

Much of the controversy now centered on whether the atomic bombing of Hiroshima and Nagasaki was the only alternative to an Allied invasion of Japan and on the number of Allied and Japanese casualties that were expected in such an invasion. Despite earlier criticism on this point, the curators continued to advance the possibility that American casualties might have been much fewer than the original postwar estimates had suggested, involving

22 Meyer, "Dropping the Bomb," *Washington Post*, 21 July 1994, C2; Harwit, "Enola Gay and a Nation's Memories," *Air & Space* (August/September 1994): 18, 20–1; Tony Snow, "Sanitizing the Flight of the Enola Gay," *USA Today*, 1 August 1994, A11; "The Mission That Ended the War," *Washington Post*, 14 August 1994, C9; Correll, "'The Last Act' at Air and Space," *Air Force Magazine* (September 1994): 58–64. Correll had earlier circulated "'The Last Act'" as "The Smithsonian Plan for the Enola Gay: A Report on the Revisions" to the publisher and staff of *Air Force Magazine*. See the copy in the OAH Files.

perhaps as few as sixty-three thousand soldiers. The higher estimates, ranging upward to five hundred thousand, had always provided moral as well as military justification for Truman's decision,
and challenging those estimates led critics, especially veterans, to
see the exhibit as an unbalanced assault on the righteousness of the
American cause. "It is totally skewed," said the Air Force Association. It "basically ignores all the figures which have been produced
to show how many people would have died invading Japan." Historians, according to Tibbets, might look "to the ashes of Hiroshima and Nagasaki to find answers for the use of those atomic
weapons." But the "real answers lay in the thousands of graves
from Pearl Harbor around the world to Normandy and back
again. The actual use of the weapons . . . was believed to be the
quickest and least costly . . . way to stop the killing." In May, the
executive committee of the American Legion adopted a resolution
objecting to an exhibit that questioned the moral and political
wisdom of dropping the atomic bombs or condemned the American airmen who carried out the last act of the war.[23]

IV

With the Air Force Association, the American Legion, and the
Retired Officers Association involved, it was not long before Congress also got involved in what had now become a political struggle to control the proposed exhibit. Republican Senator Nancy
Kassebaum of Kansas had warned the Smithsonian in the spring
not to proceed with an exhibit that offended American veterans.
Then in August, Republican Representative Peter Blute of Massachusetts led a bipartisan group of twenty-four representatives who
denounced the proposed exhibit as "anti-American." The representatives also described the exhibit script as "biased, lacking in context, and therefore unacceptable." They warned the Smithsonian
to provide "an objective accounting of the *Enola Gay* and her

23 Ian Katz, "Hiroshima Row Hits US Museum," *Guardian*, 22 July 1994, 12; "Exhibit
Plans on Hiroshima Stir a Debate," *New York Times*, 28 August 1994, A25; Allen,
"Flying into Controversy," *Phoenix Gazette*, 6 August 1994, B13. See also Larry
Miller (president of the Air Force Association of Texas), "Don't Distort History of A-
Bombing," *Dallas Morning News*, 14 August 1994, 6J; and Brian D. Smith, "Rewrit-
ing Enola Gay's History," *American Legion* (November 1994): 26–9, 68, 70.

mission," or face the consequences, which might include a congressional investigation and a reduction of federal funding for the Smithsonian.[24]

By this time leading newspapers and editorial writers had also entered the controversy, which gained fresh attention with the forty-ninth anniversary of the Hiroshima bombing in August 1994. Their involvement heightened the political stakes in the *Enola Gay* controversy. It linked that controversy to the larger "culture wars" and spelled bad news to those who thought the Smithsonian should have an independent voice in shaping historical consciousness. To be sure, an occasional commentary defended the curators at the Air and Space Museum. The *New York Times* compared them to their counterparts at the Peace Memorial Museum in Hiroshima, who had been trying in new exhibits to counter the popular perception of Japan as a victim in World War II.[25] The *St. Louis Post-Dispatch* made the same comparison. Although critical of the exhibit's original script, the *Post-Dispatch* complained more about "meddlesome" politicians who sought to impose their orthodoxy on historians. To its way of thinking, both the United States and Japan would benefit from facing the ugly brutality of war.[26] Robert Reno, a columnist for *Newsday*, was even more strident. The bombing of Hiroshima and Nagasaki, he said, was the link between a horrifying war and a host of appalling events that followed. These included the contamination of nuclear test sites, the accumulation of radioactive waste, the tens of thousands of people who were exposed to nuclear fallout, the innocent victims of radioactive experiments conducted by the Atomic Energy Commission and the American military, the billions of dollars wasted on the nuclear arms race, and more. "All in all," Reno wrote, "the Smithsonian Institution would be fully justified in mounting a major exhibit commemorating Hiroshima and the splitting of the atom as events of unspeakable malignity that have brought humanity more grief and loss than the 14th Century plagues."[27]

24 Blute et al. to Secretary Adams, 10 August 1994, OAH Files. See also Theo Lippman, Jr., editorial, *Baltimore Sun*, 15 August 1994, A6; and Dichtl, "A Chronology of the Smithsonian's 'Last Act,' " *OAH Newsletter* (November 1994): 9–10.
25 "Exhibit Plans on Hiroshima Stir a Debate," *New York Times*, 28 August 1994, A25.
26 "A Politically Correct Enola Gay?" *St. Louis Post-Dispatch*, 29 August 1994, B12.
27 Reno, "Business: Reno at Large," *Newsday*, 2 September 1994, A59.

With few exceptions, however, almost every other newspaper and editorial commentator lambasted the curators for rewriting history to denigrate the nation. Sabrina Eaton, writing for the *Plain Dealer*, repeated a charge from Republican Representative Martin Hoke of Ohio, who accused the curators of "writing revisionist history to give a black eye to the United States and somehow cast Japan in the role of victim of World War II."[28] James G. Driscoll of the Fort Lauderdale *Sun Sentinel* also denounced the "Foggy revisionists" who "distort history," as did Jeff Jacoby of the *Boston Globe*, who criticized the Smithsonian for airing revisionist points of view on such controversial issues as the "Soviet factor" or the role of race in American foreign policy. In addition, Jacoby and others hammered away at how the atomic bomb had ended the war without an Allied invasion that would have cost perhaps five hundred thousand American and two million Japanese lives.[29] The Smithsonian was more interested in "social commentary," argued Marianne Means in an editorial for the *Plain Dealer*, than in the truth that Truman's decision had shortened the war and saved lives. Means wanted to know how the country could trust an institution that postured "as moral arbiter and re-writer of history." How could it trust curators and historians who "seemed mostly interested in registering opinions framed by subsequent political and philosophical developments" – who imposed "today's morality on yesterday's war?"[30]

For the *Wall Street Journal* and its conservative allies, including Correll and *Air Force Magazine*, the *Enola Gay* exhibit was only the latest indication of the Smithsonian's "mania for revising American history."[31] They blasted the Air and Space Museum for an earlier exhibit that took a critical look at air power in the First World War and the postwar legacy of strategic bombing. They singled out the National Museum of American Art for an exhibit on the American West that supposedly debunked the pioneering

28 Eaton, "Proposed Show Irks Bipartisan Coalition," *Plain Dealer*, 13 August 1994, B7.
29 Driscoll, "Before Passing Judgment on Past Decisions It's a Good Idea to Study History," *Sun Sentinel*, 14 August 1994, G7; Jacoby, "Smithsonian Drops a Bomb in World War II Exhibit," *Boston Globe*, 16 August 1994, A14.
30 Means, "The Nation's Attic – Historian or Moralizer?" *Plain Dealer*, 27 August 1994, B9.
31 "War and the Smithsonian," *Wall Street Journal*, 29 August 1994, A10.

spirit, characterized American settlers "as rapacious brutes," and portrayed "the founding and development of America generally as a criminal capitalist venture." They also attacked the Museum of American History for celebrating the two hundredth anniversary of the U.S. Constitution with an exhibit on the internment of Japanese-Americans during World War II; for an exhibit on science in American life that focused on such "failures and dangers" as Three Mile Island, Love Canal, and acid rain; and for an exhibit on America from 1780 to 1800 that treated Indians, blacks, and Europeans as "three equally excellent cultures."[32] The *Tampa Tribune* castigated the Smithsonian's Museum of Natural History for closing a display on the "Origins of People" because it depicted the natives of ancient cultures as less worthy than Europeans – even though "European nations were further developed" than most of the people they "encountered during their explorations." The *Tribune* made the same point about the museum's decision to revise exhibits that depicted male mammals as superior to females. "The fact is that the male mammal is usually larger than the female," the *Tribune* explained. "The mate-seeking male needs to fend off competitors" while the "young-bearing female needs to be less visible to predators."[33]

According to critics in the press and elsewhere, "elite American museums" had joined modern intellectuals to redefine American history in a way that assaulted traditional values. The villains in this story were usually lumped together as revisionists, postmodernists, and politically correct thinkers who believed that objective truth was unattainable and who therefore promoted a version of truth that squared with the "current cannons of political virtue and related humbug." For the *Wall Street Journal* and conservative editorial writers like Charles Krauthammer, Robert Park, John Leo, and Pat Buchanan, "the forces of political correctness and

32 Ibid.; John Leo, "PC Propaganda at Smithsonian: More Examples," *Orlando Sentinel*, 4 October 1994, A7. See also Correll, "War Stories at Air and Space: At the Smithsonian, History Grapples with Cultural Angst," *Air Force Magazine* (April 1994): 24–9; Charles Krauthammer, "World War II Revised: Or, How We Bombed Japan out of Racism and Spite," *Washington Post*, 19 August 1994, A27; and Robert L. Park, "Science Fiction: The Smithsonian's Disparaging Look at Technological Advancement," ibid., 25 September 1994, G2.
33 "Incoming GOP Congress Should Shake Some Cages at Smithsonian," *Tampa Tribune*, 16 December 1994, 18.

historical revisionism" were "unable to view American history as anything other than a woeful catalog of crimes and aggressions against the helpless peoples of the earth."[34] Buchanan linked the *Enola Gay* exhibit to the National Standards developed by Professor Gary Nash of UCLA and other historians as a guide to teaching American and world history. Involved in both cases, Buchanan said, was "a sleepless campaign to inculcate in American youth a revulsion toward America's past." "Secure in tenure," the "UCLA crowd" and its allies in universities and museums across the country were serving a diet of "anti-Americanism" that denied the country's "greatness and glory."[35]

Other commentators picked up the same point in editorials that defended American exceptionalism against the "exhibit commissars" at the Smithsonian.[36] Ken Ringle, writing in the *Washington Post*, described the controversy as "a tug of war" between "the way mainstream America views American history and the way it is viewed in many academic circles."[37] Kevin O'Brien, in an editorial for the *Plain Dealer*, saw the *Enola Gay* exhibit as part of a larger effort by the Smithsonian and its collaborators "to change the way Americans look at the world" – to promote what he called a "paradigm shift." Whereas most Americans considered their country "the greatest nation on Earth," a nation that "has done most things right," the Smithsonian "asks us to think of . . . our country as just another name on the world map, of our culture as nothing special in comparison with others and of our political system as just one of many competing and even interchangeable options."[38] O'Brien's argument echoed a theme stressed by many veterans. As noted earlier, they, too, castigated the Smithsonian for ignoring the

---

34 Krauthammer, "World War II, Revised," *Washington Post*, 19 August 1994, A27; "War and the Smithsonian," *Wall Street Journal*, 29 August 1994, A10. See also "Context and the Enola Gay," *Washington Post*, 14 August 1994, C8; Park, "Science Fiction," ibid., 25 September 1994, G2; and Leo, "PC Propaganda at Smithsonian," *Orlando Sentinel*, 4 October 1994, A7.

35 Buchanan, "History 'Standards' Slander American Culture," *Arizona Republic*, 6 November 1994, E5. The *New York Times* rightly viewed the whole controversy as a continuation of the "culture wars" launched by political conservatives who wanted to "throttle scholarly and artistic expression" with which they disagreed. See "The Smithsonian and the Bomb," *New York Times*, 5 September 1994, A16.

36 Kevin O'Brien, "Spare the Apologies," *Plain Dealer*, 28 August 1994, C1.

37 Ringle, "At Ground Zero," *Washington Post*, 26 September 1994, A1.

38 O'Brien, "Spare the Apologies," *Plain Dealer*, 28 August 1994, C1.

unique goodness of the American cause in World War II and for
slighting the courage and self-sacrifice of the soldiers who had
fought and died in that noble venture.

Reeling from this kind of criticism, the Smithsonian decided, in
effect, to negotiate history with its critics. It decided to further revise
the script along lines suggested by the critics and to reconceptualize
the entire exhibit. The revised plan, finished in August, called for a
new section entitled "War in the Pacific: An American Perspective."
Visitors would pass through this display before entering the original
exhibit on the atomic bombing of Hiroshima and Nagasaki. Designed to contextualize the last months of the struggle, the new
section would cover four thousand square feet and include approximately fifty photographs showing events leading up to Hiroshima,
including the Japanese attack on Pearl Harbor and examples of
Japanese aggression. The new display was clearly designed to assuage critics who wanted Hiroshima and Nagasaki set against the
backdrop of the whole war, who wanted Japanese suffering balanced against the suffering caused by Japanese aggression, and who
wanted the horror of Hiroshima balanced against the horror of
Japanese atrocities in the Pacific and Asia. With the same objective
in mind, the curators revised the balance of the script as well. They
included fewer pictures of Japanese casualties, more of American.
They also reduced the number of Ground Zero images, toned down
their coverage of various historiographical controversies, and eliminated much of the speculation about why Truman dropped the
bomb. The revisions amounted to a substantial concession to the
Smithsonian's critics. "We felt that their concerns were valid," said
Harwit, "and we think this new exhibit – coupled with changes
within the original exhibition – addresses those concerns."[39]

At the same time, Harwit sought the backing of the nation's
leading historical associations in conversations in late August with
Michael Kammen, a professor of history at Cornell University,
president-elect of the Organization of American Historians (OAH),

39 "Museum Agrees to Broaden Hiroshima Exhibit," *Sacramento Bee*, 30 August 1994,
    A7. See also the copy of the August script in the OAH Files; Ken Ringle, "A-Bomb
    Exhibit Plan Revamped," *Washington Post*, 30 August 1994, C1; "Smithsonian Alters
    Plans for its Exhibit on Hiroshima Bomb," *New York Times*, 30 August 1994, A17;
    and Correll, "Three Doctors and the Enola Gay," *Air Force Magazine* (November
    1994): 8–10, 12.

and a member of the Smithsonian Council. Together they agreed that Harwit would provide Kammen and the OAH with copies of the latest script. Kammen would review the script and decide if he could write a letter of support to William Rehnquist, chief justice of the Supreme Court and chairman of the Smithsonian's Board of Regents. Harwit sent the revised script to the OAH on 2 September and Kammen followed with a letter to Rehnquist four days later. Writing in his dual capacity as president-elect of the OAH and as a member of the Smithsonian Council, Kammen told Rehnquist that he was "impressed by the historical veracity and quality" of the revised exhibit. He reminded Rehnquist that historians disagreed over such matters as the number of lives that might have been saved by bombing Hiroshima and Nagasaki. He said that it was important to convey the diversity of opinion on such controversial issues, praised the curators for doing so in a "balanced and judicious" manner, and warned that "outside interference by special interest groups, ideological partisans, and politicians" would compromise the exhibit and imperil "academic freedom."[40] A similar warning came in mid-September from the Executive Committee of the Organization of American Historians. In a resolution conveyed to the Smithsonian's Board of Regents by Professor Gary Nash of UCLA, president of the OAH, the executive committee noted that the exhibit's curators had followed "proper professional procedures" and cautioned against any congressional effort to penalize the Smithsonian for its work.[41]

If Harwit and his colleagues thought their revised script, or the support of prominent historians, would obviate the need for more fundamental changes, the initial signals were mixed at best. Tibbets considered the new section on the Pacific war a "plus factor," as did the *New York Times*, which also said that any exhibit on the atomic bombing of Japan must "reflect both the content of the debate" over Truman's decision and "its unresolved nature." The *Times* praised the revised script as balanced in this regard and as the outcome of a

40 Kammen to Rehnquist, 6 September 1994, OAH Files. See also Kammen memorandum to Arnita Jones (OAH executive secretary) and Professor Gary Nash of UCLA (OAH president), 31 August 1994, and Harwit to Jones, 2 September 1994, OAH Files. See also Kammen to the author, 20 May 1995, author's possession.
41 Nash to James M. Hobbins (Office of the Secretary, Smithsonian Institution), 19 September 1994, OAH Files.

professional process that was best left to run its course without "endless tampering" by congressional critics who would be satisfied with nothing less than "complete vilification of the Japanese and uncritical glorification of the American war effort."[42] Correll, on the other hand, attributed the revisions to constant prodding by veterans groups and other critics who continued to demand additional changes.[43] Representative Blute still wanted "a massive revision or rewrite" of the whole exhibit. "Tidying up the front hallway," as he put it, "doesn't erase the fact that the rest of the house is a mess."[44] More ominous still, Nancy Kassebaum introduced a Senate resolution denouncing the revised script as "unbalanced and offensive" and calling for further changes.[45] The same demand came from the American Legion, the nation's largest veterans group, which focused its complaint on the exhibit's reluctance to concede that the atomic bombing of Japan had saved hundreds of thousands of American lives that would have been lost in an invasion of the Japanese home islands.[46]

By the end of September it had become clear that the Smithsonian's strategy had not succeeded. The OAH's intervention had not put the museum's authority beyond question. Nor had revisions and the addition of a new display on the Pacific war assuaged its critics. In a remarkable decision, Harwit agreed to negotiate still additional changes directly with the American Legion. Meeting in late September in a windowless room in the Air and Space Museum, representatives of both sides spent two days in a line-by-line review of the script, after which the curators tried to implement the changes agreed upon. "They drafted pages while we talked," bragged Hubert R. Dagley II, a Legion official who participated in the negotiations. When it was over, the Smithsonian had agreed to erase virtually every hint of the controversy among historians over the American decision to drop the atomic bombs. In addition, the

42 "Smithsonian Alters Plans for Its Exhibit on Hiroshima Bomb," *New York Times*, 30 August 1994, A17; "The Smithsonian and the Bomb," ibid., 5 September 1994, A16.
43 Correll letter to the editor, *New York Times*, 10 September 1994, A18.
44 Ringle, "A-Bomb Exhibit Plan Revamped," *Washington Post*, 30 August 1994, C1.
45 "Senate Angry over Bomber Display," *Toronto Star*, 24 September 1994, D32. See also "Atomic Bomb Exhibit," *Houston Post*, 20 September 1994, A10; "Exhibit Called Offensive," *Pittsburgh Post-Gazette*, 20 September 1994, A6; and "Senator Criticizes Smithsonian Exhibit," *Baltimore Sun*, 20 September 1994, A6.
46 "Senate Angry over Bomber Display," *Toronto Star*, 24 September 1994, D32.

curators made the new display on the Pacific war an integral part of the exhibit and eliminated much of the last section on the postwar world, which, according to the critics, pictured Truman's decision to drop the atomic bomb as the beginning of a reckless nuclear arms race rather than the culmination of a long and costly war. The curators also agreed to reduce still further the number of photographs showing the atomic explosions over Hiroshima and Nagasaki, to eliminate some of the artifacts that captured Japanese suffering at Ground Zero, to rephrase language in order to highlight Japanese aggression, and to add language that seemed to defend the atomic bombings as the only way to end the war without an invasion of Japan that would cost hundreds of thousands of American lives. These changes were finished by the last week in October. At that point Smithsonian officials went over the new script, the fourth since January, with representatives of the Air Force Association and the Retired Officers Association at a meeting in Washington, and then flew to the American Legion's headquarters in Indianapolis to win the blessing of that group as well.[47]

It began to look as if the *New York Times* had been right: The critics would settle for nothing less than an "uncritical glorification of the American war effort."[48] The result was a strong reaction from historians, historical associations, and the organized peace movement. Leaders of the American peace movement had met with Harwit in late September and had urged him to preserve the human face of war and the integrity of the original exhibit. They were outraged when the Smithsonian "caved in" to the more compelling remonstrances of the American Legion. "They are now presenting American Legion propaganda," said John Dear of the Catholic peace group, Pax Christi USA, "an uncritical glorification of the American war effort."[49] By late October, representatives of

47 Eugene L. Meyer, "Smithsonian Bows to Critics, Revamps Atom Bomb Exhibit," *Washington Post*, 30 September 1994, A1; Neil A. Lewis, "Smithsonian Substantially Alters Enola Gay Exhibit after Criticism," *New York Times*, 1 October 1994, A10; Andrea Stone, "Wounds of War Still Color Enola Gay's Place in History," *USA Today*, 5 October 1994, A7; Arthur Hirsch, "Bowing to Pressure, Smithsonian Rewrites Its History of World War II," *Baltimore Sun*, 5 October 1994, D1.
48 "The Smithsonian and the Bomb," *New York Times*, 5 September 1994, A16.
49 Andrea Stone, "A-Bomb Exhibit Still under Fire," *USA Today*, 6 December 1994, A3. See also Joe Becker (executive director, Fellowship of Reconciliation) letter to the editor, *New York Times*, 11 October 1994, A20; and Eugene L. Meyer, "No Peace for

seventeen peace organizations had joined to protest the revisions made in the Smithsonian's original script. While the Smithsonian's curators were hammering out last-minute details with veterans groups in Washington and Indianapolis, the peace groups were demanding another meeting with the curators and were threatening to sponsor an alternative exhibit of documents and photographs that had been removed from the original script. Representatives of the Smithsonian and the peace groups met again in mid-December at the Air and Space Museum. But after a long session, Mike Fetters of the museum staff emerged to explain that further changes were inappropriate. The Smithsonian would not revise the script to include artifacts, photographs, and controversial commentary that had been removed to assuage the American Legion and other groups.[50]

Alarmed by the growing controversy, the Organization of American Historians also reasserted its position and won support from the American Historical Association (AHA). The AHA's Executive Committee unanimously endorsed the resolution passed in September by its OAH counterpart. In late October, moreover, the OAH Executive Board approved a strong resolution condemning "threats by members of Congress to penalize the Smithsonian" because of its controversial exhibit and deploring "the removal of historical documents and revisions of interpretations of history for reasons outside the professional procedures and criteria by which museum exhibitions are created." The OAH also urged immediate efforts by a number of historical societies to protect the rights and professional autonomy of museums and historical societies.[51]

Similar complaints came from various historians acting individually or in groups, including Edward Linenthal, one of the Smithsonian's original consultants. "To be called on the carpet by senators and congressmen and scolded for not doing history in a politically

Enola Gay: Exhibit Now Has Anti-War Groups Up in Arms," *Washington Post*, 21 October 1994, C2.

50 Meyer, "No Peace for Enola Gay," *Washington Post*, 21 October 1994, C2; Stone, "A-Bomb Exhibit Still under Fire," *USA Today*, 6 December 1994, A3; Meyer, "More Turbulence for Enola Gay: Peace Activists Disappointed after Smithsonian Meeting," *Washington Post*, 16 December 1994, F1; "Groups Seek Change in A-Bomb Exhibit," *Atlanta Journal and Constitution*, 24 December 1994, E8.

51 Dichtl, "A Chronology of the Smithsonian's 'Last Act,'" *OAH Newsletter* (November 1994): 10.

correct way smacks of totalitarianism," Linenthal concluded.[52] Kai Bird, another historian, wrote in the *New York Times* that the Smithsonian's curators had "agreed to censor their own historical knowledge." Bird focused particular attention on the curators' decision to increase the number of casualties that Truman and others expected from an Allied invasion of Japan. Reeling off a long list of historians who had written on the subject, he concluded that the preponderance of scholarly opinion held that the war could have been brought to an end without an Allied invasion or the atomic bombing of Japan – through diplomatic overtures, changes in the American demand for unconditional surrender, or Soviet intervention. Even had an invasion been necessary, Bird went on, historians had found no evidence that American leaders anticipated upward to a million casualties – a figure that was invented after the war.[53] Gar Alperovitz, author of one of the first revisionist histories of the atomic bombings, also denounced the Smithsonian for bowing to political pressure and provided the *Washington Post* with a similar assessment of recent historical scholarship on Truman's decision to drop the atomic bombs.[54]

By mid-November, Kai Bird and Martin Sherwin, another of the Smithsonian's original consultants, had persuaded more than sixty historians and other scholars to sign a petition that accused the Smithsonian of "historical cleansing." The new script, according to the petitioners, no longer reflected "a balanced range" of "historical scholarship." On the contrary, it presented as uncontested facts a variety of assertions that had long been challenged by historians. The petitioners urged the curators to restore some of the information deleted from the exhibit's original script, especially references to the debate in 1945 over whether the atomic bombing of Hiroshima was the only way to end the Pacific war without an invasion of Japan. On 17 November, Sherwin and eight other scholars, including Barton Bernstein of Stanford University, who

52 Stone, "Wounds of War Still Color Enola Gay's Place in History," *USA Today*, 5 October 1994, A7. See also Linenthal, "Fuss Clearly Shows Complexity of A-Bomb History," *Houston Post*, 29 November 1994, A19.

53 Bird, "The Curators Cave In," *New York Times*, 9 October 1994, section 4, 15.

54 Alperovitz, "Beyond the Smithsonian Flap: Historians' New Consensus," *Washington Post*, 16 October 1994, C3, OAH Files. See also idem, "Loading the Guns of August 1995," *Chicago Tribune*, 9 August 1994, 15; and idem letter to the editor, *Wall Street Journal*, 13 September 1994, A19.

had also been one of the Smithsonian's original consultants, met with Ira Michael Heyman, who had replaced Robert Adams as the Smithsonian's secretary. They accused the museum of completely disregarding the "historical documents and the scholarly literature on the atomic bombings." In the latest script, Bernstein announced to the press, "there is no clear statement that there is controversy surrounding the bombing of Hiroshima and Nagasaki, and that leaves Americans impoverished intellectually." Sherwin said the revised text had "nothing to do with the history, as it is known by serious historians." The Smithsonian had given in to "political pressure," and as a result the "whole presentation of history in the United States is in jeopardy."[55]

Suddenly it was the historians who were complaining that history had been appropriated by their critics and was being used to support a narrative that was more personal and political than historical. Under the weight of these complaints, Harwit decided to revise the script one more time. Responding to arguments from Bernstein, who had probably written more on the atomic bombing of Japan than any other scholar, Harwit decided to revise a portion of the script that estimated the number of casualties expected in an American invasion of Japan. The new estimate put the number at sixty-three thousand, much lower than the figure of nearly half a million included in the script approved by the American Legion. Harwit informed the Legion of the change in a letter of 9 January 1995, claiming that the higher figures were not historically accurate and had to be revised. The change touched off another firestorm. The Legion denounced the Smithsonian for backing away from its earlier agreement with the veterans and immediately withdrew its support for the exhibit. Along with other veterans groups the Legion now wanted the exhibit canceled altogether, as Legion Commander William Detweiler informed President Bill Clinton in a letter of 20 January. In Detweiler's view, there was no room in such an exhibit for "debatable information" that might

55 "Scholars Decry Exhibit on Atomic Attack: Smithsonian Accused of 'Historical Cleansing' in Bombings of Japan," *Rocky Mountain News*, 18 November 1994, A56; "Enola Gay Moves as Debate Goes On," *New York Times*, 28 November 1994, A12. See also "Hiroshima Exhibit Changes Draw Fire," *Chicago Tribune*, 18 November 1994, 20; and Eugene L. Meyer, "A-Bomb Exhibit Takes Another Hit: Academics Blast Revised Script for Beleaguered Smithsonian Show," *Washington Post*, 18 November 1994, F1.

call into question "the morality and motives of President Truman's decision to end World War II quickly and decisively by using the atomic bomb." Detweiler and other veterans wanted Harwit fired and urged Congress, dominated after the November elections by conservative Republicans, to investigate what they saw as a turn toward "political correctness" at the Smithsonian.[56]

By the end of January, Representative Blute and two other conservative Republicans had also called for Harwit's dismissal, and the historians had once again entered the fray. The National Council on Public History endorsed the resolution passed by the OAH's Executive Board in late October. Professor Eric Foner of Columbia University and a past president of the OAH, joined Nash and Kammen in a letter to Rehnquist that warned the Smithsonian's Board of Regents, on behalf of the OAH, against canceling the proposed exhibit. "We are concerned about the profoundly dangerous precedent of censoring a museum exhibition in response to political pressures from special interest groups." Such a course would, concluded the historians, send "a chilling message to museum administrators and curators throughout the United States . . . that certain aspects of our history are 'too hot to handle.'" Brigadier General Roy K. Flint, president of the Society for Military History, also spoke out on behalf of the country's military historians, who might disagree over how to interpret Truman's decision but who shared "a passionate commitment to freedom of speech and to providing the best scholarship with integrity." The Smithsonian, Flint wrote, should "stand publicly against the politicizing of scholarship in public discourse" and should do so by going forward with the planned exhibit.[57]

In the end, however, the historians were no match for the Legion

---

56 "Group Seeks Cancellation of Enola Gay Exhibit," *New York Times*, 20 January 1995, OAH Files. See also Eugene L. Meyer, "Smithsonian Stands Firm on A-Bomb Exhibit: Veterans Ask Museum to Cancel Enola Gay Plans," *Washington Post*, 19 January 1995, C1; "Legion Urges Canceling of Enola Gay Exhibit," *Los Angeles Times*, 20 January 1995, A20; Air Force Association Press Release, 20 January 1995, OAH Files; Andrea Stone, "Vets Blast A-Bomb Exhibit," *USA Today*, 20 January 1995, A1; and "The History That Tripped over Memory," *New York Times*, 5 February 1995, E5.

57 Foner, Nash, and Kammen to Rehnquist, 27 January 1995, and Flint to Rehnquist, 26 January 1995, OAH Files. See also Patricia Mooney-Melvin (president, National Council on Public History) to Smithsonian Secretary I. Michael Heyman, 16 January 1995, OAH Files; and Michael Kilian, "Enola Gay Exhibit Put on Hold Pending Smithsonian Meeting," *Houston Chronicle*, 21 January 1995, A2.

and its friends on Capitol Hill. On 24 January, Blute and his two allies were joined by seventy-eight other members of Congress in a letter to Smithsonian Secretary Heyman that demanded cancellation of the exhibit and the dismissal of Martin Harwit. The representatives also promised a congressional investigation of the entire controversy, as did Senator Bob Dole of Kansas, the new Republican majority leader in the Senate. Running for cover, Heyman suspended work on the exhibit and asked the Smithsonian's Board of Regents to take up the issue.[58] Meeting on 30 January, the board decided to cancel the original exhibit and accede to the Legion's demand that the *Enola Gay* be displayed without historical commentary. The planned exhibit of ten thousand square feet would be scrapped and the B-29 Superfortress would be displayed with little more than a plaque identifying the giant bomber and its crew. Dr. Robert K. Musil, a historian and director of Physicians for Social Responsibility, called the decision a "tragic capitulation to political pressure . . . reminiscent of the McCarthy era." Heyman viewed the results differently. Veterans and their families, he said in a statement announcing the board's decision, were expecting an exhibit that would "commemorate their valor and sacrifice." They "were not looking for analysis," and the Smithsonian, frankly, had not given "enough thought to the intense feelings such analysis would evoke."[59]

58   Eric Schmitt, "80 Lawmakers Demand Ouster of Director of Air Museum," *New York Times*, 26 January 1995, A6; "Enola Gay Controversy Continues," *OAH Newsletter* (February 1995): 3.
59   Karen De Witt, "Smithsonian Scales Back Exhibit of Plane in Atomic Bomb Attack," *New York Times*, 31 January 1995, A1, C19. On 2 May, roughly three months after Heyman canceled the original exhibit, Martin Harwit resigned as director of the National Air and Space Museum. Two weeks later the Senate Rules and Administration Committee chaired by Senator Ted Stevens of Alaska, a conservative Republican who had been a member of World War II's Flying Tigers, opened hearings on the *Enola Gay* controversy and the future of the Smithsonian. Veterans and their representatives reasserted their view that the atomic bombing of Japan had ended the war quickly and saved lives. They saw the curators as left-wing historians who were hell-bent on revising the historical record in order to advance a political agenda. Stevens and other members of the committee shared this opinion. They refused to be moved by the alternative views presented by historians and curators, accused the Smithsonian of exceeding its legal authority in presenting controversial material, and promised to help the institution get back on the right track. See "Aide Resigns Over Exhibit of Enola Gay," *New York Times*, 3 May 1995, A9; Rowan Scarborough, "Smithsonian Under Siege on Hill," *Washington Times*, 12 May 1995, A10; and Jacqueline Trescott, "Senator Warns Smithsonian on Controversies," *Washington Post*, 19 May 1995, D6.

V

The *Enola Gay* exhibit had been "caught between memory and history," wrote Edward Linenthal shortly after the exhibit was cancelled, between "the commemorative voice and the historical voice." On one side of this divide were the curators, who were "looking for analysis," to borrow Heyman's phrase. Citing their professional credentials, and backed by the authority of professional historians, they claimed a right to interpret the past in an exhibit that would challenge the historical consciousness of its viewers. They wanted viewers to wrestle with the doubts and debates that had occupied historians for half a century, to grapple with the complexities of an important historical event, and to appreciate its consequences for later generations. On the other side of the struggle were the veterans of World War II, who spoke not with the authority of the historian but with "the authority of the witness," as Linenthal put it. The veterans wanted an exhibit that squared with their collective memory, and with their sense of personal heroism and American exceptionalism. They wanted an exhibit that privileged their story over that of the Japanese, that commemorated their sacrifices in a noble cause, not the destruction at Ground Zero, and that remembered "the atomic bomb as the redemptive ending of a horrible war," not as the beginning of the nuclear arms race. This was the history recounted not only by the American Legion and other organized veterans groups, but by individual veterans in letters written to the editors of newspapers all across the country.[60]

In the end, the commemorative voice prevailed over the historical voice, in part because veterans groups could muster more political power than the historians, in part because a conservative political climate called the very practice of history into question. One of the most fascinating aspects of the *Enola Gay* controversy was the degree to which critics in Congress and the press, particularly conservative critics, discounted the authority of professional historians with whom they disagreed. Professional historians, including the curators, were dismissed as the agents of political

60 Linenthal, "Can Museums Achieve a Balance between Memory and History?" *Chronicle of Higher Education* (10 February 1995): B1–2.

correctness, multiculturalism, postmodernism, or historical revisionism — all phrases used more-or-less interchangeably in a conservative critique that ranged from the *Enola Gay* exhibit to the
National Standards for American History. If the critics needed
experts on their side of the story they pointed invariably to the
authors of popular histories, such as David McCullough, or to
military historians, who were seen as somehow uncorrupted by the
"revisionist" disease. But mostly the critics were their own experts
or found them among American veterans, whose collective memory constituted a more authentic past than the archival accounts of
professional scholars.

In this part of the story, by far the most disturbing, the memories
of American veterans became weapons not only in a vigorous
anti-intellectual assault on the practice of professional history but
also on the principle of free speech and the tradition of academic
freedom. Conservative commentators accused the curators and historians of present-mindedness while passing themselves off as defenders of historical truths, which they equated with traditional
American patriotism. Denouncing the curators for promoting a
political agenda, they demanded complete capitulation to a point
of view that was itself frankly political and that often represented
the organized interests of particular groups. This was obviously
the case with Pat Buchanan and other conservatives in the press
and in Congress, where not a single voice spoke on behalf of the
historians and the curators. But it was also the case, if less apparently so, with such critics as Richard Hallion and John Correll.

Critics often cited Hallion as the voice of military history,
though he actually spoke for the U.S. Air Force, which employed
him, and refused, according to the available record, to stand with
the Society for Military History in defending the Smithsonian's
right to interpret history. Much the same can be said of Correll,
whose employer was a professional lobby. Correll's was not the
voice of the veterans, though he claimed as much, but of professional military men who wanted the *Enola Gay* exhibit to make a
frankly political statement about the righteousness of the American cause and the blessings of air power. Correll would tolerate no
dispute with his point of view, nor even the principle that such
disputes were fundamental to the practice of history and protected

by the principle of academic freedom. Like Commander Detweiler, who told President Clinton that "debatable information" had no place in public history, Correll could not be happy until the curators accepted his position "that dropping the atomic bomb was a legitimate military action taken to end the war and save lives." Visitors to the Air and Space Museum were "not interested in countercultural morality pageants put on by academic activists," he said in words that mimicked the style of Pat Buchanan. They came to the museum to see "historic aircraft . . . cleanly presented," not to watch the curators "doubt, probe," or otherwise investigate a complex past.[61]

The *Enola Gay* controversy proved again that history is contested terrain, particularly when public presentations of the past collide with living memory. In hindsight, it is easy to wish that Neufeld, Crouch, and the other curators had tried harder, and earlier, to contextualize the atomic bombings in the long and bloody history of the Second World War. And maybe they could have struck a better balance between the narrative of Japanese suffering and the record of Japanese aggression, between the commemorative voice and the historical voice. As Heyman concluded, the curators had not thought enough about the feelings of individual veterans, who were less concerned about the politics of the *Enola Gay* controversy than they were about how their wartime sacrifices would be remembered by generations to come.

Still, the curators had been willing to share their work with the Air Force Association and other interested parties, had sought their advice, and had made adjustments accordingly. What is more, it is difficult to see how any degree of balance between history and memory would have satisfied critics like Correll, who was determined to censor all voices but his own. Second-guessing the curators also sidesteps the central issue in the *Enola Gay* controversy, on which Professor Alfred F. Young of Northern Illinois University had the last word. The issue is whether or not the nation's history can be openly and critically discussed or whether organized political pressure will encourage censorship and promote a false consciousness about the past. Historians will always

61 Correll, "Airplanes in the Mist," *Air Force Magazine* (December 1994): 2.

disagree over the past, Young wrote in the *OAH Newsletter*, but they should respect their disagreements and defend the right of public historians to represent the past without political interference.[62] Defending that right is particularly important in an age when so many critics are determined to reduce history to "bunk," to borrow a famous phrase from Henry Ford, who, like Correll, sought to build a romanticized version of the past as an alternative to the one offered by historians.

62   Young, "S.O.S.: Storm Warning for American Museums," *OAH Newsletter* (November 1994): 1, 6–8. See also Young to Nash, 21 January 1995, OAH Files.

Index

CPSIA information can be obtained
at www.ICGtesting.com
Printed in the USA
LVHW081718150120
643606LV00031B/563